Beat sound, Beat vision

Manchester University Press

Beat sound, Beat vision

The Beat spirit and popular song

Laurence Coupe

Manchester University Press
Manchester and New York
distributed exclusively in the USA by Palgrave

The right of Laurence Coupe to be identified as the author of this
work has been asserted by him in accordance with the Copyright,
Designs and Patents Act 1988.

Published by Manchester University Press
Oxford Road, Manchester M13 9NR, UK
and Room 400, 175 Fifth Avenue, New York, NY 10010, USA
www.manchesteruniversitypress.co.uk

Distributed in the United States exclusively by
Palgrave Macmillan, 175 Fifth Avenue,
New York, NY 10010, USA

Distributed in Canada exclusively by
UBC Press, University of British Columbia, 2029 West Mall,
Vancouver, BC, Canada V6T 1Z2

British Library Cataloguing-in-Publication Data is available

Library of Congress Cataloging-in-Publication Data is available

ISBN 978 0 7190 7113 3 paperback

First published by Manchester University Press in hardback 2007

This paperback edition first published 2010

Printed by Lightning Source

Contents

To Marina Warner

Acknowledgements

I am grateful to the colleagues who have helped, in various ways, to ensure that this book got written: Berthold Schoene, Jeff Wainwright and Sue Zlosnik. Thanks are due also to Matthew Frost at MUP for his enthusiastic encouragement and good-humoured support. Finally, I am indebted, as always, to my wife, Margaret – not forgetting our friends, Pauline and Simon Butler.

A note on usage

When I refer to the 'Beat' movement I use a capital letter to distinguish it from other possible meanings of the word, in the same way that I would use a capital R for the 'Romantic' movement. However, if writers quoted use lower case, then I remain faithful to their usage.

I spell 'counterculture' as one word, in accordance with the increasing custom to absorb prefixes (cf, 'postmodernism'). However, if writers quoted prefer to use either two separate words ('counter culture') or hyphenation ('counter-culture'), then I remain faithful to their usage.

In order not to overwhelm the reader with italics, I do not treat terms used in Eastern religion as 'foreign', but simply place them in quotation marks: eg, 'dharma' not *dharma*. However, if writers quoted use italics, then I remain faithful to their usage.

When I use the word 'materialist' I generally mean it in both senses usually given in the dictionary, because the Beats seem to me to have done likewise: '1. a tendency to consider material possessions and physical comfort to be more important than spiritual values. 2. the opinion that nothing exists but matter and that consciousness and will are wholly due to material agency' (OED). The Beats rebelled against North American civilisation of the post-war period, not only because it seemed to them to be dedicated chiefly to commerce and consumption, but also because it consistently suppressed genuine spirituality (despite its official adherence to Christian belief). Wherever I make a departure from this double usage, I try and draw attention to it.

Last, I should point out that I have opted to write in the first person, rather than in the academic convention of the impersonal third, as (a) I feel it is more appropriate to the subject matter, and (b) I am making a personal intervention in this area of interest, for good or ill.

Introduction

This is not, strictly speaking, a book about music: I am neither a musicologist nor a pop journalist. Nor is it a wide, equal survey of an era: I am not a cultural historian. Still less is it a work of critical theory: I am not setting out to expose the hidden agenda of literature and popular song. Rather, it is a series of reflections on ideas addressed by certain songwriters who came to prominence in the 1960s. These ideas, I argue, derive from the literary phenomenon known as the Beat movement. My premiss is that the 'Beat vision' of the 1950s lies behind the 'Beat sound' of the following decade. Taking my cue from Jack Kerouac, the effective founder of the movement, I understand 'Beat' as meaning primarily 'beatific'. The implications of this will be spelt out as we proceed, but for now I should emphasise that the overriding assumption of the book is that the Beats initiated a new concern with spirituality, the effects of which became evident in some of the more adventurous popular music.

Having said that, I need to offer another proviso: this book is not meant to be an exhaustive study in influence; my aim is rather more modest than that. If readers think of this as a series of related insights rather than as a continuous narrative, exposition or overview, they might yet find that it proves revealing. Because it is Beat writing that is the source of the 'vision', it is fitting that at least two chapters should each concentrate on a figure associated with the movement. I choose Alan Watts because he was the first person to understand the implications of Beat spirituality. I choose Jack Kerouac because he was, to my mind, the most important and influential Beat writer. Allen Ginsberg and Gary Snyder feature throughout, but I have excluded William Burroughs because he does not appear to me to exemplify Kerouac's translation of 'Beat' as 'beatific'.[1]

As for popular song, I have confined myself to artists who came to prominence in the 1960s, the decade in which spirituality gained a new relevance thanks to the Beat writers. This chronological limit means that I cannot include such Beat-inspired figures as Tom Waits and Patti Smith – each of whom would otherwise merit attention. But to return to the matter in hand: no account of sixties songwriters can afford to exclude either Bob Dylan or the Beatles; but here I have deliberately made them central because they exemplify, in their different ways, the complexity of the Beat legacy. Dylan is the focus of a whole chapter because he is a notoriously difficult artist to classify, having something of Keats's 'chameleon poet' about him: I believe that this difficulty may best be overcome by relating him sequentially to Kerouac and Ginsberg, each of whom has his own special understanding of what Beat spirituality involves. The Beatles, though they include three different songwriters, seem to me to make most sense if related collectively to Ginsberg. Again, had I attempted to produce separate essays on Jim Morrison, Joni Mitchell, Leonard Cohen, Donovan, the Incredible String Band, Van Morrison and Nick Drake, this book would have become unwieldy; I trust that discussing them together in the context of the concerns of Gary Snyder will convey the depth and extent of the influence of Beat spirituality on popular song in our chosen period.

*****

Despite half a century of commentary on the Beat movement, there is still a good deal of confusion over the meaning of the word 'Beat'. It is generally acknowledged that it refers to the 'beat' of bebop music, admired so much by the Beat generation. Again, most commentators know that it can also refer to the condition of being 'dead beat' or 'beat down', as used by Herbert Huncke, the New York vagrant adopted as a role model by the young Beats in the mid-1940s: 'Man, I'm beat.'[2] But there is a third meaning which is too often overlooked, the implications of which we will be exploring. For it is important from the start to take seriously what Kerouac, the founder of the movement, declared in February 1958:

> Beat doesn't mean tired, or bushed, so much as it means *beato*, the Italian for beatific: to be in a state of beatitude, like St Francis, trying to love all life, trying to be utterly sincere with everyone, practising endurance, kindness, cultivating joy of heart. How can this be done in our mad modern world of

multiplicities and millions? By practising a little solitude, going off by yourself once in awhile to store up that most precious of golds: the vibrations of sincerity.[3]

Kerouac continued to insist throughout his writing career that the Beat generation was 'basically a religious generation'.[4] Indeed, his definition of the function of literature left no room for doubt on this score: to teach 'religious reverence' for 'real life'.[5]

To define 'Beat' as 'beatific' is to suggest that the purpose of Beat writing is to view the world under the aspect of 'beatitude', or blessedness – which is only another way of saying that one should treat 'real life' with 'religious reverence'. Put in more abstract, academic terms, we might say that its purpose is to reveal the 'sacred' in the 'profane'. Here we should pause to clarify those last two terms. The first is not a problem: it is synonymous with 'holy': to have a sense of the sacred is to have a sense of 'religious reverence'. The second term needs slightly more explanation, particularly as these days it is used interchangeably with 'obscene'. Going further into its etymology, however, we discover that it derives from the Latin *profanus*, which means 'before (i.e. outside) the temple' (OED). That is, it is the contrary term to 'sacred': it covers all that is normally excluded from our idea of holiness. It is not, however, a state to be starkly opposed to the sacred: to be contrary is not the same as to be opposite.

According to the historian of religions, Mircea Eliade, as far back as we go into the archaic past we find that humanity has had a religious sense, and has sought a 'manifestation of the sacred' as a release from the sense of being trapped in a merely profane realm. However, *homo religiosus* ('religious man': Eliade's name for our species) has always understood that the sacred and the profane exist in a reciprocal relationship. For example, the sacred may be thought to manifest itself in some ordinary object (a stone, a tree) or in a specially designated human being (Krishna, Jesus). The point is that 'in each case we are confronted by the same mysterious act – the manifestation of something of a wholly different order, a reality that does not belong to our world, in objects that are an integral part of our natural "profane" world'.[6] There is, then, a dialectic at work: the sacred, while transcending the profane, can only reveal itself within the profane; again, unless there were a mode of experience deemed profane, the need to apprehend the sacred would make no sense. I would suggest that the Beat writers and the sixties songwriters whom we will be discussing may be seen as attempting to provide manifestations of the sacred. More particularly, the Beat impulse is to transform profane time into sacred time, and to transform profane space into sacred space. Here and now one can 'hold infinity in the palm of your hand / And eternity in an hour'.[7] Those are the words of the first of the major English Romantic poets, William Blake, whom the Beats regarded as a model of the artist as visionary. Leaving him aside for the time being, we might summarise the endeavour of the Blake-inspired Beats as being to develop, in the words of Jon Lardas, a 'theology of experience', by which divinity might be known in the very act of living.[8]

The Beat ideal, then, is the beatific vision. That ideal stands opposed to the materialism of contemporary civilisation: 'materialism', that is, in both senses of the word – the denial of spirit and the pursuit of possessions. But a question now arises: how far was the desire of the Beat generation to manifest the sacred fulfilled by the 'love generation' which claimed the Beats as its mentors? If we attend strictly to etymology, then it is striking that one of the key words associated with the later generation was 'psychedelic'. This epithet was used mainly in relation to drugs such as LSD and mescalin, use of which would lead to a 'psychedelic experience', usually involving bizarre phenomena, vivid colours, swirling patterns and so forth. However, the term itself has wider and perhaps deeper importance, which resonates with Eliade's account of the dialectic of the sacred and the profane. The adjective 'psychedelic' derives from two ancient Greek words: *psyche* (soul, spirit, mind) and *delos* (clear, manifest). 'Psychedelic' means, then, 'making the spirit manifest'. That is, it refers to the very process described by Eliade. Hallucinatory drugs rather than a genuine 'theology of experience' may have formed the main means to this in the period of 'flower power'; but the impulse was certainly in keeping with Kerouac's ideal of the 'beatific' vision. Nor should we be coy about acknowledging that the Beat generation had early on been more than willing to use drugs such as cannabis and alcohol in pursuit of that vision. Moreover, Allen Ginsberg became a great enthusiast for LSD in the late sixties – a period when he was hailed as a guru of the counterculture. Of course, that does not mean that the 'beatific' vision is reducible to the level of a recreational diversion – particularly not one which has proved so disastrous in so many cases.

If we are thinking sociologically, however, there is an important distinction to be made between the 'Beat' fifties and the 'hippie' sixties. Strictly speaking, the earlier movement, constituting a small group of writers and a significant but nonetheless small following of imitators, or 'beatniks' (as they were popularly and derisively known), is best described as a 'subculture'. What arose in the following decade, for good or ill, was a mass movement based on the international language of rock music, which was far more accessible to young people than the modern jazz favoured by the Beats: this movement became known as the 'counterculture'. Kerouac was alarmed and alienated by this development, but his friend Allen Ginsberg embraced it. Either way, the songwriters who became icons of the counterculture saw themselves as the heirs of the Beats. How they regarded the counterculture is another matter: Bob Dylan, for example, more or less disowned it around 1966–67.

Having raised this issue, it should be admitted that for many commentators the spiritual continuity is more important than the sociological hiatus. Paul Heelas, for example, in his study, *The New Age Movement*, sees the Beat legacy as being formative of what he calls in his subtitle 'the sacralization of modernity':

> Lines etched on the triangular granite columns of the Jack
> Kerouac Commemorative Park capture an important aspect
> of the beat [sic] movement: 'When you've understood this
> scripture, throw it away. If you can't understand this scripture,
> throw it away. I insist on your freedom'. Alternative, highly
> expressive, concerned with pushing forward the boundaries of
> consciousness, the beats were basically intent on creating
> a western *sadhana* or 'way'. ... The beat movement remained
> small: until, that is, it flowed into the counter-culture with its
> hippies. The 1960s witnessed the most significant turn to inner
> spirituality to have taken place during modernity. The upsurge
> was almost entirely bound up with the development of the
> counter-culture.[9]

For him, the ethos that was inherited could be summarised as follows: 'people should be free to express their authentic nature, [and this] ensured that capitalism, the forces of law and order, the educational establishment, indeed any form of self-control which thwarted self-expressivity, came under attack.'[10] While this was liberating for those with the opportunity to thus express themselves, Heelas implies that it had a dangerous tendency towards narcissism. He does not state his case in those terms, but he certainly queries the validity of what he calls 'Self-spirituality'.[11]

On the other hand, Theodore Roszak, one of the first commentators to use the term 'counter culture' (for him, two words), was consistently sanguine about the spiritual advances of the sixties. In his seminal work, *The Making of a Counter Culture*, written in 1970, he praised the courage of the disaffected youth of contemporary North America and Europe to 'investigate the non-intellective consciousness'. He elaborates upon this insight as follows, invoking the spiritual wisdom of the East, to which the counterculture seems to him to be chiefly indebted:

> This emerges primarily from the strong influence upon the young of Eastern religion, with its heritage of gentle, tranquil, and thoroughly civilized contemplativeness. Here we have a tradition that calls radically into question the validity of the scientific world view, the supremacy of cerebral cognition, the value of technological prowess; but does so in the most quiet and measured of tones, with humor, with tenderness, even with a deal of cunning argumentation. If there is anything off-putting to the scientific mind about this tradition, it does not result from any unwillingness on the part of the Eastern religions to indulge in analysis and debate. It results, rather, from their assertion of the intellectual value of paradox and from their conviction that analysis and debate must finally yield to the claims of ineffable experience. Oriental mysticism comprehends argumentation; but it also provides a generous place for silence, out of wise recognition of the fact that it is with silence that men confront the great moments of life. Unhappily, the Western intellect is inclined to treat silence as if it were a mere zero: a loss for words indicating the absence of meaning. However sternly one may wish to reject the world view of Lao-tzu, of the Buddha, of the Zen masters, one cannot fairly accuse such figures of lacking intellect, wit, or humane cultivation. Though their minds lay at the service of a vision that is incompatible with our conventional science, such men are the prospective participants of neither a lynch mob nor a group-grope party. Fortunately, their example has not been lost on our dissenting young; indeed, it has become one of the strongest strains of the counter culture.[12]

For Roszak, the hippies followed on from the Beats in a necessary revolt against what he called 'the technocratic society', a hierarchical civilisation in which those with control of technology, who could thereby further material 'development', had the power. A rediscovery

of spirituality was intrinsic to the alternative visi⟨
is surely correct, in that the Beat writers – notah
and above all Snyder – had always insisted o
sense of the sacredness of the earth. Green thi⟨.
Beat vision right from the start, given that it wa⟨
ecologically inclined religions of the East; and the co⟨
certainly took its cue from the Beats in this respect.
One other dimension of the spiritual continuity of Beat movement
and counterculture should be mentioned. This is what the anthropologist Victor Turner refers to as the challenge to 'structure' (social hierarchy and inequality) by 'communitas' (an alternative way of living,
focussed on the idea of genuine fellowship). For Turner, the groups
which represent 'communitas' must of necessity be 'liminal', existing
on the threshold of the given society (Latin, *limen*, threshold), and will
thereby have a strong sense of being transitional. For Turner, writing at
the end of the sixties, there is no need to look far to find a contemporary example:

> In modern Western society, the values of communitas are
> strikingly present in the literature and behavior of what came to
> be known as the 'beat generation,' who were succeeded by the
> 'hippies' ... [These] 'opt out' of the status-bound social order
> and acquire the stigmata of the lowly, dressing like 'bums,'
> itinerant in their habits, 'folk' in their musical tastes, and
> menial in the casual employment they undertake. They stress
> personal relationships rather than social obligations ... The
> 'sacred' properties often assigned to communitas are not
> lacking here, either: this can be seen in their frequent use
> of religious terms, such as 'saint' and 'angel,' to describe
> their congeners and in their interest in Zen Buddhism. The
> Zen formulation 'all is one, one is none, none is all' well
> expresses the global, unstructured character earlier applied to
> communitas. The hippie emphasis on spontaneity, immediacy,
> and 'existence' throws into relief one of the senses in which
> communitas contrasts with structure. Communitas is of the
> now; structure is rooted in the past and extends into the future
> through language, law, and custom.[13]

This idea of spirituality as alternative, liminal, marginal, transitional
and immediate, and as focussed on those who identify with the weak
and the dispossessed, is a theme to which we will return when we
discuss Kerouac's idea of the 'fellaheen' (see Chapter 2).

It was indicated above that Kerouac's ideal of the beatific vision certainly continued to mean something to the 'love generation'. But what also has to be borne in mind is the contrast between the minority subculture of the 1950s and the mass counterculture of the 1960s. The latter was, as we have said, focussed on rock music. There may appear to be an irony in the fact that a movement designed to foster an alternative idea of community should have been inspired by the music of millionaire songwriters. But rock was the primary medium of the movement, and there seems to me to be little point in trying to disentangle the movement and the music. Indeed, most of the Beats were well-disposed towards the innovations in popular song that were made during the sixties. Ginsberg above all continued for long after to regard that generation of songwriters as supremely important. In 1981 he praised the 'evolution of rhythm and blues into rock'n'roll into high art form, as evidenced by the Beatles, Bob Dylan, and other popular musicians influenced in the late 1950s and '60s by beat generation poets' and writers' works.'[14] If a major Beat writer saw such artists as extending the Beat aesthetic, they certainly merit a place in the present study.

As to the details of the connection between the Beat writers and what we might now call the Beat songwriters, let us refer briefly to Bruce Cook's account, written at the close of that decade, of what happened in the sixties to the relationship between poetry and popular song. He begins by proposing that the Beat writers' attempt to make literature accessible by means of performance with a jazz accompaniment did not work very well because jazz had by then become too self-conscious and esoteric. But though rock music may have sounded crude in its early 'rock'n'roll' days, it proved itself extremely versatile as it developed, gradually becoming perfectly compatible with the popularisation of poetry. In doing so, it realised the Beat aim:

> It was, after all, when the fad for the Beat Generation was at its height that popular music was going through these throes of transformation that eventually brought forth rock in its present sound and shape. The Beats had led them a couple of steps in the right direction. There was, as noted, the poetry-with-jazz experiment. Unsuccessful though it may have been in practice, the *idea* was a good one. It suggested a return to the old conception of poetry as song, and it indicated possibilities for rock that the square world could not then even conceive. But music aside, it was also important that so much of the poetry called Beat was written for the human voice. It made use of old

bardic devices of chant and simple rhythmic repetition to stir audiences.[15]

Whether or not we concede that jazz was the wrong kind of music to accompany the kind of poetry the Beats were producing, we can perhaps agree with Cook that the broad aim of aligning literature and music was valid, and that the sixties songwriters went a long way to realising that aim. In short, 'the Beat vision' and 'the Beat sound' are complementary.

There we have the main aspects of our study. The most important is the equation between the 'Beat' vision and the 'beatific' vision. Illuminating that is the differentiation between the 'sacred' and the 'profane', and the dialectical relationship between them. Consequent upon both is the question of the continuity between the Beat generation and the counterculture of the 1960s. Essential to understanding that is a willingness to trace elements of the 'beatific' vision within popular song. These factors may not always be explicitly restated in any systematic way, but they will certainly be either assumed or alluded to in what follows.

* * * * *

Before we can discuss the Beats' place in the visionary tradition, we have to get our bearings and define our terms. All being well, the former should stem from the latter. Timothy Freke, a respected authority on world religions, makes a useful differentiation between three words that are often used interchangeably. These are 'religion', 'spirituality' and 'mysticism'. It is true that the Beats themselves often did so, as do proponents of the 'New Age' movement which owes so much to them. We, however, have to try to be more careful. That said, it is often difficult to maintain the differentiation, especially when summarising a Beat writer's position. Kerouac, for example, often treats the first and third as synonymous.

Here, then, is the essence of Freke's threefold definition. 'Religion is concerned with rituals, observances, creeds, and codes of social morality. ... Religion is the outer form of spirituality.' In this light, religion may well form the basis of a spiritual way of life, but one may be religious without being interested in spirituality: that is, one may follow the letter but miss the spirit. 'Spirituality is the inner content of all religions, but it does not necessarily have to have a religious context. Spirituality is about setting out on a personal search for answers to the most profound questions of life.' This search is ultimately 'a journey of awakening to who we really are'. But this in turn takes us to a third level of understanding. 'Mysticism is the deepest level of spirituality. It teaches that reality is an indivisible Whole appearing as many parts.' This idea of apprehending the 'Whole' amidst the diversity of life is key: 'Although we think of ourselves as separate individuals, this is an illusion. We are not the transitory mortal beings we take ourselves to be.' In the depths of mystical experience, we understand that we are in reality 'one with the Oneness'.[16]

Obviously, the above is a simplification; but it is a useful starting point. Again, if anyone is going to clarify these issues, Freke, who has written several studies making Eastern wisdom accessible to Western readers, is qualified to do it. We will therefore rely on him also in making a survey of the specific religions from which the Beats took spiritual inspiration in their quest for the beatific vision – a vision which borders on the sphere of mysticism. Of course, if any readers are familiar with these traditions, they are welcome to skip the next section of this chapter.

* * * * *

It should be said from the outset that Freke's assumption is that all of these traditions coincide on essentials: hence his discovery of the idea of 'the One' in the five faiths outlined here. Specialists may object that this overrides important distinctions, but my instinct is that his comprehensive, inclusive approach will help those comparatively new to this area of study to get their bearings. Any necessary revisions may be made as appropriate.

We begin with *Hinduism*, which is the oldest of the major religions. Strictly speaking, the term 'Hinduism' is misleading, as it suggests a uniform body of beliefs rather than a complex wisdom comprehending the various strands of thought which developed throughout the Indian subcontinent from the beginning of the second millennium BC. But the word must suffice, so long as it is understood as a term of convenience. Freke offers the following summary:

> Hinduism is rooted in the ancient Vedas, the oldest sacred
> writings of humanity. Yet, despite its great age, Hinduism
> remains a vibrant living tradition, still producing exceptional
> saints and sages today. It is a broad and inclusive religion made
> up of many cults that, although they perform different spiritual
> practices and even propound contradictory philosophies, are all

understood as approaches to the one transcendent Truth.
This is why the Indians call their faith simply the 'santana
dharma' – the eternal doctrine. In recent decades Hinduism
has had a profound influence on spirituality in the West. (p. 20)

To this we should add that the culmination of Hinduism is the sophis-
ticated reflection on the Vedas in the texts known as the Upanishads,
the basis of the philosophy known as 'Vedanta'. It is with Vedanta that
the idea of the One underlying the many is articulated most clearly.

But what does it involve to realise the One? Here we need to clarify
the key Hindu principles by which the human being is connected to the
cosmos:

The essential teaching of Hinduism is that the 'jiva' – the
individual personal self – is not our true identity. Through
spiritual practice we can realize our true identity as the
Atman or Higher Self. Through further spiritual awakening
we can come to the enlightened realization that 'Atman is
Brahman' – the Self is God. Our consciousness is an expression
of the one Consciousness of the Universe. (p. 20)

The route to such a realisation, of which there are many, is called a
'yoga'. The two most important of these paths to enlightenment are
'Gnana' and 'Bhatki':

Gnana is ... a path of the head that emphasizes philosophical
understanding, meditation, and the study of scripture. Through
this path seekers understand that the world is an illusion, that
they have no individual identity, and that in truth God is all
that exists. Bhakti is a path of the heart that emphasizes
worship, prayer, and surrender to God. Bhaktas lose themselves
in all-consuming ecstatic devotion to God, until they transcend
their separate identities and become one with their Beloved.
Although the paths of Bhakti Yoga and Gnana Yoga are quite
different in approach, their essential purpose is identical – to
nurture a spontaneous experience of enlightenment. (p. 20)

The tension between these alternatives – specifically the path of
contemplation ('head') and the path of devotion ('heart') – has its
parallel in other religions. Usually, the idea is that they are complementary rather than exclusive. Indeed, attention to one at the expense of
the other is understood to be the source of imbalance.

One characteristic of Hinduism which Freke does not discuss, but which is worth emphasising here, is that it is, strictly speaking, a form of theism. Let us be clear about this. Most readers will be familiar with the Krishna Consciousness movement, famous for its members' ritual chanting of 'Hare Krishna' on many a city high street. Now, Krishna is the incarnate form of Vishnu; and Vishnu is part of that trinity of deities – the others being Shiva and Brahma – which is in turn the personified expression of absolute reality, Brahman, the Godhead. Thus, for the Hindu mystic, the aim is to attain oneness with that reality, which he may choose to approach through the mediatory form of Krishna. But insofar as Hinduism adheres to terms such as 'Godhead' (Brahman) and 'god' (Brahma), it is theistic. That development from Hinduism which we know as Buddhism, to which we must now turn, is by contrast non-theistic since, though it posits an absolute reality (Buddha-nature, or Buddha-mind), it does not speak of this as the 'Godhead'; nor is the Buddha a god.

Having referred to it, let us now give a brief account of *Buddhism*, which also originated in India, at a later date. Indeed, it may be said to have emerged out of Hinduism in a manner analogous to the way Christianity emerged out of Judaism. Its founder began within the spiritual context of Hinduism, but then set out to formulate his own path to enlightenment – while being reluctant to describe his philosophy as a religion. As Freke explains:

> Buddhism was inspired by an Indian sage named Siddhartha Guatama (b. 560 BCE), more commonly known by the title of 'Buddha'. He was not concerned with metaphysical speculation, but with guiding his students toward the experience of enlightenment. The Tibetan word for Buddhist is 'nangpa', which means 'insider'. Buddhism is about looking inside to discover the essential nature of the mind. (p. 32)

The Buddha's starting point was that life necessarily involves 'dukkha', which is often translated as 'suffering'. However, it is more accurately thought of as 'anxiety', or 'dis-ease'. The Buddha realised the full challenge of 'dukkha' when he left his father's palace, where he had been sheltered from anything painful, and saw in turn a sick man, an old man and a dead man. He determined to find the answer to human misery. This led him to formulate the idea of 'samsara':

> Buddhism teaches that our lives are full of suffering because we mistakenly believe ourselves to be a body that is born to die.

But in reality there is no separate 'self' at all. In fact, there
are no separate individual entities, because all things are so
intimately interrelated that nothing has any independent
existence. The world of separate things is an illusion, which
Buddhists call 'samsara', and the idea of ourselves as separate
beings is part of that illusion. (p. 32)

The goal of Buddhism is to see through the illusion of 'samsara', and
awaken to that reality which lies behind it:

Enlightenment is the experience of 'nirvana' – the
'extinguishing' of the illusion of the self. This is a blissful
state of being pure Consciousness. This is our true identity
or Buddha-Nature. We are the Mind of the Universe. Yet
Buddhism does not reject the illusionary world of appearances.
It teaches that, since all is One, 'samsara is nirvana and nirvana
is samsara.' The world is an appearance in Consciousness, but
Consciousness is only experienced because of the appearances.
(p. 32)

We can now see the affinities between Buddhism and the Hinduism
from which it derived: the aim is to get beyond the illusion of the ego
to the truth of the One. However, Buddhism does not accept the idea
of an essential, eternal soul or Self, 'Atman': enlightenment comes
when one abandons all ideas of permanence and embraces impermanence, having understood that all phenomena are 'empty' of separate,
substantial being. This idea of giving up the comfort of persistent
identity is what makes Buddhism seem pessimistic to some, but it is
more fairly described as liberating:

The experience of abandoning the illusion of being an
individual self is often compared to a drop of water dissolving
back into the mighty ocean. This metaphor can seem to imply
that we are going to be annihilated, which does not sound
particularly appealing. But this is a complete misunderstanding.
Buddhism teaches that the separate self cannot cease to be
because it never existed. It was merely a transitory illusion.
The enlightened are not lost in the overwhelming vastness
of the Ocean of Being. They know that there has only ever
been the Ocean. The separate self is like a wave upon the sea
that, although apparently distinct, is actually no more than a

disturbance on the surface of the water. Relinquishing the
illusion of separateness is not annihilation. It is the knowledge
that our essential being cannot possibly die. When the wave
crashes onto the shore, the ocean is not diminished, and we
are that ocean. (p. 32)

Realisation of the 'Buddha-nature' beyond one's own individual,
phenomenal life is not too remote from the Hindu idea of Brahman as
the reality underlying everything. But again we should remind
ourselves that Buddhists usually wish to query the notion that there is
an Atman which finds fulfillment in identification with Brahman. For
that is the error of essentialism, which Buddhism wishes to avoid. Or,
to put the same point in the terms we used earlier: if Hinduism is a
form of theism, then Buddhism is a form of non-theism. But what is
common is the idea of an ultimate unity underlying all apparently
distinct phenomena.

This idea also was developed in China, about the same time as
Prince Gautama was determining to find his own path to enlightenment in India. Here we are referring to the spiritual philosophy known
as *Taoism*, which is said to originate in a text known as the *Tao Te
Ching*, attributed to a reclusive sage called Lao Tzu (or Lao-Tse). The
key idea is that of 'Tao' or 'Way':

> Tao is 'the way it is', 'the way life works', the natural unfolding
> of existence. Tao is the fundamental Nature of Reality, the
> underlying Oneness, the great Ocean of Being, the Primal
> Source. ... Taoism is about learning to live in harmony with
> Tao by abandoning the futile attempt to control the tides of
> perpetual transformation and instead to go with the flow of
> life. Taoism is known as the 'Way of Water' because Taoists
> seek to embody the yielding qualities of water. Like water,
> which flows around any obstacle it confronts, they seek to
> accommodate rather than confront problems. Like water, which
> is soft and weak yet has the power to wear away hard rocks,
> they trust in the strength of acceptance and perseverance rather
> than effort and force. Like a river rushing to the ocean, Taoists
> seek to transform their lives into a journey back to Tao. (p. 30)

That journey, as with Buddhism, necessitates the abandonment of the
sense of being an isolated individual. One has to let go of the idea of
an independent, intending self:

A central practice of Taoism is the cultivation of the state of
'wu wei'. This phrase is often translated as 'not doing', but the
Taoist sages are not encouraging us to do nothing. This is
obviously an impossibility for a human being. They want us to
recognize that there is in reality 'no doer'. All that we do and
think and feel is an expression of Tao through a particular body
and mind. To live truly in harmony with Tao is to be in the
state of 'wu wei' in which we have no sense of being a separate
individual to interfere with the natural organic unfolding of
existence. (p. 30)

As with Hinduism and Buddhism, the aim is the apprehension of, and
absorption in, the One. In both those religions, there is a subtle understanding of the relationship between unity and multiplicity, between
the One and the many. But it is Taoism that is particularly associated
with the idea of dynamic interaction: the 'Way' works by virtue of a
cosmic dialectic:

Taoism teaches that everything in life has its complementary
pole – day and night, male and female, seer and seen, subject
and object, yes and no, pleasure and pain, quality and quantity,
life and death. Taoists call this omnipresent polarity that
underlies all of life 'Yin' and 'Yang'. The constant flux we call
reality is created by the process of Yin and Yang perpetually
changing into each other. This fundamental rhythm of life is
symbolically represented by the familiar Yin\Yang symbol in
which the dark Yin segment is shown with a white spot of
Yang, and vice versa. Yin and Yang are united in the circle of
Tao. Although Yin and Yang are opposites, they are also
comple-mentaries that can only exist together. They are like two
ends of one piece of string. They are the dual expressions of the
paradoxical Oneness of Tao. (p. 30)

Thus we come to the fourth of our Eastern religions, the one that
the Beats have become especially associated with, despite the ambivalence of more than one of them towards it and despite the awkward
fact that practitioners frequently deny that it is a religion at all. I refer
to *Zen*:

Zen is a synthesis of Indian Buddhism and Chinese Taoism. Its
founder was an Indian Buddhist named 'Bodhidharma' or
'Knower of the Way'. In the 6th century CE he journeyed from

India to China where he founded a school of Buddhism known
as 'Ch'an', which in 12th-century Japan acquired the familiar
name 'Zen'. Zen is a vibrant and anarchic approach to
spirituality, which emphasizes direct experience and
irreverence toward religious formalities. This has led to it being
enthusiastically embraced by many modern seekers, often
outside a specifically Buddhist context. (p. 34)

This last insight will be worth bearing in mind as we proceed. Many of
the assumptions of the counterculture derive from Zen, even though
those who articulate them may have little or no knowledge of either
Chinese or Japanese wisdom.

If Zen is a form of Buddhism, it is one that has been purified of the
speculative element in the original Indian system of thought
constructed in the name of the Buddha. Indeed, it is scarcely a system
at all:

Zen is not an organized set of teachings. It is about discovering
who we are. Master Bassui reduced Zen teachings to one
phrase: 'Seeing one's own nature is Buddhahood.' Zen is not a
philosophy. Zen is about emptying the mind of thoughts and
experiencing the mind itself. The empty mind is our true
Buddha-Nature. In the emptiness of pure Consciousness there is
no sense of being a separate individual, but rather of being One
with all that is. (p. 34)

Zen is often referred to as 'the religion of no religion', since it asks us
to abandon all our ideas about the sacred and to learn to respond as
naturally as possible to the profane world. Then, miraculously, we will
realise that the sacred and the profane are the same.

Again we return to that idea of an all-embracing unity of being,
which our egos prevent us apprehending. But Zen warns us not to
expect to come to this apprehension through conceptual understanding. We have to trust in what is known as 'beginner's mind'; we have
to be open to reality, not seeking to fit it into our preconceptions, even
those about the nature of Zen:

There is a story of a young student who visited master Dokuon
hoping to show off his understanding of Zen. In an erudite
manner he proudly expounded Buddhist teachings for some
time, eventually concluding, 'In reality nothing exists.' Master

Dokuon sat silently smoking, ignoring the pupil who became increasingly agitated. Suddenly Dokuon whacked him with his bamboo pipe, making him yell with anger. 'If nothing exists,' inquired the master with a smile, 'where did this anger come from?' (p. 34)

The willingness on the part of the master to shock and outrage the student is typical of Zen, especially the school known as 'Rinzai-shu', which is dedicated to sudden enlightenment; this uses 'koans', or 'mind games', such as 'What is the sound of one hand clapping?', as well as the provocative aggression exemplified by Dokuon. By way of balance, we should acknowledge that there is another school, the 'Soto-shu', which allows for the more gentle, gradual path of 'silent illumination'; this is based chiefly on meditation.[17]

There, then, are the four major Eastern kinds of wisdom in which the Beats took an interest: Hinduism, Buddhism, Taoism and Zen. It would be misleading, however, to leave our survey of religion there, as it might imply that mystical wisdom is confined to religions of the East. As Freke points out, *Christianity* is a rich source of inspiration, even though that source has been overlooked, misunderstood or denied:

Christianity began as a minor group of Jewish mystics, but has become the most influential religion of all time. Fundamentalist Christians claim that Jesus Christ is the one and only Son of God and that only those who acknowledge his historical death and resurrection can be saved. Despite this tendency toward exclusivity and division, Christianity has also given rise to many great saints and sages who have taught the perennial spiritual philosophy of Unity. Today many are seeking to rediscover the mystical essence of Christianity, which, throughout its history, the religious authorities have persistently attempted to suppress. (p. 26)

We will have more to say about the hidden, mystical tradition of Christianity in our next chapter. But for now, we can see how it merits a place in our survey of those religions which offered the possibility of spiritual enlightenment to some of the more important members of the Beat movement – even though not all concurred as to which was the most important. Jack Kerouac, for example, was never wholly convinced by Zen, and ultimately opted for Christianity. Gary Snyder, on the other hand, mistrusted Christianity and has remained committed to Zen ever since. More attention will be paid to these matters as we proceed.

By way of an addendum to this summary, it should be acknowledged that Islam also has a richly spiritual tradition, especially that associated with Sufism. Sufis devote themselves to pursuing direct communion with Allah. They believe this to be possible in this life, whereas conventional Islam teaches that it is only possible after death and judgement. Sufism, then, would be a classic case of a spirituality which is rooted in a religion, but which reaches towards a mysticism which lies beyond orthodoxy. However, we will not be alluding any further to Islam in this study, for the simple reason that neither the three Beat writers who will provide our focus nor the songwriters who follow on from them show a particular interest in it.

*＊＊＊＊

Finally, I must briefly anticipate an objection to a twofold assumption of this book: that popular song is worth taking seriously, regardless of its status in our society as commercial entertainment, and that it is a valid medium for the exploration of the spiritual traditions outlined above. With regard to the first, I am trying to avoid the twin dangers of the academic approach to 'pop'. The first of these, associated with literary studies, is the dismissal of 'pop' as trivial and insubstantial: some readers may recall a longwinded debate some years ago, based on the motion that 'Dylan is not as good as Keats'. The second of these, associated with cultural studies, is the embrace of 'pop' as a subject worthy of investigation, but chiefly as a manifestation of what the philosopher Theodor Adorno called 'the culture industry'. The assumption here would be along the lines of 'Dylan is no better than Britney Spears', since they both are marketed within the same capitalist system. I am caricaturing both tendencies, of course: there are several shades in between the two extremes. However, what seems to be the case is that, apart from a brief vogue in the 1960s for celebrating 'the poetry of rock', it has habitually been thought to be naïve to attribute significance to the lyrics of popular songs, or to read them with the attention one would give a poem. Granted, there is a good case to be made for not analysing lyrics as words on the page, even if one admires them, since their poetry is a poetry of performance. However, I would defend the practice, given that meanings are often lost when one attends too closely to musicology. Sometimes, one has to ponder the subtleties of expression on the semantic level before restoring the text to its mode of delivery.

In the present context, that means taking into account a focus on spirituality – which in turn involves an awareness of the spiritual traditions outline above. Here we broach the other side of our twofold assumption: popular song as a means of exploring spiritual traditions. Those traditions are, as we have seen, broadly Eastern. The question, then, is: how far do songwriters who draw on them misrepresent them? That question is raised by John Hutnyk in his stimulating and challenging work, *Critique of Exotica*. There he queries the phenomenon of 'world music', relating it to the onset of economic 'globalisation'. Put starkly, his argument is that, from the Beatles to the present, the East has been appropriated, incorporated and so homogenised – its diversity being smoothed over in the interests of easy consumption. Discussing a 1990s band called Kula Shaker, which drew on Hindu myth and iconography, Hutnyk finds them guilty of 'the souveniring of sound and culture'. More broadly, he condemns 'the saccharine multiculturalism of the Global Jukebox'. Of all artists considered, he finds Madonna most culpable. Promotional videos for the album *Ray of Light* include 'decontextualised symbols of Hinduism floating in ethereal new age mush with embarrassingly clunky *bharatanatyam* dance imitations'.[18] Thus far, I am in agreement: the cynical opportunism of artists such as Madonna cannot be defended. However, I must demur when Hutnyk includes songwriters such as George Harrison in his critique, seeing him as merely representative of 'whiteness in crisis'.[19] It seems unfair to dismiss him in the same manner as one might (justifiably) dismiss Madonna. Even granted his initial sentimentalisation of the East, Harrison's work as a whole surely represents a sincere engagement with Indian culture (particularly music) and the Hindu religion (in which he was initiated). He did not earn the respect of the classical Indian musician and composer, Ravi Shankar, for nothing. But then again, according to the 'exotica' argument, Shankar himself would have to be found guilty of 'essentialising' his own tradition for Western consumption – no matter how 'authentic' his art might seem.

In citing Hutnyk's work, I am acknowledging its importance. Its challenge is an important one, and we must be careful not to take the Eastern 'turn' of popular song for granted. The present study is intended to provide some sort of context for it, in its discussion of the spiritual significance of the Beat movement. Ultimately, though, one has to decide whether to give it the benefit of the doubt or not. I would be inclined to do so; Hutnyk would not. He makes this clear in the following statement on the ideological alternatives available in the late 1960s:

If the counterculture movement was the exoticisation of the West by means of incense-burning easternisation, the threat to global capitalist power came in those days from the anti-imperialist struggle also most effectively articulated by Maoists in the East (and Black Panthers wielding little red books in East Compton). The East of the revolutionary movement was a rather different East than that admired by joss-stick poet Ginsberg and bed-protestor Lennon – one based on a long tradition of struggle and organisation, of dedicated fighters using whatever means necessary in the cause of throwing off the yoke of imperial power.[20]

Though he admits that the latter movements 'did not succeed in precipitating revolutions in the West', he nonetheless makes it clear that he regards them as having the advantage of political clarity and commitment. By contrast, the stance of Ginsbserg and Lennon seems to him to be vague and whimsical – and so condemned to futility. However, I would suggest that, bearing in mind the evils of Maoism and the 'revolutionary' cult of violence, readers might be prepared to give credence to the worldview represented by Ginsberg and Lennon, despite its absurdities and contradictions. The Beat vision and the Beat sound still have something to teach us.

Notes

1 I am aware that John Tytell takes Kerouac, Ginsberg and Burroughs to be kindred spirits, and that John Lardas considers them worth comparing and contrasting as spiritual writers, but I consider Burroughs' vision to be demonic rather than beatific. See John Tytell, *Naked Angels: Kerouac, Ginsberg, Burroughs* (New York: Grove Press, 1976); see John Lardas, *The Bop Apocalypse: The Religious Visions of Kerouac, Ginsberg, and Burroughs* (Illinois: Illinois University Press, 2001).
2 Jack Kerouac, 'Beatific: The Origins of the Beat Generation' (1959), in Ann Charters (ed.), *The Portable Jack Kerouac* (New York: Viking Penguin, 1995), p. 568.
3 Jack Kerouac, 'Lamb, No Lion', in *The Portable Jack Kerouac*, pp. 562–3.
4 Quoted in Stephen Prothero, 'Introduction', in Carole Tonkinson (ed.), *Big Sky Mind: Buddhism and the Beat Generation* (New York: Riverhead Books, 1995), p. 6.
5 Jack Kerouac, *Satori in Paris* (New York: Grove Press, 1966), p. 10.
6 Mircea Eliade, *The Sacred and the Profane: The Nature of Religion* (New York: Harcourt, 1959; 1987), pp. 11–12.
7 William Blake, 'Auguries of Innocence', in David V. Erdman and Harold Bloom (eds), *The Complete Poetry and Prose of William Blake* (New

York: Doubleday, 1988), p. 490. As Blake is quoted frequently during this book, his spelling has been amended whenever his use of capital letters might create confusion; capitals have been reserved where they seem to serve the function of emphasis.

8 Lardas, *The Bop Apocalypse*, p. 16.
9 Paul Heelas, *The New Age Movement: The Celebration of the Self and the Sacralization of Modernity* (Oxford: Blackwell, 1996), pp. 49–50.
10 Heelas, *The New Age Movement*, p. 50
11 Heelas, *The New Age Movement*, p. 49.
12 Thedore Roszak, *The Making of a Counter Culture: Reflections on the Technocratic Society and its Youthful Opposition* (London: Faber and Faber, 1970), pp. 82–3.
13 Victor Turner, *The Ritual Process: Structure and Anti-Structure* (Chicago: Aldine, 1969; 1997), pp. 112–13.
14 Allen Ginsberg, 'A Definition of the Beat Generation', *Deliberate Prose: Selected Essays 1952–1995* (New York: HarperCollins, 2000), p. 239.
15 Bruce Cook, *The Beat Generation* (New York: Charles Scribner's Sons, 1971), p. 223.
16 Timothy Freke, *Spiritual Traditions* (New York: Sterling Publishing Co., 2001), pp. 152–3. Further references to this edition are given after quotations in the text.
17 Eric Chaline, *The Book of Zen: The Path to Inner Peace* (Gloucester, MA: Fair Winds Press, 2003), pp. 46–59.
18 John Hutnyk, *Critique of Exotica: Music, Politics and the Culture Industry* (London: Pluto Press, 2000), pp. 88, 113 (note 35), 120.
19 Hutnyk, *Critique of Exotica*, p. 92.
20 Hutnyk, *Critique of Exotica* , pp. 183–4.

1 'This is IT':
Alan Watts and the visionary tradition

Western writers and artists have been looking to the East for inspiration since at least the eighteenth century. In the United States a decisive moment came in the middle of the nineteenth century when Ralph Waldo Emerson discovered the Hindu scriptures in translation, and conveyed his enthusiasm to his protégé, Henry David Thoreau. Both men became associated with the school of thought known as Transcendentalism, which effectively fused English Romanticism and Eastern mysticism. The Transcendentalists, as the name implies, thought of themselves as religious thinkers, not just literary writers or cultural commentators (though they were both of these). But it is significant that their idea of religion was formed mainly by their study of texts such as the Bhagavad Gita rather than the New Testament. Their preference for Hinduism over Christianity led to their being regarded as subversives, or even heretics. At best, they were accused of superficiality, of dabbling in Eastern thought instead of engaging with the profundities of the pilgrim fathers' favoured religion. In truth, they were not opposed to Christianity, but they objected to what they saw as the spiritual impoverishment fostered by the dominant church, namely the Unitarian – Emerson famously referring more than once to 'corpse-cold' Unitarianism. In discovering the potential in Hinduism, and in celebrating the idea that the sacred could be apprehended by letting go of dogma, they had a profound impact on the spirituality of the following century. Perhaps their most important influence – one that is routinely overlooked – was on the Beat movement.[1]

The mystical philosophy espoused in Emerson's essay, 'The Over-Soul' (1841) – which posited an affinity between humanity and divinity, with nature as the bridge – was particularly important. Here Eastern wisdom, particularly the speculations of Hinduism, is made accessible to educated North Americans in enthusiastic but elegant prose which is rhetorically very powerful:

> The Supreme Critic on the errors of the past and the present,
> and the only prophet of that which must be, is that great
> nature in which we rest, as the earth lies in the soft arms of the
> atmosphere; that Unity, that Over-soul, within which every
> man's particular being is contained and made one with all
> other; that common heart, of which all sincere conversation is
> the worship, to which all right action is submission; that
> overpowering reality which confutes our tricks and talents,
> and constrains every one to pass for what he is, and to speak
> from his character, and not from his tongue, and which
> evermore tends to pass into our thought and hand, and
> become wisdom, and virtue, and power, and beauty. We live
> in succession, in division, in parts, in particles. Meantime
> within man is the soul of the whole; the wise silence; the
> universal beauty, to which every part and particle is equally
> related; the eternal ONE.[2]

Never had the idea of the One been rendered so attractive to Western ears. Emerson made mystical experience seem the most natural thing in the world. Indeed, it is fitting that he should do so, as he had understood from his immersion in Hindu scriptures that the divine was perpetually manifesting itself in nature, if only we would open our eyes:

> And this deep power in which we exist, and whose beatitude is
> all accessible to us, is not only self-sufficing and perfect in every
> hour, but the act of seeing and the thing seen, the seer and the
> spectacle, the subject and the object, are one. We see the world
> piece by piece, as the sun, the moon, the animal, the tree; but
> the whole, of which these are the shining parts, is the soul.
> Only by the vision of that Wisdom can the horoscope of the
> ages be read, and by falling back on our better thoughts, by
> yielding to the spirit of prophecy which is innate in every man,
> we can know what it saith. Every man's words, who speaks
> from that life, must sound vain to those who do not dwell in
> the same thought on their own part. I dare not speak for it.
> My words do not carry its august sense; they fall short and
> cold. Only itself can inspire whom it will, and behold! their

speech shall be lyrical, and sweet, and universal as the rising
of the wind. Yet I desire, even by profane words, if I may not
use sacred, to indicate the heaven of this deity, and to report
what hints I have collected of the transcendent simplicity and
energy of the Highest Law.[3]

Note the implicit dialectic between the sacred and the profane realms,
which mysticism works to realise. Note too the trust in the power of
language to articulate the divine: even 'profane words' may communicate 'the Highest Law'.

There is a chapter in Thoreau's *Walden* (1854) entitled 'Higher
Laws', which may indicate the author's commitment to the Transcen-
dentalist ideal. Indeed, the book is an account of Thoreau's retreat into
rural solitude at Walden Pond in Massachusetts in order to live authentically and discover his spiritual being, which he had undertaken at the
instigation of Emerson himself. *Walden* celebrates the contemplation of
natural beauty and the giving-up of false, materialistic goals. It is
clearly informed by that reverence for Eastern wisdom which his
mentor had encouraged, as in the following passage:

I have read in a Hindoo [sic] book, that there was a king's son,
who, being expelled in infancy from his native city, was brought
up by a forester, and, growing up to maturity in that state,
imagined himself to belong to the barbarous race with which he
lived. One of his father's ministers having discovered him,
revealed to him what he was, and the misconception of his
character was removed, and he knew himself to be a prince. 'So
soul,' continues the Hindoo philosopher, 'from the circumstances in which it is placed, mistakes its own character, until
the truth is revealed to it by some holy teacher, and then it
knows itself to be Brahme [ie, Brahman].' I perceive that we
inhabitants of New England live this mean life that we do
because our vision does not penetrate the surface of things. ...
Men esteem truth remote, in the outskirts of the system, behind
the farthest star, before Adam and after the last man. In eternity
there is indeed something true and sublime. But all these times
and places and occasions are now and here. God himself culminates in the present moment, and will never be more divine in
the lapse of all the ages. And we are enabled to apprehend at
all what is sublime and noble only by the perpetual instilling
and drenching of the reality that surrounds us.[4]

Thoreau clearly follows on from Emerson, nowhere more so than in the ease with which he moves from esoteric wisdom to everyday reality. He accepts and extends Emerson's idea of nature as bridge between human and divine. The difference is that he has a much more practical interest in the ways of the natural world. That is, his 'theology of experience' is rooted in his response to his environment. One cannot imagine Emerson himself undertaking the kind of rural frugality of which *Walden* is largely a report. Nor would he have been capable of the book's close observation of the behaviour of animals, the appearance of trees, the sound of birds and so forth.

That said, we do need to acknowledge the influence of both writers on the Beats, even if Thoreau's seems the more obvious. In his account of the 'Beat spirit', Mel Ash asserts: 'Ridiculed in his time for his image of himself as a gigantic meditative "transparent eyeball" that saw and observed all without critical comment, Emerson prefigured the Beat / Buddhist alliance of a hundred years later and laid important groundwork for this very American tradition of questioning the unquestionable and shaking up "polite society".'[5] As for Thoreau, Ash provides more than enough evidence of his influence: 'Probably the most "Beat" of his time, eschewing formalities, disdaining "proper" appearance, dismissing money-based economy, avoiding most forms of "respectable" work and fascinated with nature, poetry and Eastern mysticism, Thoreau, like other early American Beats like Whitman, is now treasured as a national icon.'[6]

That other 'early American Beat' deserves a special mention. It is not only his own debt to Transcendentalism, and his own commitment to finding the sacred in the profane, that counts. It is also his audacious use of open form in verse, and his capacity to celebrate his own experience without inviting the charge of egotism. His poetry is paradoxically both highly personal and universal, both particular and general. This stems from his orientation towards mysticism, particularly nature mysticism. Here is the opening of 'Song of Myself' (1855), a definitive exposition of his 'theology of experience':

I celebrate myself, and sing myself,
And what I assume you shall assume,
For every atom belonging to me as good belongs to you.

I loafe and invite my soul,
I lean and loafe at my ease observing a spear of summer grass.
My tongue, every atom of my blood, form'd from this soil,
    this air,

Born here of parents born here from parents the same, and
    their parents the same,
I, now thirty-seven years old in perfect health begin,
Hoping to cease not till death.

Creeds and schools in abeyance,
Retiring back a while sufficed at what they are, but never
    forgotten,
I harbor for good or bad, I permit to speak at every hazard,
Nature without check with original energy.[7]

With such utterances in mind, we might concur with Ash's assessment
of the poet: 'Whitman is one of the primary Beat ancestors, a man who
eagerly embraced Eastern mysticism, refused gender roles, and advocated a wide-open political vision, all earmarks of Beat ethics.' Again:
'Whitman foresaw two roads for American culture, one lit by spirituality, art, literature, simplicity, loving comradeship, robust health, and
the other, he said, consisting of "solely materialistic bearings" that
must be firmly countered with the elimination of repressive Puritan
ideals.' Thus, Ash feels able to conclude: 'The Beats and their heirs of
the twentieth century stand in an unbroken line of descent from the
"Gentle Gray Bard" of New York, standing watch and calling alarm,
providing a corrective culture of resistance to the headlong rush to the
modern religion of "progress."'[8]
    If Whitman is the main literary ancestor of the Beats, and above all
of Ginsberg's, it is imperative that we do not infer from our first quotation that his stance is one of irresponsibility. Far from it: his repudiation of orthodox religion and his embrace of a new, free-flowing
spirituality involves a sustained engagement with the deeper currents of
Eastern mysticism. This is evident in the following lines from his
'Passage to India' (1870), which celebrates Hindu-Buddhist wisdom as
part and parcel of a North American revival of mysticism. It is in many
ways a poetic version of Emerson's 'Over-Soul':

O Thou transcendent!
Nameless—the fibre and the breath!
Light of the light—shedding forth universes—thou centre of
    them!
Thou mightier centre of the true, the good, the loving!
Thou moral, spiritual fountain! affection's source! thou
    reservoir! ...
Thou pulse! thou motive of the stars, suns, systems,

That, circling, move in order, safe, harmonious,
Athwart the shapeless vastnesses of space!
How should I think – how breathe a single breath – how speak
   if, out of myself,
I could not launch, to those, superior universes?[9]

Such confidence in the possibility of expanding vision, unfettered by dogma, was indispensable to the Beats. They learnt from Whitman how to open their minds to the possibilities of the cosmic Self, of the Atman which is also Brahman – or, to use an alternative vocabulary, to wake up to their Buddha-nature.

It was not Whitman, however, but Thoreau who proved to be the specific catalyst for Beat spirituality. In 1953, Jack Kerouac read *Walden*, and it stimulated him to seek out the Hindu scriptures for himself. However, at that time there was still considerable confusion in the West over the distinction between Hinduism and Buddhism (as there had been in the era of the Transcendentalists), so Kerouac ended up taking home Dwight Goddard's *A Buddhist Bible* (1932) from the library instead of the Upanishads. The significance of this moment should not be underestimated:

> Kerouac's reading of *Walden*, and later of Buddhist teachings,
> clearly marked a new era in his life, but it also marked a new
> era in the life of the nation, since Kerouac's awakening to
> Buddhism stirred similar searches in other members of the
> Beat Generation, and in the hippies of the sixties, thus helping
> to bend postwar counterculture eastward. Just as Kerouac, in
> a mood of desolation over a lost love and a large pile of
> unpublished manuscripts, had turned to Thoreau and to
> Buddhist texts, many young people, disenchanted with Cold
> War America and the atomic age issued in by World War II,
> sought solace in Kerouac's *The Dharma Bums* (1958). In turn,
> *The Dharma Bums* soon proved itself capable of marking new
> eras in individual lives, thus sparking something of the rucksack
> revolution of wondering 'Zen lunatics' that it had prophesied.[10]

Other writers associated with this spiritual turn were Allen Ginsberg, Gary Snyder, Philip Whalen and Anne Waldman. Essentially, each of these concurred with Kerouac when he declared: 'The Beat Generation is a religious generation.'[11] For example, Ginsberg defended the controversial title poem of *Howl and other poems* (1956) as a 'protest' in the original sense of 'pro-attestation, that is, testimony in favor of Value'. Of the volume as a whole, he simply said: 'The poems are religious and I meant them to be.'[12] As Stephen Prothero has stated: 'What united the work of the early Beats and defined them as a movement was not so much a common political stance or even a shared literary style but a distinctly spiritual quest for a "new consciousness".'[13]

Their chief resource on that quest was Buddhism, discovered accidentally by Kerouac and then conveyed to Ginsberg, but consciously sought out by Snyder. It would be misleading, however, to think of the Beats as focussing narrowly on one spiritual path. For they were prophetic in their very capacity to find good in each and every religion: without the Beats, we would not have, for good or ill, the spiritual eclecticism of the New Age. But unlike some of their imitators, they were serious and committed students. Kerouac, who was brought up a Roman Catholic, was deeply knowledgeable about Christianity, particularly its mystical dimension. Both Kerouac and Ginsberg, as students at Columbia University in the mid-forties, undertook the study of the Gnostic religion, which had overlapped with early Christianity. Ginsberg made a systematic study of Hinduism and Buddhism, not forgetting the Judaism of his own upbringing. Moreover, his devotion to the radical Christian poet, William Blake, necessitated his study of the mystical element in Christianity. Snyder, less interested than either Kerouac or Ginsberg in Christian salvation, was the Beat poet most strongly identified with Buddhism, even though he never lost his sympathy for both Hinduism and for Native American religion. He went so far as to spend several years in a Zen Buddhist monastery in Japan.

Zen it was that became popularly associated with the Beat movement, mainly because it was the focus of the novel by Kerouac already mentioned, *The Dharma Bums*, which centered on a fictional representation of Snyder's spiritual practice. But as we shall see in our discussion of Kerouac, there was by no means unanimous endorsement of Zen by all the Beats. True, Whalen was to become an initiate of the San Fransisco Zen Center; and Snyder remains a Zen practitioner at the time of writing. But though Zen certainly influenced Ginsberg's poetic technique, his interest in the philosophy was intermittent, and he made his vows as a Tibetan Buddhist in 1972. As for Kerouac, he was consistently and increasingly interested in Christianity, maintaining and deepening his dedication to the figures of Jesus and the Virgin Mary – preferring it finally to Buddhism, whether Zen, Tibetan or otherwise.

It is worth mentioning that Ginsberg and Kerouac were East Coast Beats, while Snyder and Whalen were West Coast Beats; and it was on the West Coast that Buddhism first established itself in the United States. Asian immigrants at the end of the nineteenth century brought a new religious awareness with them, and in their wake came Buddhist teachers such as D. T. Suzuki, a specialist in Zen. His hugely influential *An Introduction to Zen Buddhism*, based on articles published over the previous two decades, appeared in 1949 – just three years before Snyder came to settle in the San Francisco Bay area. Interest in Japanese culture had increased, ironically, as a result of the enforced American encounter with it in World War II, and the Beats – especially the West Coast Beats – were the main beneficiaries.

The Beat movement is, then, undoubtedly part of a general spiritual turn that took place in the middle of the twentieth century, while being hugely indebted to the example of the Transcendentalists, who made a similar turn a century earlier. We have noted that Emerson and Thoreau tended to equate spirituality with Eastern religion; however, both they and Whitman were deeply sympathetic to the spirit of early Christianity, and habitually invoked Jesus as a spiritual guide. For example, Emerson in 'The Over-Soul' writes: 'if [a man] would know what the great God speaketh, he must "go into his closet and shut the door", as Jesus said. … He must greatly listen to himself, withdrawing himself from all the accents of other men's devotion.'[14] The idea of invoking Jesus was to counter the dead weight of Christendom, which had distorted and reified his message, turning him into a reflection of its false social hierarchy:

> The position men have given to Jesus, now for many centuries
> of history, is a position of authority. It characterizes themselves.
> It cannot alter the eternal facts. Great is the soul, and plain. It
> is no flatterer, it is no follower; it never appeals from itself. It
> always believes in itself. … Behold, it saith, I am born into the
> great, the universal mind.[15]

Emerson's understanding that the essence of Christianity is mystical wisdom rather than theological doctrine, and that Jesus proclaimed the possibility of communing with the One, would certainly chime with the Beats' attitude. Giving their primary attention to Buddhism, they yet understood that what the philosopher Leibniz had called 'the perennial philosophy' – that central body of spiritual knowledge central to all religions – necessarily encompasses the resources of Christianity also.[16]

In this respect, they concurred also with Alan Watts. It is to his relationship with the Beats that we now turn.

*****

In the course of the summary of spiritual traditions in the Introduction,
having charted the turn to the East, and having made a synopsis of
Eastern religion, it seemed appropriate to recall that the dominant religion of North America, namely Christianity, has itself a rich mystical
tradition. We might go further now, and say that it overlaps at many
points with the philosophy of Hinduism, Buddhism, Taoism and Zen.
One man who was especially well placed to understand this was Alan
Watts (1915–73). An Englishman raised in the Anglican faith, he early
on developed an interest in Buddhism – though this did not prevent his
taking holy orders in the church. Thus we have the intriguing phenomenon of a Christian priest writing a book entitled *The Spirit of Zen* in
1935, when scarcely anybody in England had heard of Buddhism, let
alone Zen. More fascinating still is the fact that Watts eventually
settled in the United States and became, in turn, an Episcopalian minister and a founder member of the American Academy of Asian studies
in San Francisco in the early 1950s – Gary Snyder being one of his first
pupils. Not long after, Watts produced one of the most influential
studies in Eastern spirituality published in the twentieth century, *The
Way of Zen* (1957). It must have been read by Snyder, and therefore
must have had an impact on the other Beats, coming as it did just as
they were taking their turn to the East.

But an equally important book of his, published ten years previously, was *Behold the Spirit* (1947). The work of someone still broadly
committed to Christianity, it sought to recover the wisdom of Jesus
Christ, which Watts took to have been suppressed over the centuries by
the Christian church. Subtitled 'A Study in the Necessity of Mystical
Religion', it argues that early Christianity was mysticism pure and
simple, offering its followers a means to union with the Godhead, and
that much of the doctrine that later adhered to it was alien to its original formulation. As Emerson reacted against 'corpse-cold' Unitarianism, so Watts begins from the assumption that 'Church religion is
spiritually dead'. Its members require a much greater sense of fulfilment than they get from its vacuous moralising: 'They want God
himself by whatever name he may be called; they want to be filled with
his creative life and power; want some conscious experience of being at
one with Reality itself, so that their otherwise meaningless and

ephemeral lives may acquire an eternal significance.' There again, they 'cannot be expected to know that the Church has in its possession under lock and key (or maybe the sheer weight of persons sitting on the lid), the purest gold of mystical religion.'[17]

This determination to liberate the mysticism which lies at the heart of all great religions characterises Watts's career as a writer. Accused by many of being boundlessly eclectic, he insisted that each religion illuminated all the others, and that Christianity would benefit most from such comparative revelation. Certainly, it had nothing to fear, whatever his Episcopalian colleagues might have thought. At the same time, Watts was suspicious of those who were superficial in their approach to religion. A voracious scholar himself, albeit one capable of wearing his learning very lightly, he was interested in people who genuinely yearned to 'behold the spirit', not in people whose spirituality was subject to fashion. Yet it must be conceded that he himself was perhaps partially responsible for the modish approach to choosing a spiritual path which he saw developing in his later years.

In 1958, thanks largely to the efforts of Suzuki and of Watts, the spiritual path which was very much in vogue was that of Zen Buddhism. In that year, a special number of the *Chicago Review* appeared, entirely dedicated to the subject.[18] The Beats were well represented. The issue featured Kerouac's 'Meditation in the Woods', an extract from his new novel, *The Dharma Bums*. Again, though both Philip Whalen and Gary Snyder thought of themselves of that time as representatives of the San Francisco poetry scene rather than of a specific Beat movement, their inclusion along with Kerouac seemed appropriate. Whalen contributed a Zen-style poem, while Snyder contributed a description of life in a Japanese monastery. Heading the list of contents was an essay intriguingly entitled 'Beat Zen, Square Zen, and Zen'; its author was none other than Alan Watts. This essay was meant to be controversial – it queried the assumptions of the 'Beat' approach to Buddhism – but Watts could scarcely have predicted that it would still be a key reference point half a century later for debates about the way a 'counterculture' may appropriate Eastern religion. In a sense, we are still trying to catch up with it.

Scarcely had Watts seen his essay published in the *Chicago Review* than he felt that it needed expanding. He decided to incorporate some commentary on *The Dharma Bums*, which he had now had a chance to read, together with some general reflections about Zen and art. This expanded version appeared the following year as a pamphlet published, significantly, by City Lights Press: the same press as had

published Ginsberg's *Howl and other poems*, and which was closely
identified with the Beat movement. It was this version that Watts chose
to reprint in a subsequent volume of essays. The title of that volume
was *This is IT and Other Essays on Zen and Spiritual Experience*.[19] We
will return to that title in due course, to register its significance.

It is interesting to note that in the short prefatory statement which
Watts provided for the reprint, he went out of his way to emphasise
that the essay was not written from any official position. In particular,
he denied that he was a representative of 'square' Zen, as had been
suggested by at least one commentator. The fact that Watts, regarded
in orthodox Buddhist circles as a vulgar populariser, felt obliged to
deny that he was a traditionalist only conveys the confusion and
controversy surrounding the Zen influence at that time. Watts himself
could not be clearer:

> [I]n matters of this kind, I am temperamentally not a joiner.
> I do not even style myself a Zen Buddhist. The aspect of Zen
> in which I am personally interested is nothing that can be
> organised, taught, transmitted, certified, or wrapped up in any
> kind of system. (p. 79)

Of course, in making this statement, he runs the risk of appearing to
identify with the spirit of 'beat' Zen – which the original essay queries
as much as it does that of 'square' Zen. (Watts, it should be pointed
out, always uses lower case for both terms.)

There again, the premiss of the essay is that Zen is so beautifully
simple that it is bound to invite competing interpretations. On the one
hand, there will be those who yearn for the strict ritual and rules of
formal Japanese Zen. On the other hand, there will be those who
cannot believe their luck, as the Zen ideal of spontaneity seems to offer
them an excuse for avoiding all restraints. He invokes the earlier
Chinese form of Zen to make his point, emphasising that its natural-
ness should not be confused with irresponsibility:

> How remote from the regimen of the Japanese Zen monastery
> are the words of the great T'ang master Lin-chi:
>
> > In Buddhism there is no place for using effort. Just be
> > ordinary and nothing special. Eat your food, move your
> > bowels, pass water, and when you're tired go and lie down.
> > The ignorant will laugh at me, but the wise will understand.
>
> Yet the spirit of these words is just as remote from a kind of

Western Zen which would employ this philosophy to justify a very self-defensive bohemianism. (p. 84)

Watts has to strike a very delicate balance throughout the essay, differentiating carefully between true Zen and the uses to which it is put. But what is 'true Zen'? Already we have seen Watts imply that it is not the excessive formality of the Japanese development of the practice which is best imported, but rather the original Chinese Zen or 'Ch'an'. Moreover, just as the latter's sense of organic spontaneity gives it an advantage over the self-conscious, almost neurotic, codification which subsequently took place in Japan, so does 'Ch'an' offer a corrective to earlier, ascetic systems, whether Buddhist or Hindu:

> Here is a view of the world imparting a profoundly refreshing
> sense of wholeness to a culture in which the spiritual and
> material, the conscious and the unconscious, have been
> cataclysmically split. For this reason the Chinese humanism
> and naturalism of Zen intrigue us much more strongly than
> Indian Buddhism or Vedanta. ... The ideal man of Indian
> Buddhism is clearly a superman, a yogi with absolute mastery
> of his own nature, according perfectly with the science-fiction
> ideal of 'men beyond mankind.' But the Buddha or awakened
> man of Chinese Zen is 'ordinary and nothing special'; he is
> humorously human like the Zen tramps portrayed by Mu-ch'i
> and Liang-k'ai. (p. 86)

That would seem to justify 'beat' Zen, rather more than 'square', perhaps. But we must not jump to conclusions.

For Watts's next point is that the distinction between 'beat' and 'square' is itself symptomatic of the wrong approach to Zen. It is necessary to avoid misreading it in terms of a false dichotomy:

> [But] the Westerner who is attracted by Zen and who would
> understand it deeply must have one indispensable qualification:
> he must understand his own culture so thoroughly that he is no
> longer swayed by its premises unconsciously. ... He must be
> free of the itch to justify himself. Lacking this, his Zen will be
> either 'beat' or 'square', either a revolt from the culture and
> social order or a new form of stuffiness and respectability. For
> Zen is above all the liberation of the mind from conventional
> thought, and this is something utterly different from rebellion

against convention, on the one hand, or adapting foreign conventions, on the other. (p. 90)

For Watts, true Zen takes us beyond the two complementary errors of the self-conscious rejection of rules and the self-conscious adherence to rules. It avoids the extremes of 'square' Zen (religion without spirituality) and of 'beat' Zen (spirituality as fashion or opportunism). He turns his attention now to the nature of 'beat' Zen, seeking to do justice to the intentions of those writers associated with it, but reserving his right to criticise Kerouac in particular for his rather cavalier approach:

> Beat Zen is a complex phenomenon. It ranges from a use of Zen for justifying sheer caprice in art, literature, and life to a very forceful social criticism and 'digging of the universe' such as one may find in the poetry of Ginsberg, Whalen, and Snyder, and, rather unevenly, in Kerouac, who is always a shade too self-conscious, too subjective, and too strident to have the flavor of Zen. When Kerouac gives his philosophical final statement, 'I don't know. I don't care. And it doesn't make any difference' – the cat is out of the bag, for there is a hostility in these words which clangs with self-defence. But just because Zen truly surpasses convention and its values, it has no need to say 'To hell with it,' nor to underline with violence the fact that anything goes. (p. 92)

Being self-consciously and defiantly unconventional is no more representative of true Zen than is obsessive adherence to form.

The Beat writer whom Watts regards as the most important exception to the trend which he sees represented by Kerouac is Gary Snyder. Indeed, claims Watts, to appreciate his authenticity one has to disassociate the man himself from his fictional depiction by that other Beat:

> It is generally known that *The Dharma Bums* is not a novel, but a flimsily fictionalized account of the author's experiences in California in 1956. To anyone who knows the milieu described, the identity of each character is plain and it is no secret that Japhy Ryder, the hero of the story, is Gary Snyder. Whatever may be said of Kerouac himself and of a few other characters in the story, it would be difficult indeed to fit Snyder into any stereotype of the Bohemian underworld. He has spent

a year of Zen study in Kyoto, and has recently (1959) returned for another session, perhaps for two years this time. (p. 100)

In short, 'Snyder is, in the best sense, a bum' (p. 100). He encapsulates the spirit of liberation, which is Zen – beyond 'beat' or 'square' distortions.

But Watts is determined to play fair, and he has no sooner queried Kerouac's intentions than he makes a generous concession:

In *The Dharma Bums*, however, we are seeing Snyder through Kerouac's eyes, and some distortions arise because Kerouac's own Buddhism is a true beat Zen which confuses 'anything goes' at the existential level with 'anything goes' on the artistic and social levels. Nevertheless, there is something endearing about Kerouac's personality as a writer, something which comes out in the warmth of his admiration for Gary, and in the lusty, generous enthusiasm for life which wells up at every point in his colourful and undisciplined prose. This exuberant warmth makes it impossible to put Kerouac in the class of the beat mentality described by John Clelland-Holmes – the cool, fake-intellectual hipster searching for kicks, namedropping bits of Zen and jazz jargon to justify a disaffiliation from society which is in fact just ordinary, callous exploitation of other people. (p. 101)

Though Watts may seem to damn Kerouac with faint praise here, it is important to recognise that his true target is not so much the Beat writers as the gathering of 'beatniks' which surrounds them. The word 'beatnik', a coinage of the late 1950s derived from the Russian spacecraft, Sputnik, was already being used widely, and here Watts cannot resist it. Referring to 'a number of weak imitators and hangers-on' who are seeking justification for a 'shiftless existence', he sees their behaviour as countenancing 'the stereotype of the "beatnik," with his phony Zen' (p. 99). This is a point Watts confirms in a talk given on the radio in 1959, in which he distinguishes between the Beat movement proper and the superficial scene surrounding it. He does so in such a way as to vindicate the former:

[If] you set out to do what you really want to do, you may lose a lot of friends but you will not lose a single friend who is worth having. In the same way, a movement like the Beat [sic] way of life, for instance, or one interested in Oriental

philosophy may be made vulnerable to ridicule because of its
hangers-on, but they will not do it any real harm, and they will
not lose it any friends worth having.[20]

To return to Watts's main essay: no sooner has Watts offered his
damning characterisation of a current trend which justifies itself as an
extension of the 'beat' ideal, than he feels obliged to note the complementary error encouraged by the 'square' camp. He is being very
careful to maintain a judicious stance:

> If square Zen falls into any serious excess it is in the direction
> of spiritual snobbism and artistic preciousness, though I have
> never known an orthodox Zen teacher who could be accused of
> either. These gentlemen seem to take their exalted office rather
> lightly, respecting its dignity without standing on it. The faults
> of square Zen are the faults of any spiritual in-group with an
> esoteric discipline and degrees of initiation. (p. 104)

Being 'temperamentally not a joiner', of course, Watts is perhaps being
as much sceptical as judicious; but it is difficult to fault his logic, either
here or elsewhere in the essay.

Certainly, he succeeds in steering a middle way between extremes –
appropriately enough, in this Buddhist context – in approaching his
conclusion. He suggests that the dialogue between the two Western
variants on Zen may yet prove fruitful, if we are prepared to make
allowances:

> Indeed, it is possible that beat Zen and square Zen will so
> complement and rub against one another that an amazingly
> pure and lively Zen will arise from the hassle. For this reason I
> see no really serious quarrel with either extreme. There was
> never a spiritual movement without its excesses and distortions.
> The experience of awakening which truly constitutes Zen is too
> timeless and universal to be injured. The extremes of beat Zen
> need alarm no one since, as Blake said, 'the fool who persists in
> his folly will become wise.' As for square Zen, 'authoritative'
> spiritual experiences have always had a way of wearing thin,
> and thus of generating the demand for something genuine and
> unique which needs no stamp. (p. 106)

Interestingly, the appeal to Blake here would tend to put him in the company of the Beats, for whom the great Romantic poet was not only a model of an artistic visionary but something of a spiritual authority. Not that Watts could ever be accused of relying on authorities. More frequently, his way of resolving an issue is to use humour and paradox – typical Zen tactics. Here he rounds off his argument by invoking a principle which Zen took up from Taoism: *wu-shih*, 'nothing special' or 'no fuss'. For 'no fuss' inevitably suggests its contrary:

> But Zen is 'fuss' when it is mixed up with Bohemian affectations, and 'fuss' when it is imagined that the only proper way to find it is to run off to a monastery in Japan or to do special exercises in the lotus posture for five hours a day. And I will admit that the very hullabaloo about Zen, even in such an essay as this, is also fuss – but a little less so. Having said that, I would like to say something for all Zen fussers, beat or square. Fuss is all right, too. If you are hung on Zen, there's no need to try to pretend that you're not. If you really want to spend some years in a Japanese monastery, there is no earthly reason why you shouldn't. Or if you want to spend your time hopping freight cars and digging Charlie Parker, it's a free country.
>
> In the landscape of spring there is neither better nor worse;
> The flowering branches grow naturally, some long,
>   some short. (pp. 109–10)

Finally, then, the Beats are vindicated, or at least excused. Yes, they are guilty as charged, of committing the error of self-conscious spirituality; but for them to start worrying about whether this offends against Zen would only be a greater offence against Zen. So let the Beat branch flower in its own sweet way.

                                                    * * * * *

Throughout his essay, 'Beat Zen, Square Zen, and Zen', Watts makes a show of his impartiality. One cannot help but suspect, however, that his invective against Kerouac, even while being qualified by his comments about Kerouac's relationship with Snyder, is not wholly disinterested. Perhaps *The Dharma Bums* itself offers a clue. Towards the end of the novel, during the description of the party given for Japhy Ryder (the fictional equivalent of Gary Snyder), there is a cameo appearance by one Arthur Whane (the fictional equivalent of Alan

Watts), a self-proclaimed expert on Buddhism. The party is taking place both inside and outside of a friend's rural shack. Outside there is a bonfire, towards which the narrator, Ray Smith, wanders in the course of the evening:

> Arthur Whane was sitting on a log, well-dressed, necktie and suit, and I went over and asked him 'Well, what is Buddhism? Is it fantastic imagination magic of the lightning flash, is it plays, dreams, not even plays, dreams?'
>
> 'No, to me Buddhism is getting to know as many people as possible.' And there he was going around the party real affable shaking hands with everybody and chatting, a regular cocktail party.[21]

It is hard to believe that Watts would not have been piqued by this depiction, as Kerouac is implying that he is something of a spiritual charlatan. Perhaps the expanded version of 'Beat Zen, Square Zen, and Zen' is Watts's spirited rejoinder.

For the irony is that just as Watts expressed doubts about the Beats' spiritual authenticity, so would others express doubts about his – especially regarding the work done during the 1960s. He came to favour a playful, provocative style of writing, which effortlessly incorporated elements from all the major religions. Effortlessness – lack of 'fuss' – was the key. For Watt's persistent theme was the absurdity of trying, or even wanting, to reach a state of enlightenment. For to set out towards a goal is to be trapped in two prisons: that of the ego and that of time. Hence in his preface to *This is IT* he explains its title as follows:

> [T]he essays here gathered together have a common point of focus – the spiritual or mystical experience and its relation to ordinary material life. Having said this, I am instantly aware that I have used the wrong words; and yet there are no satisfactory alternatives. Spiritual and mystical suggest something rarefied, otherworldly, and loftily religious, opposed to an ordinary material life which is simply practical and commonplace. The whole point of these essays is to show the fallacy of this opposition, to show that the spiritual is not to be separated from the material, nor the wonderful from the ordinary. We need, above all, to disentangle ourselves from habits of speech and thought which set the two apart, making it impossible for us to see that *this* – the immediate, everyday, and

present experience – is IT, the entire and ultimate point for the
existence of a universe.

As his friend Krishnamurti would put it: 'Truth is a pathless land.'[22]
Enlightenment is here and now: what prevents us achieving it is our
desire to get from where we are to some perfect state that lies some-
where ahead of us. No wonder Watts was so scathing about both
'square' Zennists and the beatniks who attached themselves to the Beat
scene, given their insistence on going through the motions of Zen
without seeing what was already there, right in front of their eyes. If
his critique seemed harsh, it was (he would surely say in retrospect)
because he wanted them to wake up and stop acting out a pseudo-
spiritual dream.

As Watts worked out the implications of his insight, his mode of
expression became more and more audacious. A typical title is *The
Book: On the Taboo Against Knowing Who You Are* (1966). A typical
pronouncement is that made in the preface of that work:

> This book explores an unrecognized but mighty taboo – our
> tacit conspiracy to ignore who, or what, we really are. Briefly,
> the thesis is that the prevalent sensation of oneself as a separate
> ego enclosed in a bag of skin is a hallucination which accords
> neither with Western science nor with the experimental
> philosophy-religions of the East – in particular the central and
> germinal Vedanta philosophy of Hinduism. This hallucination
> underlies the misuse of technology for the violent subjugation
> of man's natural environment and, consequently, its eventual
> destruction.[23]

One should not overlook the serious point Watts is making here about
the relationship between the illusion of the separate, substantial self
and the exploitation of the earth. One might yet demur, however, about
his appropriation of religious concepts. If pressed as to whether his
position was Hindu, Buddhist or Christian, Watts became increasingly
evasive. What he was after was a sense of the spirit, not membership
of any religious organisation. But people could be forgiven for wonder-
ing whether he was entitled to be so high-handed in his random appropriation of ideas.

Watts addressed this very question in his autobiography, written in
1972 and published the following year, that of his death. He is here
reflecting on his relationship with the Beat movement and with the
counterculture generally:

What we were doing in San Francisco in the 1950s must,
of course, be seen in the context of America's military
involvements in Japan, Korea, and then Vietnam, for these
exploits were bound to bring the cultures of those areas back
home. My own interest in this cultural encounter was peculiar,
in the sense that I was not simply a fact-seeker, like a historian
or journalist, nor a missionary trying to convert Westerners to
Buddhism, though I have been taken for that. No one, however,
has ever accused me of being a scholarly Orientalist.
I am more often considered a popularizer of Zen, Vedanta,
and Taoism, who often twists the facts to suit his own views.[24]

It is as if Watts knew how to criticise his own methodology long before
any commentator attempted to do so. His capacity for self-awareness
is exemplified here by his detailed consideration of the twofold case
against himself:

One reason for this impression [of being a populariser] is that
my style of writing does not lend itself to the tortuous course of
interminable qualifications, reservations, and drawing of fine
distinctions. But I am well aware of them when I leave them
out, and can (and do) refer those who want the fine points to
the proper sources, and can, furthermore, produce the necessary
scholarly evidence for my conclusions if asked. Another is that I
am not interested in studying, say, Buddhism in terms of what
most Buddhists think about it – that is, as an anthropological
phenomenon. I am interested in the work of those who are, and
have been, its most creative exponents, and, above all, in the
actual nature of the inner experiences which they describe. ...
It is [therefore] believed in some circles that I have seriously
misrepresented Zen by failing to bring out, and indeed even
questioning, the importance of the discipline of za-zen – or
sitting in meditation for long hours – as the royal road to
Buddhist enlightenment.[25]

Perhaps the most interesting aspect of such moments of reflection is
Watts's ability and willingness to defend himself with ease against
charges that might appear to be similar to those he levelled at the Beat
writers. With the wisdom of hindsight, he is able to see how close he
must have seemed to them, despite his strictures:

It is therefore also said – perhaps with truth – that my easy
and free-floating attitude to Zen was largely responsible for
the notorious 'Zen boom' which flourished among artists and
'pseudo-intellectuals' in the late 1950s, and led on to the
frivolous 'beat Zen' of Kerouac's *Dharma Bums*, of Franz
Kline's black and white abstractions, and of John Cage's silent
concerts. From the beginning, I was never interested in being
'good at Zen' in the sense of mastering a traditional discipline,
as for example, in studying the piano with Schnabel to the
point where my recordings of the Beethoven sonatas would be
indistinguishable from his. ... What I was after was, therefore,
not so much discipline as understanding ...[26]

The Beats might have said as much themselves in their own defence.

At about the same time that Watts was setting down his recollections of the counterculture, Theodore Roszak published his account of
its origins. It is interesting to note that *The Making of a Counter
Culture* includes a chapter entitled 'Journey to the East ... and Points
Beyond: Allen Ginsberg and Alan Watts'. Taking his assessment of the
former first, but keeping Watts always in mind, we may note that he
explicitly defends Ginsberg, and therefore the phenomenon of 'beat'
Zen, from the charge of spiritual insensitivity:

Perhaps what the young took Zen to be has little relationship
to that venerable and elusive tradition; but what they readily
adopted was a gentle and gay rejection of the positivistic and
the compulsively cerebral. It was the beginning of a youth
culture that continues to be shot through with the spontaneous
urge to counter the joyless, rapacious, and egomaniacal order
of our technological society. This is another way of saying that,
after a certain point, it becomes little better than pedantic to
ask how authentically 'Buddhist' a poem like Ginsberg's
Sunflower Sutra (1955) is. Perhaps not very. But it is a poem
of great tenderness, expressing an unashamed wonder for
the commonplace splendors of the world. It asserts a sensibility
that calls into question the anthropocentric arrogance with
which our society has gone about mechanizing and brutalizing
its environment in the name of progress. And it is a
commentary on the state of what our society regards as its
'religion' that the poet who still commands the greatest
attention among our youth should have had to cast about for

such an exotic tradition from which to take inspiration in expressing these beautifully humane sentiments.[27]

Unfortunately, Roszak does not attempt to elucidate the poem referred to, so we should add the following information. Included in the controversial *Howl and other poems*, it is based on William Blake's 'Ah! Sunflower'. That poem meant a great deal to Ginsberg, who claimed to have had the auditory hallucination of hearing Blake himself read it aloud – what he referred to thereafter as his 'Blake vision'.[28] The very title, 'Sunflower Sutra', fuses the poetic canon of the West (Blake is the first great Romantic) with the religious philosophy of the East ('sutra' is a Buddhist term for a sermon). It celebrates natural beauty, which becomes the more intense in the context of the degradation of the manmade environment: 'and the gray Sunflower poised against the sunset, crackly bleak and dusty with the smut and smiled and smog and smoke of olden locomotives in its eye ...'[29] Posterity has favoured this poem, which has become a classic example of locating the sacred in the profane. It confirms Kerouac's ideal of conveying 'religious reverence' for 'real life'. It is, in short, a striking instance of the 'Beat vision' as 'beatific vision', with which we are concerned throughout this study, and which we will be clarifying further in the next chapter.

Roszak's defence of Ginsberg might have seemed indulgent to those who were still suspicious of the Beats at the time he wrote, but it is worth noting that of the two figures whom he celebrates for taking a 'Journey to the East' it is Watts whom he acknowledges as the more significant, even though he assumes he is open to the same kind of charges as are levelled at the Beats:

> Of the two, I think it is Watts whose influence has been the more widespread, for often at the expense of risking vulgarization, he has made the most determined effort to translate the insights of Zen and Taoism into the language of Western science and psychology. He has approached his task with an impish willingness to be catchy and cute, and to play at philosophy as if it were an enjoyable game. It is a style easily mistaken for flippancy, and it has exposed him to a deal of rather arrogant criticism: on the one hand from elitist Zen devotees who have found him too discursive for their mystic tastes (I recall one such telling me smugly, 'Watts has never experienced satori'), and on the other hand from professional philosophers who have been inclined to ridicule him for his

popularizing bent as being, in the words of one academic, 'The Norman Vincent Peale of Zen.'[30]

Norman Vincent Peale was a minister in the Dutch Reformed Church who regularly broadcast his sermons on radio and television; he was the most effective populariser of Christianity in the USA at that time apart from Billy Graham. The author of the best-selling book, *The Power of Positive Thought* (1952), which endorsed the Christian message as a means of improving one's quality of life, he was a pioneer of spiritual self-help. Roszak's point is that for Watts to be compared with him is to be accused of superficiality and opportunism.

However, as Roszak has already hinted, he regards such a comparison as unfair. His real doubts are not about Watts's apparent lack of academic rigour but about the kind of people who do not approve of Watts:

It is the typical and inevitable sort of resistance anyone
encounters when he makes bold to find a greater audience for
an idea than the academy or any restricted cult can provide –
and it overlooks the fact that Watts' books and essays include
such very solid intellectual achievements as *Psychotherapy East
And West*. Too often such aristocratic stricture comes from
those who have risen above popularization by the device of
restricting themselves to a subject matter that preserves its
purity only because it has no conceivable relevance to anything
beyond the interests of a small circle of experts.[31]

Roszak is determined to make a case for Watts – also for Ginsberg – as a proponent of a genuine, if unorthodox, spirituality. The point to note, in the light of our previous discussion, is that Ginsberg the Beat poet and Watts the popularising theorist of religion are taken to be speaking the same language – suspect to some, but most welcome to Roszak, advocate of the counterculture.

In fact, Watts and the Beats were to grow very close throughout the 1960s. Having made his corrective to 'beat' Zen, Watts was not anxious to alienate potential allies in his campaign to spread his wide-ranging, cross-cultural, trans-religious message. His retrospective assessment of the Beat writers in his autobiography is positively benign. Thinking of 1960 as a particularly significant year, he recalls:

[I]t will be remembered that this was when – in San Francisco
in particular – there were the first signs of an astonishing

change of attitude among young people which, despite its
excesses and self-caricatures, had spread far over the world
by the end of the decade. In a way, it started with the Beat
Generation, and though I appear under a pseudonym in
Kerouac's *Dharma Bums*, Jano [Watts's wife] and I were *in* this
milieu rather than *of* it, and I was somewhat severe with it in
my essay *Beat Zen, Square Zen, and Zen* which had appeared
in the *Chicago Review* in 1958. But Jack Kerouac, Lawrence
Ferlinghetti, and especially Gary Snyder and Allen Ginsberg,
were now among our friends. Jack – a second Thomas Wolfe –
was a warm and affectionate dog who eventually succumbed
to the bottle, but the others were more serious artists and,
speaking at least of Gary and Allen, more disciplined yogis.[32]

With Kerouac having been benignly put in his place, Watts proceeds to
celebrate Ginsberg in particular:

Allen is a rabbinic *sadhu* who can at need transform himself
into an astute and hardheaded lawyer, and only this
combination of fearless holiness, blazing compassion, and
clear intellect has prevented him from being jailed or shot
long ago. There was a night in Gavin's apartment when we
chanted sutras together for hours, Allen ringing the time
with his little Indian finger-cymbals, and through this purely
sonic communion, with the glee that Allen puts into it, we
somehow reached each other more deeply than in verbal
exchanges. There was a time, too, when we chanted the
Dharani of the Great Compassionate One all the way down
New York's Second Avenue in a Volkswagen bus.[33]

Watts increasingly shared Ginsberg's tendency to showmanship,
though he never committed himself to any of the numerous political
causes which the poet advocated and supported – for example, the
resistance to the Vietnam War, or the defence of the environment
against capitalist exploitation and pollution. That, of course, is not to
say that he did not care about the latter: we have only to think of the
preface to *The Book*, quoted earlier.

Indeed, it was his insight that a genuine spirituality has ecological
implications, and that concern for the earth should be central to one's
writing, that makes his affinity with Snyder seem so appropriate. As we
know from the 'Beat Zen' essay, he was particularly impressed by

Snyder early on, exempting him from the judgement he made of the Beats generally. Snyder seemed to him to have truly internalised Zen rather than adopted its vocabulary for effect, as Kerouac seemed to him to have done. More generally, as became evident in the sixties, we can see their affinity quite clearly. For, just as Watts was no respecter of religious tradition wherever it sought to repress mystical wisdom, so Snyder did not let his own Buddhist faith prevent him from criticising Buddhism. There is a striking moment in his poem, 'Mother Earth: Her Whales': 'And Japan quibbles for words on / what kinds of whales they can kill? / A once-great Buddhist nation / dribbles methyl mercury / like gonorrhea / in the sea.'[34] Such moments are substantiated by several prose statements, notably this paragraph from Snyder's essay, 'Buddhism and the Possibilities of a Planetary Culture':

> Historically, Buddhist philosophers have failed to analyze out the degree to which ignorance and suffering are caused or encouraged by social factors, considering fear and desire to be given facts of the human condition. Consequently the major concern of Buddhist philosophy is epistemology and 'psychology', with no attention paid to historical or sociological problems. … Institutional Buddhism has been conspicuously ready to accept or ignore the inequalities and tyrannies of whatever political system it found itself under. This can be death to Buddhism, because it is death to any meaningful function of compassion. Wisdom without compassion feels no pain.[35]

It will be evident from this, a representative quotation, that we cannot simply identify Gary Snyder with Japhy Ryder, the fictional version of him offered by Kerouac in *The Dharma Bums*. There, Ryder/Snyder is presented as largely indifferent to the imperative of compassion. In fact, Snyder's use of his talents as a Buddhist has meant an expansion of concern, taking in people and planet alike. Again, this has involved action as well as words – a move which Watts never favoured. But the common interest evident in their writings is certainly to honour nature as sacred, and to query any religion which fails to do so. In this sense, too, their vision is ultimately non-Biblical, insofar as the account of creation in the Book of Genesis is habitually read as sanctioning human domination over the earth.[36] Watts, however, is more sympathetic to Christianity than is Snyder, as he finds its hidden, mystical wisdom congenial.

With Watts becoming more and more sympathetic to both Ginsberg and Snyder, he was now genuinely open to the legacy of the Beat writers, manifest in the 1960s. Like them, he was even willing to acknowledge a genuine advance, simultaneously spiritual and social. In short, he welcomed the move from a minority subculture to a mass counterculture:

The Beat Generation was aggressively dowdy and slovenly, and lacked *gaiete d'esprit*. Patrons of the Coexistence Bagel Shop on Grant Avenue went about in shaggy blue jeans with their feet bare and grimy and their hair in pony-tails, and over-use of marijuana made them withdrawn and morose, even if internally beatific. (The style appeared again at the end of the decade, after the collapse of Haight-Ashbury and the dispersion of the Flower Children.) But in the circles in which we were then moving – in San Francisco, Los Angeles, and New York – something else was on the way, in religion, in music, in ethics and sexuality, in our attitudes to nature, and in our whole style of life. We took courage and began to swing. For there was an energy in the air that cannot entirely be attributed to the revelations of LSD, an energy which manifested itself on the surface as color and imagination in clothing, in a rebirth of poetry, in the rhythms of rock-and-roll and in fascination for Hindu music, in social gatherings where people were no longer afraid to touch one another and show affection (so that even men greeted one another with embraces), and in a general letting down of hair, both figurative and literal. One by one I watched this change coming over my friends as if they had been initiated into a mystery and were suddenly 'in the know' about something not expressly defined.[37]

Watts goes on to offer a catalogue of the phenomena that struck him as significant. Taking 1960 as his signpost, he reflects:

This was before the founding of Esalen in Big Sur and the proliferation of growth centers, before the Hippies and the Flower Children and the great days of the *San Francisco Oracle*, before Maharishi Mahesh turned on the Beatles to Transcendental Meditation, before Bob Dylan brought serious poetry back into popular music, and before Timothy Leary and Richard Alpert scared Harvard and the nation at large with LSD and the slogan, 'Turn on, tune in, and drop out.'[38]

He is sketching a broad change of consciousness, but not entirely a random one. He seems to believe that the Beats opened what Blake had called 'the doors of perception' – an act which proved decisive for the *Zeitgeist.*

Blake's phrase comes from his *Marriage of Heaven and Hell* (1793), which gave Aldous Huxley the title for his account of his experience with psychedelic drugs.[39] It was then left to Leary to come up with the idea that LSD could save the United States from terminal materialism and militarism. If enough people took the drug, the American consumer culture and the Vietnam War would both become unnecessary.[40] While Watts includes this campaign in his catalogue of shifting consciousness, quoted above, his own attitude to drugs was ambivalent. In *The Joyous Cosmology* (1962), he advocated LSD as a potential cure for the malaise of modernity; but as the decade came to its close, and as he saw the consequences of widespread drug consumption in the Haight-Ashbury area and elsewhere, he decided that Leary's optimism was unfounded.[41]

Nevertheless, Watts was, on the whole, very willing to be identified with the counterculture generally, and especially with those Beats who embraced it. In January 1967, he agreed to participate in an event announced as a 'Human Be-In', staged in Park Stadium, San Francisco. The announcement in the *Berkeley Barb* read as follows:

> The spiritual revolution will be manifest and proven. In
> unity we shall shower the country with waves of ecstasy and
> purification. Fear will be washed away; ignorance will be
> exposed to sunlight; profits and empire will lie drying on desert
> beaches; violence will be submerged and transmuted to rhythm
> and dancing.[42]

Watts's biographer describes the event:

> On the morning of January 14, Snyder, Ginsberg, Watts,
> and others performed *pradakshina*, a Hindu rite of
> circumambulation at the polo field. It was a fine day, and
> from early in the morning people began walking from all over
> the city toward the meadow. Tens of thousands were there,
> some with banners, some in robes and exotic clothing, others in
> denims. ... Speakers, rock bands, and Shunryu Suzuki-roshi of
> the San Francisco Zen Temple meditating on the platform and
> holding up a flower passed the afternoon. ... At sunset Gary

Snyder blew on a conch shell, Allen Ginsberg led a chant, and
the crowd drifted away, some of them to build fires, chant, and
pray on Ocean Beach. An unexpected spin-off from the Be-In
was the comment of Police Chief Thomas Cahill. 'You're sort of
the love generation, aren't you?" he asked a delighted group
from the Haight, a title which was instantly claimed.[43]

Disillusionment with the 'love generation' was soon to follow,
however, as the drug culture escalated, becoming corrupt, sordid and
destructive. But despite his own disaffection from Leary's propaganda,
Watts continued until his death in 1973 to celebrate the idea of a new
age, involving a radical shift in consciousness, quite other than the cult
of material 'improvement'.

In a journal entry entitled 'What On Earth Are We Doing?', written
in October 1971, and included in his penultimate book, *Cloud-
Hidden, Whereabouts Unknown* (published 1974), Watts declared:

I simply do not understand the goals and rewards of the
Western Way of Life, apart from such side-effects of the project
as anesthesia for dentistry (which can just as well be effected by
hypnosis). What is the point of Progress if the food is tasteless,
the housing absurd, the clothing uncomfortable, the religion
just talk, the air poisoned by Cadillacs, the work boring, the
sex uptight and mechanical, the earth clobbered with concrete,
and the water so chemicalized that even the fish are abandoning
existence?[44]

These questions all pointed to the answer that he consistently gave:
that the main spiritual challenge was to stop looking forward to
salvation in the future and to stop seeking God in the beyond: indeed,
to stop wanting anything at all. For that would be to remain trapped
inside the desiring, restless ego, rather than to realise that 'I' am
inseparable from 'IT': nature, cosmos, the whole, the divine, the One.[45]
Once we have understood that, we see that we do not need to 'do' or
to 'have' anything, just to 'be' (though that by no means implies indifference, apathy or nihilism). On the occasion of the founding of the
Zen Mountain Centre in Los Padres National Forest, he wrote:

It is for us in America to realise that the goal of action is
contemplation. Otherwise, we are caught up in mock progress
which is just going on toward going on, what Buddhists call

samsara – the squirrel cage of birth and death. That people are getting together to buy this property for meditation is one of the most hopeful signs of our time.[46]

If we had not attributed the quotation, we might almost have thought it was Ginsberg or Snyder speaking.

* * * * *

What, then, are we to make of the philosophy of Alan Watts? Different commentators have made different emphases, but perhaps we can infer a broad consensus running through these. According to Philip Wheelwright, Watts's philosophy is rooted in the tradition of the American Transcendentalists, which takes mysticism to be the most important goal of religion; it is a repudiation of the alternative American tradition of pragmatism, which tends to justify religion in terms of psychological effects.[47] According to David K. Clark, its goal is 'nonduality', beyond all false divisions such as subject and object, humanity and nature, 'I' and 'IT'; this state is best expressed through Hinduism, whose theism for Watts is much closer to pantheism (all is Brahman) than to conventional Christian theism (God is wholly other, and entirely distinct from his creation).[48] According to Michael C. Brannigan, its chief aim is to overcome the confusion between the word and the world, between the false ego and the true Self, and to celebrate the eternal present.[49] According to David Stuart, it involves going beyond dogmatic Christianity – but not Jesus Christ – in giving up God for the Godhead; and it was because this philosophy chimed with the times that Watts became the guru of the counterculture.[50] Certainly, all agree that he is the prophet of a spirituality which comes naturally and, beyond that, a mysticism which is our birthright. As for religion, it is a matter of choice: that is, we are free to opt for any available mode of expression. Watts moves freely in his own work among Hinduism, Buddhism, Taoism, Zen and mystical Christianity.

Having said that, it is probably fair to say that it is Hinduism which provides him with his key terms, as Alan Keightley observes:

> Watts's elaboration of the meaning of the Hindu *Tat Tvam Asi* (that art thou) lies at the centre of his approach in showing his readers that they may feel themselves as one particular focal point where the whole universe is expressing itself; the only real self is the whole. But he is also fond of using the phrase

sat-chit-ananda … Watts translates this phrase as 'the which
than which there is no whicher' to stress that – if only we could
see it – our ordinary state of life now is the ultimate state of
bliss. We are standing right now in the middle of the Beatific
Vision [sic].[51]

As we know, and as we shall confirm at more length as we proceed, the
beatific vision is implicit in the Beat vision, especially as espoused by
Kerouac. Perhaps Watts and he concur after all.

Again, by way of balance, we might consider Watts's increasing
preoccupation with Taoism. His final project, unfinished at his death
but published nonetheless after being completed by his friend Al
Chung-lian Huang, was a book called *Tao: The Watercourse Way*
(1975). This preoccupation with Taoism brought him very close to
Snyder:

> [O]ne of the central aims of Alan Watts' philosophical output
> was to interpret the Taoist outlook as a viable option for the
> West. Watts, like many other people, found it almost impossible
> to be a Christian out of doors. The traditional forms of
> Christian thought seemed so contrary to the forms of nature.
> Nevertheless, Watts and other writers have suggested ways in
> which Christianity can become sensitive to the Taoist vision.
> Christians may then behave less like those who 'have dominion'
> and, to use Gary Snyder's words, learn 'to live lightly in the
> earth.'[52]

Watts thereby not only comes close to Snyder, but also articulates the
values of the 'love generation'. As R. C. Zaehner notes, the Taoists had
reacted against the Confucian aim 'to regulate, improve, and exploit
Nature, and to adapt Nature to the new situation created by the emer-
gence of man as a rational and social animal'. Confucianism for
Zaehner has a 'curiously modern ring, for it seems to inaugurate an era
of progress, organization, science and technology'. It was against this
trend that the Taoists reacted: 'they were quite literally the drop-outs
of their time – anti-intellectual, anti-organization, anti-status-seeking,
anti-moralist.' The *Tao Te Ching*, he surmises, 'might be taken as the
hippies' charter'.[53] It was, we might add, also Watts's charter by the
end of his writing career.

We have come quite a distance from Watts's indictment of 'beat'
Zen to Watts's role as guru of the counterculture. But it is certainly

a role he took seriously. Nor does it mean the abandonment of his former values. Looking around him in May 1971, he asked dramatically:

> Whatever happened to the hippies? During the late sixties
> one had the impression that the ordinarily drab scene of
> American life is about to blossom into an easy-going colourful
> exuberance. ... There were even prospects of a truly swinging
> religion with meditation, chanting and joyous ritual,
> unorganized and set free from the unproductive guilt hangups
> of the Judeao-Christian conscience. ... [But now] the attitude is
> silent – even surly – and the music has just turned up the
> volume. ... Love' has become 'fuck'.[54]

This shrewd assessment of the decline in countercultural values is from an essay entitled 'Consider the Lilies', included in *Cloud-Hidden*. We might recognise the Biblical allusion: 'And why take ye thought for raiment? Consider the lilies of the field, how they grow: they toil not, neither do they spin: And yet I say unto you, That even Solomon in all his glory was not arrayed like one of these' (Matthew 42: 28–29). It is typical of Watts to invoke Jesus when addressing the current conduct of the hippies. For him, Christianity – the suppressed, mystical content of Christianity – may be enlisted in his cause as appropriately as Taoism. He even has another essay in the same volume which asks the question, 'Was Jesus a Freak?' – the answer to which is that those hippies who have become 'Jesus freaks' would do well to ponder his mystical message of identity with the Godhead rather than dubious doctrines about his being the unique 'son of God'. For 'Jesus is the particular instance and expression of a wisdom which was also, if differently, realized in the Buddha [and] Lao-Tzu ...'[55]

Meanwhile, Watts has to deal with the current crisis of the counter-culture. So 'Consider the Lilies' goes on to address the possible reasons for disillusionment and cynicism:

> This sagging of spirits may reflect simple depression at the
> endless and sickening war, at the realization that it may be
> too late to do anything about ecological catastrophe, and at
> the difficulty of finding employment even in the sterile busy-
> work of government and the big corporations. The temptation
> to free enterprise in dope is almost irresistible, but there can be
> too much pot – like too much booze or too much religion – and

the result is not a profound mystical contemplation but the
most ordinary lethargy.[56]

Significantly, the only hope Watts can see amidst the current squalor is
the awakening of a love of nature. He notices that there has been 'an
appreciable migration of hippies from the streets to the countryside in
an attempt to love and cultivate the earth at first hand'. But he warns
that such a move will be doomed to failure, unless there is a correspon-
ding revival of the inner life: 'If the earth is man's extended body, to be
loved and respected as one's own body, those who do no greening of
themselves will hardly bring about the greening of America.'[57] To do
this, they have to rediscover the flowing, mystical way of Jesus rather
than the inflexible, dogmatic project of conventional Christianity. Thus
he builds to his conclusion, typically invoking the Tao in the same
breath as the Gospels. For him they speak the same language, which
has become newly relevant in the age of 'flower power':

> I wish, then, that hippies would once again consider the lilies –
> for the very reason that they are frail and frivolous, gentle and
> inconsequential, and thus have those very qualities of vegetative
> wisdom so despised by those who have wills of iron and nerves
> of steel to fight the good fight and run the straight race. As
> Lao-tzu put it two thousand years ago:
>> Man at his birth is supple and tender, but in death
>>   he is rigid and hard.
>> Plants when young are sinuous and moist, but when old are
>>   brittle and dry.
>> Thus suppleness and tenderness are signs of life,
>> While rigidity and hardness are signs of death.
>
> For I feel that we would go better with this wiggly world if we
> thought in terms of roots and branches, vines and creepers,
> fronds and fiber, rather than in sterile angularities of metal and
> quartz in which the genius of life has not yet arisen, and in
> which energy may stutter and hum but has not yet learned to
> feel. At least then let me hope – dear children – that there are
> seeds in your dirty fingernails, and that you will again come out
> with flowers.[58]

The man who had lectured the Beats now found himself lecturing the
hippies. But thanks to his wit and lightly worn learning he became
immensely popular with all those seeking an alternative to Western

materialism. Whether he was conscious of drawing on, and expanding, the rich legacy of the Transcendentalists, it is hard to say: there are scarcely any citations of Emerson, Thoreau or Whitman in his writings. Perhaps they struck him as rather too self-conscious in their spirituality. His own recurrent message to his readers – which might account for his success with the hippies – was that the best way of gaining enlightenment was to cease wanting to gain enlightenment. 'This is IT.' However, that insight did not prevent him producing a score of books, simultaneously entertaining and erudite, which beguiled his readers into contemplating, and even savouring, the paradox involved. His inimitable contribution to the visionary tradition is surely not in doubt.

Notes

1 See Stephen Prothero, 'Introduction', in Carole Tonkinson (ed.), *Big Sky Mind: Buddhism and the Beat Generation* (New York: Riverhead Books, 1995), pp. 5–10.

2 Ralph Waldo Emerson, 'The Over-Soul', *Essays* (London and Glasgow: Blackie & Son, 1940), pp. 212–13.

3 Emerson, 'The Over-Soul', pp. 213–14.

4 Henry David Thoreau, *Walden*, in Carl Bode (ed.), *The Portable Thoreau* (New York: Penguin, 1975), pp. 438–40.

5 Mel Ash, *Beat Spirit: The Way of the Beat Writers as a Living Experience* (New York: Putnam, 1997), p. 34.

6 Ash, *Beat Spirit*, p. 35.

7 Walt Whitman, 'Song of Myself', in Francis Murphy (ed.), *The Complete Poems* (London: Penguin, 2004), p. 63.

8 Ash, *Beat Spirit*, pp. 32–3.

9 Whitman, 'Passage to India', *The Complete Poems*, p. 435.

10 Prothero, 'Introduction', *Big Sky Mind*, p. 2.

11 Quoted in Prothero, 'Introduction', *Big Sky Mind*, p. 6.

12 Quoted in Prothero, 'Introduction', *Big Sky Mind*, p. 8.

13 Prothero, 'Introduction', *Big Sky Mind*, p. 11.

14 Emerson, 'The Over-Soul', p. 234.

15 Emerson, 'The Over-Soul', p. 235.

16 See Aldous Huxley, *The Perennial Philosophy* (New York: Harper & Row, 1945; 1970).

17 Alan Watts, *Behold the Spirit: A Study in the Necessity of Mystical Religion* (New York: Vintage, 1947; 1971), p. 15.

18 See *Chicago Review* 12 (Summer 1958).

19 Alan Watts, 'Beat Zen, Square Zen, and Zen', in *This is IT and other Essays on Zen and Spiritual Experience* (London: Rider & Co, 1960; 1978), pp. 77–110. Further references to this edition are given after quotations in the text.

20 Alan Watts, 'The Beat Way of Life', in Mark Watts (ed.), *Zen and the Beat Way* (Enfield: Eden Grove Editions, 1997), p. 25.
21 Jack Kerouac, *The Dharma Bums* (London: Penguin, 1959; 2000), p. 163.
22 Krishnamurti, *Commentaries on Living: Second Series* (London: Gollancz, 1958), p. 64.
23 Alan Watts, *The Book: On the Taboo Against Knowing Who You Are* (New York: Random House/Vintage, 1966; 1989), p. ix.
24 Alan Watts, *In My Own Way: An Autobiography 1916–1965* (London: Jonathan Cape, 1973), p. 261.
25 Watts, *In My Own Way*, p. 261.
26 Watts, *In My Own Way*, p. 262.
27 Thedore Roszak, *The Making of a Counter Culture: Reflections on the Technocratic Society and its Youthful Opposition* (London: Faber and Faber, 1970), p. 137.
28 See Allen Ginsberg, 'What Way I Write', in *Deliberate Prose: Selected Essays 1952–1995* (New York: HarperCollins, 2000), p. 255. The 'Blake vision' will be discussed in more detail in Chapter 4. For an account of its importance in understanding Ginsberg, see Paul Portuges, *The Visionary Poetics of Allen Ginsberg* (Santa Barbara: Ross-Erikson Publishers, 1978).
29 Allen Ginsberg, 'Sunflower Sutra', in *Selected Poems 1947–1995* (London and New York: Penguin, 1997), p. 60.
30 Roszak, *The Making of a Counter Culture*, p. 132.
31 Roszak, *The Making of a Counter Culture*, pp. 132–3.
32 Watts, *In My Own Way*, p. 309.
33 Watts, *In My Own Way*, p. 309.
34 Gary Snyder, 'Mother Earth: Her Whales', in *No Nature: New and Selected Poems* (New York: Pantheon Books, 1992), p. 236.
35 Gary Snyder, 'Buddhism and the Possibilities of a Planetary Culture', in *The Gary Snyder Reader: Prose, Poetry, and Translations* (Washington: Counterpoint, 1999), p. 41.
36 See Alan Watts, *Nature, Man and Woman* (New York: Vintage Books, 1958; 1991), pp. 51–69. For an interesting discussion about whether the Bible might be read in a more ecological perspective, see Tom Hayden, *The Lost Gospel of the Earth: A Call for Renewing Nature, Spirit, & Politics* (San Francisco: Sierra Club Books, 1996).
37 Watts, *In My Own Way*, p. 311.
38 Watts, *In My Own Way*, pp. 311–12.
39 See Aldous Huxley, *The Doors of Perception* (1954), repr. *The Doors of Perception* and *Heaven and Hell* (Harmondsworth: Penguin, 1959).
40 See Barry Miles, *In the Sixties* (London: Pimlico, 2003), pp. 87–90.
41 See Monica Furlong, *Zen Effects: The Life of Alan Watts* (Woodstock, Vermont: Skylight Paths Publishing, 2001), pp. 168–72.
42 Quoted in Furlong, *Zen Effects*, p. 181.
43 Furlong, *Zen Effects*, pp. 181–2
44 Alan Watts, *Cloud-Hidden, Whereabouts Unknown: A Mountain Journal* (New York: Vintage, 1974), p. 127.
45 See 'This is IT', *This is IT*, pp. 15–40.

46 Quoted in Furlong, *Zen Effects*, p. 185.
47 See Philip Wheelwright, 'The Philosophy of Alan Watts', in *Sewanee Review* 61 (1953), pp. 493–500.
48 See David K. Clark, *The Pantheism of Alan Watts* (Illinois: Inter-Varsity Press, 1978).
49 See Michael C. Brannigan, *Everywhere and Nowhere: The Path of Alan Watts* (New York: Peter Lang, 1988).
50 See David Stuart, *Alan Watts* (New York: Stein and Day, 1983).
51 Alan Keightley, *Into Every Life a Little Zen Must Fall: A Christian Philosopher Looks to Alan Watts and the East* (London: Wisdom Publications, 1986), pp. 76–7.
52 Keightley, *Into Every Life a Little Zen Must Fall*, pp. 167–8.
53 R. C. Zaehner, *Drugs, Mysticism and Make-Believe* (London: Collins, 1972), pp. 129–30.
54 Watts, *Cloud-Hidden*, p. 110.
55 Watts, *Cloud-Hidden*, p. 150.
56 Watts, *Cloud-Hidden*, p. 110.
57 Watts, *Cloud-Hidden*, p. 111.
58 Watts, *Cloud-Hidden*, pp. 111–12.

2 'Go moan for man': Jack Kerouac and the beatific vision

Of the three main Beats whom we are considering in this study, it is Kerouac who merits a complete chapter to himself. Not only does he give us our understanding of 'Beat' as 'beatific', but also he gives us the fullest sense of what literature as spiritual quest might involve – more so even than do Ginsberg and Snyder. The trouble is that this aspect of Kerouac's achievement is all too often glossed over: there is still a tendency for interest in him to be confined to his bohemian image and his reputation as untutored genius. My aim here is to make a case for him as a substantial writer with serious concerns, and in particular to encourage interest in his preoccupation with spirituality.

Having said that, we should not therefore discount such matters as his innovative style and his nonconformist stance. Indeed, what is interesting is that his reinvigoration of literary culture by drawing on possibilities previously ignored in popular culture, both as a writer and a man, is inseparable from his spiritual quest. To understand this, we need to be alert to the connotations of the word 'Beat'. We have already addressed these briefly in the Introduction; now we must examine them in detail. Our main task, then, is to consider carefully in turn the following three aspects of Kerouac's work, showing how the third proceeds logically from the first two:

1 His development of a new style of writing inspired by jazz – particularly 'bebop' – and blues. This is 'beat' in the musical sense.
2 His fascination with the oppressed and dispossessed, with the figure of the hobo, tramp or bum. This is 'beat' in the sense of weary or worn down.
3 His conviction of a new kind of spiritual revelation, made possible by the first two dimensions. This is 'beat' in the sense of 'beatific'.

*****

Everybody who knows anything about the Beat movement knows that in the late 1950s Jack Kerouac often used to recite poems and extracts from his novels to the accompaniment of a piano or small band. Whether or not we agree with Bruce Cook that this enterprise was flawed, it is probably fair to say that it was thanks to his example that artists such as Bob Dylan and Leonard Cohen felt able to develop their own kind of 'poetic' popular song. But that was some time ahead. As we know, Kerouac's own particular enthusiasm was jazz: in particular, the form which had developed in the previous decade, namely 'bebop', because it gave him a model of improvisation for his own writing. Indeed, it is often said, with some validity, that Kerouac's literary style is a bebop style. While we have to be careful to avoid a glib labelling, it is probably accurate to say that Kerouac found his voice not only through reading Henry David Thoreau but also through listening to Charlie 'Bird' Parker. It is important to mention Parker by name, and to be specific about the kind of music by which Kerouac was influenced. We must avoid the danger of identifying Kerouac's Beat innovation in writing with the 'free jazz' which succeeded bebop, and which is associated chiefly with the name of Ornette Coleman.[1] For Kerouac was no more interested than was Parker in out-and-out experimentation. Their common interest was in taking a given idiom – whether music or language – and revivifying it by letting in more experience, more energy and, where possible, more ecstasy.

We can gain a sense of how Kerouac early on acquired the 'Bird'-like confidence to test the boundaries of language by reminding ourselves of a famous sentence from *On the Road* (1951, published 1957):

> But then they danced down the streets like dingledodies, and I shambled after as I've been doing all my life after people who interest me, because the only people for me are the mad ones, the ones who are mad to live, mad to talk, mad to be saved, desirous of everything at the same time, the ones who never yawn or say a commonplace thing, but burn, burn, burn like fabulous yellow roman candles exploding like spiders across the stars and in the middle you see the blue centerlight pop and everybody goes 'Awww!'[2]

For Kerouac this style of writing is the appropriate medium through which he can demonstrate the possibility of locating the sacred within the profane. The purpose of the prose is revelation.

The same is true of the poetry. It is significant that when Parker is honoured in *Mexico City Blues*, Kerouac's sequence of poetic 'choruses' (1955, published 1959), he is represented as nothing less than a visionary, who allows us to understand ourselves, our world and our fate in the eternal moment of his genius. The poet has Parker 'whistling' his listeners 'on to the brink of eternity'.[3] The musician therefore deserves to be honoured as a holy man, a guru, a model of spiritual liberation: 'Charley [sic] Parker, pray for me – / Pray for me and everybody / In the Nirvanas of your brain ...'[4] He is addressed as if he offers not only Christian salvation ('pray for me') but also Buddhist liberation ('Nirvanas'). This audacious shift of allusion is peculiarly effective: nirvana being the 'blowing out' of the flame of egotism, it is appropriately invoked in honouring a man who is famous for blowing or 'whistling' on a saxophone.

Just as important as the invocation of Parker's name and spirit is Kerouac's attempt to produce the equivalent of the music he admires within his poetic form. But we must not overlook the fact that the volume's title promises its reader a sequence of 'blues' songs; nor must we evade the difficulty this creates. Which musical form is it exactly that is inspiring Kerouac here: the bebop of Parker or the blues of someone like Leadbelly? Chorus 221, which plays with the latter's name, suggests that Kerouac sees them as closely related: 'Old Man Mose / Early American jazz pianist / Had a grandson / Called Deadbelly ...'[5]

Gerald Nicosia has defended Kerouac's merging of genres, arguing that his instinctive insight is that jazz and blues emerge from a common source of popular imagination:

> It may seem that Kerouac is confusing blues with bop, but actually he is perceiving their consanguinity. The day Charlie Parker died, he lamented that 'many of the young guys coming up didn't know or had forgotten their foundation – the blues.' Blues, Parker affirmed, was 'the basis of jazz.' Above all, what makes Kerouac's poems blues is that their diction and structure are dictated directly by his feelings.[6]

But the impact of the blues on Kerouac ran deeper still. For he not only instinctively responded to the way it used language to convey the immediacy and richness of experience, but he also found in it a complete vision of life. As Dennis McNally explains, reflecting on Kerouac's youthful discovery of the musical form:

> [The blues] is the freedom sound, the call of those displaced from Mother Africa, the cry of the people who can't go home again. The blues were inspired not by an abstract ideal but by the sound of the human voice, choked with tears or ripped by rage, but always the voice. 'Blues truth,' as [the] critic [Michael Lydon] later wrote, 'runs counter to hysterical confidence in progress, machines, and human power. It is a darker, more fateful, though ultimately more relaxed and humorous truth that has its own sober and sensual comfort.' As Memphis Slim once remarked, when it all comes down, 'you gotta go back to Mother Earth.'[7]

The question Kerouac was addressing, then, was how to articulate this 'blues truth'.

* * * * *

Memphis Slim's remark is echoed by Sal Paradise's reflection in *On the Road* that 'the earth is an Indian thing. As essential as rocks in the desert are they in the desert of "history"...'[8] Against the technological materialism of the contemporary United States, Kerouac looked to the ecological spirituality of the Native Americans. Similarly, he found in the blues an alternative way of articulating what it meant to be human: an idiom which transcended the comfortable consumer civilisation of mainstream America. As to the fate of that worldview and of that civilisation, Sal Paradise foresees that 'when destruction comes to the world of history and the Apocalypse of the Fellahin returns once more, as so many times before, people will still stare with the same eyes from the caves of Mexico as well as from the caves of Bali, where it all began and where Adam was suckled and taught to know.'[9] In returning to our common humanity ('Adam'), and in identifying with the oppressed and dispossessed ('the Fellahin') rather than subscribing to the inhuman and unnatural cult of progress ('history'), we are in a position to receive a new revelation ('Apocalypse'). Such a vision requires a restoration of authentic speech, since our words have been compromised and corrupted by our commercial civilisation: hence Kerouac's urge to speak 'blues truth' and to produce a kind of writing which is as close as possible to the inspired improvisation of bebop. For blues and jazz comprise for him the 'roots' music which will restore the power of the word. In *Visions of Cody*, which involves an audacious reworking of part of *On the Road*, written only a year later, Kerouac manages to fuse his love of vernacular language, his compassion for his fellow human beings and his visionary impulse:

> At the junction of the state of Colorado, its arid western one, and the state line of poor Utah I saw in the clouds huge and massed above the fiery golden desert of eveningfall the great image of God with forefinger pointed straight at me through halos and rolls and gold folds that were like the existence of the gleaming spear in His right hand, and sayeth, Go thou across the ground; go moan for man; go moan; go groan; go groan alone go roll your bones, alone; go thou and be little beneath my sight; go thou, and be minute and as seed in the pod, but the pod the pit, world a Pod, universe a Pit; go thou, go thou, die hence; and of [this world] report you well and truly.[10]

Far from being an affectation, the Beat idiom is for Kerouac a way of releasing possibilities of language which are also possibilities of humanity, culture and spirit. 'Go moan for man' embodies not only despair but also hope: the hope implicit in 'blues truth'. In finding ecstatic expression for one's downtrodden state, one transcends it: one moves from resignation to revelation.

The obvious echo in such passages as the one just quoted is the Bible; and Kerouac's Christianity is a topic which we will need to address. But for now, we should not overlook the importance of another influence, Oswald Spengler's *The Decline of the West*.[11] Published in two volumes (1918 and 1922), and shortly after translated into English (1926 and1928), Spengler's account of how civilisations rise and fall had a huge impact not only on Kerouac but also on his friends William Burroughs and Allen Ginsberg. In particular, they were impressed by his confirmation of their suspicion that the civilisation in which they lived was on the verge of collapse, and they were encouraged by his cyclical model of history to look for signs of an alternative culture emerging from its decline.

With Spengler, they saw 'civilisation' and 'culture' as contrary terms. With Spengler too, they identified the living culture with the 'fellaheen' (or 'fellahin') – the outcasts of the dying civilisation. Originally an Arabic term, referring to the peasantry, it became in Spengler's model the shorthand for those of the dispossessed who had been granted an alternative vision, and could see beyond the moribund West. For Kerouac, the culture of the fellaheen was implicit in the language of blues, bebop and Beat. Indeed, the fellaheen themselves were those who had been worn down by the given civilisation; but thereby they were released from its constrictions, as they had no investment in it. As Allen Ginsberg later recalled concerning the significance of the word 'Beat': 'the point [is] that you get beat down to a certain nakedness where you are actually able to see the world in a visionary way'.[12] No wonder Victor Turner thought of the Beats and their successors the hippies when he was trying to illustrate the idea of 'communitas', that spiritual sense of community which arises by way of corrective to the social hierarchy of 'structure'.

Kerouac himself articulates this possibility in his article, 'About the Beat Generation' (1957). There he begins by explaining that the word 'beat' [sic] was used by Ginsberg, John Clellon Holmes and himself in the later 1940s to designate 'a generation of crazy, illuminated hipsters, suddenly rising, roaming America, serious, curious, bumming and hitchhiking everywhere, ragged, beatific, beautiful in an ugly graceful new way'. In this light he can offer the following cryptic definition: 'beat, meaning down and out but full of intense conviction'.[13] But he is aware that sceptical commentators will need a more substantial account. Here he invokes Spengler:

> Even in this late stage of civilization when money is the only thing that really matters to everybody, I think perhaps it is the Second Religiousness that Oswald Spengler prophesied for the West (in America the final home of Faust), because there are elements of hidden religious significance in the way, for instance, that a guy like Stan Getz, the highest jazz genius of his 'beat' generation, was put in jail for trying to hold up a drug store, suddenly had visions of God and repented (something gracefully Villonesque in that story) ...[14]

Speculating further, he cites other examples of spiritual revelation which have taken their recipients beyond 'Bourgeois-Bohemian Materialism', and he draws what is for him an inevitable conclusion:

> A. G.'s [Allen Ginsberg's] visions in Harlem and elsewhere of the tearful Divine Love, W. S. B.'s [William Burroughs'] reception of the word that he is the One Prophet, G. S.'s [Gary Snyder's] Buddhist visions of the vow of salvation, peotl

visions of all the myths being true ... J. K. 's [Jack Kerouac's]
numerous visions of Heaven, the 'Golden Eternity,' bright light
in the night woods ... (all taking place, a definite fact, in the
midst of everyday contemporary life in the minds of typical
members of my generation whom I know), reappearances of the
early Gothic Springtime feeling of Western mankind before it
went on its 'Civilization' Rationale and developed relativity, jets
and superbombs and supercolossal bureaucratic totalitarian
benevolent Big Brother structures – so, as Spengler says, when
comes the sunset of our culture [i.e., civilisation] (due now,
according to his morphological graphs) and the dust of civilized
striving settles, lo, the clear late-day glow reveals the original
concerns again, reveals a beatific indifference to things that are
Caesar's, for instance, a tiredness of that, and a yearning for, a
regret for, the transcendent value, or 'God' again, 'Heaven', the
spiritual regret for Endless Love ...[15]

Here, we must pause to note his usage of that word, 'beatific': we
have already had 'ragged, beatific, beautiful'; now we have 'beatific
indifference', in the sense of a high-minded disinterestedness which
contrasts with the gross, aggressive materialism of contemporary north
America. Kerouac's commissioned topic is 'the Beat Generation', but
he makes sure that the reader is in no doubt about the spiritual dimension of a movement which, he is all too aware, some might see as a
passing literary or cultural fad. For Kerouac, the Beat phenomenon can
only be understood in the context of the fellaheen; and the fellaheen
are those who are not only 'beat' (worn down, weary) but also
'beatific' (blissful, blessed). Indeed, they are granted the 'beatific' vision
precisely because they are 'beat'.
    As for what that vision involves, let John Lardas provide a
summary:

Spengler's premise that there were immutable laws of history,
and that those who understood the nature of the laws were
capable of prophecy, or at the very least were privileged, was
of great appeal to the Beats. In Spengler, they found an
epistemology in which to place their millennial hope, an
alternative religious vocabulary that replaced the scientific
lexicon of empiricism and causality with that of intuition. ...
Spengler's cosmological frame of reference was one of
correspondence, a model that assumes no radical break between

knower and known, subject and object, or sacred and profane.
He declared in no uncertain terms the existence of a universal
spirit active in both history and the individual and also
connecting the two. Because no barriers separated the universal
from the human community, the macrocosmic from the
microcosmic, the same universal laws governed each; structure
and movement in one were replicated in the other. ... In
recognizing the overlap between macrocosmic universality and
microcosmic particularity, the Beats looked to this world for
answers to their most profound questions. By evaluating and
taking note of the world around them, they hoped to gain
insight into the cosmos and its logic.[16]

In other words, Spengler taught the Beats, as did the Transcendentalists also, that the very life they were living was their means to revelation of the divine. It was from him that they learned their 'theology of
experience'. The majority might not be able to see or understand this,
being blinded by dead conventions; but the 'fellaheen' had just the sort
of free, intuitive spirituality that made revelation possible.

It is worth noting how consistent Kerouac was in evoking spiritual
concerns when discussing his literary technique. For example, he
continued to insist throughout his writing career that his 'spontaneous
prose' was not a matter of bohemian affectation or hedonistic indul-
gence, but stemmed from this 'beatific' sense. In 1967, he defended his
technique by invoking the Buddha, who had advised his followers to
answer questions 'with no recourse to discriminative thinking', trust-
ing in 'the enlightening nature of pure Mind Essence'. Jesus, too, is
enlisted to the cause, with Kerouac quoting Mark 13:11: 'Take no
thought beforehand what ye shall speak, neither do ye premeditate: but
whatsoever shall be given you in that hour, that speak ye: for it is not
ye that speak, but the Holy Ghost.' Having invoked two great spiritual
masters, Kerouac was anxious to make the link with artistic practice:
'Mozart and Blake often felt they weren't pushing their own pens,
'twas the "Muse" singing and pushing.'[17] In short, he was aligning the
Beat movement with a model of divine inspiration. No wonder he
would always insist that the Beat generation was 'basically a religious
generation'.[18] No wonder he would see the function of literature as
teaching 'religious reverence' for 'real life'.[19]

Despite such consistency, Kerouac's spirituality has too often been
overshadowed by an emphasis on the apparent celebration of unre-
strained hedonism in fiction such as *On the Road*. But even a passing

acquaintance with that novel and with a small sample of his other work will be sufficient to remind us of his seriously spiritual preoccupations. These become even more explicit in the statement which we quoted in the Introduction, which comes from his article of the following year, 'Lamb, No Lion' (1958):

> Beat doesn't mean tired, or bushed, so much as it means *beato*, the Italian for beatific: to be in a state of beatitude, like St Francis, trying to love all life, trying to be utterly sincere with everyone, practising endurance, kindness, cultivating joy of heart. How can this be done in our mad modern world of multiplicities and millions? By practising a little solitude, going off by yourself once in awhile to store up that most precious of golds: the vibrations of sincerity.[20]

As if he had not made his belief in the spiritual dimension of a literary movement clear, Kerouac wrote and published yet another article on this theme in the following year. In 'Beatific: The Origins of the Beat Generation' (1959), we read:

> I am not ashamed to wear the crucifix of my Lord. It is because I am Beat, that is, I believe in beatitude and that God so loved the world that he gave his only begotten son to it. ... No, I want to speak *for* things, for the crucifix I speak out, for the Star of Israel I speak out, for the divinest man who ever lived who was a German (Bach) I speak out, for sweet Mohammed I speak out, for Buddha I speak out, for Lao-tse and Chuang-tse I speak out, for D. T. Suzuki I speak out ... why should I attack what I love out of life. This is Beat.[21]

In both of these last two quotations, we will note that Christianity, far from being rejected in the name of what he dubs 'Bourgeois-Bohemian Materialism' – that denial of the spirit which is simultaneously an enslavement to the consumer ideology of Western civilisation – is reaffirmed and validated within the context of the Beat commitment to genuinely alternative values. The voluntary embrace of poverty and simplicity – the willingness to identify with the fellaheen – is sanctioned by the example of Jesus Christ and his imitators. Similarly, the courage to stand apart, to live on the margins of society, is seen as perfectly in keeping with the Christian way. The 'Beat' vision is the 'beatific' vision.

* * * * *

Kerouac's background was French-Canadian, working-class and Roman Catholic. Though his family had moved to Lowell, Massachusetts, before he was born, he was still christened Jean-Louis (Jack being a name acquired later) and brought up speaking French before he acquired any English. His family knew financial hardship, and he was brought up to expect life to be difficult. He was much affected by the early death of his saintly brother Gerard, whose religious faith had sustained him during his long, painful illness. Dennis McNally speculates about his mood as he prepared for his first Holy Communion:

> Complex, terrifying, and fulfilling, the Church's sacraments
> embraced the whole of life, from Baptism at birth and
> Confirmation in childhood to the rite of Marriage and the
> Extreme Unction of death. Of all the sacraments, however, none
> was more important than the Eucharist, when the body of
> Christ was present during the holy sacrifice of the Mass.
> Sunday after Sunday for fourteen years, he listened to the priest
> and joined the parish in the whispered replies. Like rolling
> thunder, the refrains of the Mass swept him out of his body and
> into his soul. For they celebrated a mystery, fueled by the
> majesty of Latin.[22]

Kerouac's early immersion in the mysteries of the Catholic faith informed much of his later thinking. For example, he maintained his devotion to the Virgin Mary; nor did he ever forget St Teresa of Lisieux, whom McNally describes as 'a late nineteenth-century Carmelite nun who had preached the "little way" of simplicity and perfection in the ordinary tasks of life, "of spiritual childhood, the way of trust, and absolute self-surrender".'[23]

One of the chief fascinations of Kerouac's work is the tension in it between the Catholicism of his childhood faith and the Eastern wisdom which he discovered as a young man. For he was probably the first of the Beat generation to turn to the East for spiritual insight, stimulated by his reading of Thoreau's *Walden*.[24] He was attracted in particular to Buddhism, primarily because 'the first noble truth', that all life is 'dukkha' (anxiety, 'dis-ease', dislocation, suffering) made perfect sense to him. The agony and death of Gerard gave the young Jack a strong sense of the vulnerability of the human individual, which never left him. Again, he sustained a serious injury while attending Columbia

College, New York, on a football scholarship: for the rest of his life, he was plagued by phlebitis of the knee. The Buddha's insight that the pursuit of pleasure is doomed to failure – the illusory project of an illusory ego – and that our time is far better spent in becoming aware of our own impermanence and in alleviating the suffering of others, informed most of Kerouac's central body of work. He began reading Buddhist literature in late 1953 and began writing about it the following year. Nor is it a coincidence that it was about the same time that he started using the word 'Beat' in the sense of 'beatific'.[25] Again, we should be aware that his turn to Buddhism seemed to him to be sanctioned by his reading of *The Decline of the West*, with its cyclical model of history. In an interview he gave to the journalist Mike Wallace in 1958, we can infer the paradoxical fusion of pessimism and ecstasy that he experienced thanks to reading Buddhism in light of Spengler, and vice-versa:

> Wallace: You mean beat people are mystics?
> Kerouac: Yeah, it's a revival prophesied by Spengler. He
>   said that in the late movements of Western civilization
>   there would be a great revival of religious mysticism. It's
>   happening.
> Wallace: What do the mystics believe in?
> Kerouac: Oh, they believe in love ... and ... all is well ... we're
>   in heaven now really.
> Wallace: You don't sound happy.
> Kerouac: Oh, I'm tremendously sad, I'm in great despair.
> Wallace: Why?
> Kerouac: Oh, it's a great burden to be alive.[26]

There is the typically playful evasiveness of Kerouac to contend with here, which always made him such an awkward interviewee; but there can surely be little doubt that that final statement was heartfelt.

Anyone who has any doubt that Kerouac is a seriously religious writer could do worse than spend half an hour browsing through *Some of the Dharma*, his collection of ruminations on the Buddha's teachings, or 'dharma' (truth, law). Though this was not published until many years after his death, it was for Kerouac his most important task between 1954 and 1956 – more so even than his fiction. The following pronouncements will give something of its flavour: 'Life is nothing but a short vague dream encompassed round by flesh and tears' ... 'I don't want to be a drunken hero of the generation suffering everywhere, with everyone – I want to be a quiet saint living in a shack in solitary meditation of universal mind' ... 'I believe in emptiness; I do not believe in things'.[27]

Kerouac's immersion in Buddhism has to be borne in mind when assessing both his poetry and his fiction. We have already quoted from *Mexico City Blues*, but here we should reemphasise its spiritual dimension. Indeed, another Beat poet, Michael McClure, has declared that work to be 'the finest long, religious poem of the 20th century'.[28] Allowing for some hyperbole here, we can yet admit the validity of McClure's challenge. But we must not look for the measured, formal quality of T. S. Eliot's masterpiece of contemplative verse, *Four Quartets*, a work which is more usually described in such terms. In *Mexico City Blues* one has a strong sense of what in Zen Buddhism is called 'beginner's mind'. Kerouac's spiritual insight is expressed with the relief of a realisation that comes to him even as the words tumble forth, though we must then acknowledge in retrospect the artifice necessarily involved: 'The wheel of the quivering meat conception / Turns in the void expelling human beings, / Pigs, turtles, frogs, insects, nits ...' His list goes on with apparent randomness, but the penultimate insight makes it cohere: 'All the endless conception of living beings / Gnashing everywhere in Consciousness / Throughout the ten directions of space ... / Illuminating the sky of one Mind ...' It is with a typically dramatic turn of thought, however, that Kerouac brings the poem back to its starting point: '*Poor*! I wish I was free / of that slaving meat wheel / and safe in heaven dead.'[29]

This is an audacious way of depicting Buddhist principles, but it is in keeping with the Buddhist injunction not to evade the facts of death and decay whilst in the midst of life and fruition. It is at once an acknowledgement of 'samsara' (the cycle of death and rebirth, the wheel of existence) and a celebration of 'sunyata' (the emptiness of all phenomena). What we take to be substantial entities are really manifestations of the Buddha-mind. Nothing lasts, so one should not put one's trust in anything. But we might note that while the poem might seem orthodox enough up to the final three lines, as far as a Buddhist is concerned, there is yet something peculiarly and poignantly non-Buddhist about its coda. One cannot help but infer a personal pressure behind the exposition of the dharma: those last lines perhaps betray Kerouac's very particular desire to join his brother Gerard in another, higher realm; and the use of the word 'heaven' suggests a desire to translate Buddhist thought into Christian language.

Thus, when his friend Gary Snyder told Kerouac in 1956 that he ought to write a 'sutra', or short Buddhist discourse, he set out to demonstrate the compatibility of Buddhism and Christianity. It took Kerouac a while to complete his 'sutra', but *The Scripture of the Golden Eternity* (1960) seems to flow easily between the two poles. It contains many utterances such as these: 'The awakened Buddha to show the way, the chosen Messiah to die in the degradation of sentience, is the golden eternity.'[30] That is, Jesus the Messiah and Gautama the Buddha are aspects of the same divine being; and their common message seems to be that so are we all. The reader is told in no uncertain terms: 'You are the golden eternity, because there is no me, no you, only one golden eternity.'[31]

Kerouac's attempt to fuse two faiths, long before the 'New Age' fashion for the eclectic sampling of world religions, is a bold one – almost impossible, some might say. Where conventional Christian theology adheres to a 'theistic' doctrine, by which we are to understand that there is one creator-God, Buddhism is strictly speaking 'non-theistic', having no notion of a God and very little interest in the origin of the world. Yet here is Kerouac rendering them compatible in language that is at once simple and tantalising. He moves dexterously between the Buddhist idea of nirvana and the Christian idea of salvation, foregrounding all the while the elusive nature of such concepts:

> Do you think the emptiness of the sky will ever crumble away?
> Every little child knows that everybody will go to heaven.
> Knowing that nothing ever happened is not really knowing that nothing ever happened, it's the golden eternity. ... Nothing was ever born, nothing will ever die.[32]

This is the language of mystical paradox: Heaven is what awaits us after we are released from this life by death, but neither of these contrary states has any real existence. That which is unborn – Buddha-mind, 'golden eternity' – cannot die.

Kerouac might be said to have got his taste for paradox from the Zen practice of the master setting for his pupils a 'koan', a short puzzle or riddle that forces them to get beyond their rational minds and to apprehend the true nature of existence. 'What is the sound of one hand clapping?' is one of the more well-known examples of this form. 'Does a dog have Buddha-nature?' – with the proviso that one must answer neither yes nor no – is another.[33] Kerouac himself offers us his own koan-like aphorisms in the course of this sutra. For example: 'When you've understood this scripture, throw it away. If you can't

understand this scripture, throw it away. I insist on your freedom.'[34]
But on the whole, the spirit of Zen does not inform Kerouac's heavily
Christian Buddhism. Indeed, he expresses his doubts about the Zen
idea of 'sudden attainment' early on. In *Some of the Dharma* he deems
it 'shallow' and 'naïve', countering it with the insistence that if time is
unreal, then so must be the moment within time that such attainment
is achieved. 'The truth is already in the Mind,' he reminds us.[35]

Kerouac's attitude to Buddhism is a complex topic. But we might
gain some purchase on it if we consider that Buddhist practice might
be seen as the putting into action of two basic principles: 'prajna'
(insight) and 'karuna' (kindness); in other words, meditation and
morality; or again, contemplation and compassion. Enlightenment
comes to those who are prepared both to dwell on the impermanence
of all things and to dedicate themselves to the welfare of others.
Looking back to the Introduction, we may note a parallel here with
Hinduism, which we saw as allowing for two paths towards realisation
of the Godhead: 'Gnana Yoga' (head) and 'Bhakti Yoga' (heart). Different schools of Buddhism seem to emphasise one principle more than
the other. Kerouac was consistently of the opinion that, if there was a
choice, it was better to love others than to absorbed in the inner life.
Rightly or wrongly, he came to identify the latter pursuit with Zen,
which he regarded as too narrow and too self-conscious, even while it
offered models of thought from which he could benefit.

Our key reference point here must be the novel which Kerouac
wrote the year after the publication of *On the Road*, and published the
following year, namely *The Dharma Bums* (1959).[36] Typically, it begins
with an image of hard travelling as a way of indicating a spiritual
calling. The narrator, Ray Smith, is hitching a ride on a train to San
Francisco: 'Hopping a freight out of Los Angeles at high noon one day
in late September 1955 I got on a gondola and lay down with my duffel
bag under my head and my knees crossed and contemplated the clouds
as we rolled north to Santa Barbara' (p. 7). The spiritual dimension is
introduced almost immediately, when the presence of the little old
'bum' who hops the freight at the same time prompts Ray to reflect on
the words in the Diamond Sutra concerning charity and to offer to
share his food with him. In doing so, he later realises, he is acting as a
'Dharma Bum' [sic] (p. 8).

In a sense the whole novel is a debate between the side of Buddhism
which emphasises compassion, represented by Ray, and the side of
Buddhism which emphasises contemplation, represented by the friend
he is soon to make, Japhy Ryder. Japhy is the central figure of the

novel: 'The little Saint Teresa bum was the first genuine Dharma Bum I'd met, and the second was the number one Dharma Bum of them all and in fact it was he, Japhy Ryder, who coined the phrase' (p. 12). Japhy lives frugally in San Francisco, as much in the spirit of Zen as possible – a spirit which does not exclude a taste for alcohol and sexual experimentation, however. Ray, by contrast, is much more anxious about following what he regards as a proper Buddhist code of conduct, involving self-denial and charity. The novel explores the tension between Zen freedom and orthodox restraint.

While there is little doubt that Japhy is a fictionalised representation of Kerouac's friend, the poet Gary Snyder, it is by no means clear that Ray stands for Kerouac himself. There is frequently an ironic distance between the author and the narrator. However, one can certainly see traces of the author's spiritual concerns in the narrator's dispute with Japhy over the validity of Zen. Even though Kerouac's work is indebted to the Zen emphasis on paradox, Ray's objection to what goes with it in practice is probably sanctioned by Kerouac, on the evidence of his other writings:

> 'Lissen, Japhy,' I said, 'I'm not a Zen Buddhist, I'm a serious Buddhist, I'm an oldfashioned dreamy Hinayana coward of later Mahayanism,' and so forth into the night, my contention being that Zen Buddhism didn't concentrate on kindness so much as on confusing the intellect to make it perceive the illusion of all sources of things. 'It's *mean*,' I complained. 'All those Zen Masters throwing young kids in the mud because they can't answer their silly word questions.' (p. 15)

It is unlikely, however, that the author would have been as confused as the narrator about the relationship between 'Hinayana' ('the lesser vehicle') and 'Mahayana' ('the greater vehicle'). The latter was a reform movement within Buddhism which arose around 380BC, in reaction against the former's exclusivity, in order to widen the relevance of Buddha's wisdom to lay people as well as monks. The confusion seems to have been included in order to humanise the narrator, whom Kerouac does not want us to regard as wholly reliable.

Sympathising with Ray, while aware of his weaknesses, the reader must yet be given a sense of how inspiring the ideas and the presence of Japhy are to all who meet him. It is his vision of a 'rucksack revolution' that the rest of the novel seems to endorse:

a world full of rucksack wanderers, Dharma Bums refusing to
subscribe to the general demand that they consume production
and therefore have to work for the privilege of consuming, all
that crap they didn't really want anyway ... I see a vision of a
great rucksack revolution, thousands or even millions of young
Americans wandering around with rucksacks, going up to
mountains to pray, making children laugh and old men glad,
making young girls happy and old girls happier, all of 'em Zen
Lunatics who go about writing poems that happen to appear in
their heads for no reason ... (p. 83)

There can be little doubt, despite the doubts cast on this beatific future
by other characters – notably Rosie Buchanan, the depressive girlfriend
of Ray's friend Cody Pomeray, who eventually commits suicide after
predicting a police state rather than a 'rucksack revolution' – that this
manifesto conveys much of Kerouac's own faith in the future at the
time of writing. Compare it with his own account of the novel,
provided as the jacket copy for the original Viking hardback edition:

Dharma is the Sanskrit Word for Truth. It may also be
translated as The Duty, or The Law. *The Dharma Bums* is a
surprising story of two young Americans who make a
goodhearted effort to know the Truth with full packs on their
backs, rucksack wanderers of the West Coast, hiking and
climbing mountains to go and meditate and pray and cook
their simple foods, and down below living in shacks and
sleeping outdoors under the California stars. ... [This] is the
ancient Way of all the wild prophets of the past, whether St
John the Baptist in the West or the holy old Zen Lunatic
Hanshan in the East. ... In this new novel, Jack Kerouac
departs from the 'hipster' movement of the Beat Generation
and leads his readers towards a conception of 'continual
conscious compassion' and a peaceful understanding truce
with the paradox of existence.[37]

It might almost be Japhy speaking – were it not for the allusion to John
the Baptist. Even here, we should not overlook Kerouac's assumption
of the compatibility of Buddhist and Christian thinking.

In this light, it would seem that the author endorses his narrator's
search for an inclusive worldview in which both of these have
their place: that is, a version of the idea of a 'perennial philosophy', a

mystical wisdom common to all religions. Ray seeks what he calls 'the truth that is realisable in the dead man's bones and is beyond the tree of Buddha as well as the cross of Jesus' (p. 115). In order to attain that truth, he knows that he has fully to understand the meaning behind both symbols. Gautama demonstrates the possibility of enlightenment for all humanity by meditating under the 'bodhi' (enlightenment) tree; thus, he becomes Buddha. Jesus saves humanity from sin by dying in agony on the cross; thus, he becomes Christ. Both are inspiring icons, equally valid, and Ray's aim is to reconcile them in the service of an inclusive wisdom. Whether he achieves this is another matter. The novel ends ambiguously. With Japhy having left to spend time in a Japanese monastery, Ray follows his advice to serve as fire lookout on Desolation Peak in the Cascade Mountains. The closing paragraph of the final chapter has Ray on the one hand invoking the spirit of the absent Japhy, thus implicitly affirming the non-theism of Zen Buddhism, and on the other hand declaring his adherence to the theism of Christianity: 'Down on the lake rosy reflections of celestial vapour appeared, and I said "God, I love you" and looked up to the sky and really meant it. "I have fallen in love with you, God. Take care of us all, one way or the other."' (p. 204).

If Ray fails to find and formulate an inclusive wisdom, incorporating both Buddhist and Christian traditions, Japhy's persistent limitation, evident throughout the novel, is his blind spot when it comes to the latter. When he and Ray come across a black, evangelical Christian woman preaching on the streets of San Francisco's Chinatown, Ray is pleased, not only because of what she's saying but because of her delivery, which reminds him of Ma Rainey, the early jazz/blues singer. But Japhy can only grumble, 'I don't like all that Jesus stuff she's talking about', to which Ray retorts: 'What's wrong with Jesus? Didn't Jesus speak of Heaven? Isn't Heaven Buddha's nirvana?' Refusing to make any concession, Japhy condescendingly replies: 'According to your own interpretation, Smith' (p. 97).

Lest we be in any doubt about Kerouac's own perspective, we should note his self-summation in the biographical note which serves as an introduction to his volume of travel writing, *Lonesome Traveler* (1960]: 'Am actually not "beat" [sic], but strange solitary crazy Catholic mystic.' And he adds: 'Final plans: hermitage in the woods, quiet writing of old age, mellow hopes of Paradise (which comes to everybody anyway) ...'[38] Certainly, in the years following the publication of *The Dharma Bums*, his Roman Catholicism came to figure more and more centrally in his work. Perhaps the most important fictional instance of this comes towards the end of his novel *Big Sur* (1961, published 1963). Closely based on Kerouac's own experience, it charts the alcoholic breakdown of its narrator-protagonist, Jack Duluoz. It is in the midst of this despair and darkness that a vision of salvation is granted:

> I see the Cross [sic], it's silent, it stays a long time, my heart goes out to it, my whole body fades away to it, I hold out my arms to be taken away to it, by God I am being taken away my body starts dying and swooning out to the Cross, standing in a luminous area of the darkness, I start to scream because I know I'm dying but I don't want to scare Billie or anybody with my death scream so I swallow the scream and just let myself go into death and the Cross: as soon as that happens, I slowly sink back to life ... 'I'm with you, Jesus, for always, thank you' – I lie there in cold sweat wondering what's come over me for years my Buddhist studies and pipesmoking assured meditations on emptiness and all of a sudden the Cross is manifested to me – My eyes fill with tears – 'We'll all be saved ...'[39]

Such a moment of spiritual crisis might invite comparison with the writings of St John of the Cross, the sixteenth-century Catholic mystic who had to undergo his 'dark night of the soul' as the necessary prelude to revelation.[40]

Allowing for some distance between author and narrator, we must yet acknowledge that Kerouac himself turned increasingly to the cross rather than the bodhi tree in the last decade of his life. Two years before his death, when asked during an interview why he had never written a book about Jesus, he replied curtly: 'All I *write about* is Jesus.'[41] At the same time, we should note the consistency of concern underlying the shift from Buddhism back to Christianity. When he declared in the Buddhist-influenced *Mexico City Blues* that he wished to be 'safe in heaven dead', he was anticipating the kind of Christianity that he would come to adopt. His turn to the cross is surely the expression of a more and more intense obsession with death – not only that of Jesus, but also that of Gerard, and ultimately his own. Kerouac seems increasingly to have equated death with salvation itself.

The temptation here is to explain away Kerouac's increasing focus on death as a morbid consequence of his alcoholism. Even Allen Ginsberg, who was always grateful to his friend for introducing him to Buddhism, and who did more than anyone to honour his memory (founding the 'Jack Kerouac School of Disembodied Poetics' in 1974, for example), may have encouraged this error. In his retrospective assessment of Kerouac's later years, he offered a wholly pathological interpretation:

> As Jack grew older, in despair and lacking the means to calm his mind and let go of the suffering, he tended more and more to grasp at the Cross [sic]. And so, in his later years, he made many paintings of the Cross, of cardinals, popes, of Christ crucified, of Mary; seeing himself on the Cross, and finally conceiving of himself as being crucified. He was undergoing crucifixion in the mortification of his body as he drank.[42]

This observation probably has much truth in it, but we would surely be mistaken to take it as the key to Kerouac as religious writer. It is an explanation, but it does not necessarily make for understanding.

A more judicious approach would be to reflect that, while Kerouac's fixation on the cross no doubt was fuelled by a personal sense of pain, and while it may have prevented him attaining the balanced, inclusive spirituality sought by his fictional character, Ray Smith, it is spiritually valid. That is, it is consistent with his longstanding preoccupation with the nature of suffering. Moreover, it is in keeping with both Christianity and Buddhism, insofar as both of these warn against the error of clinging to one's individual life. Perhaps the more relevant here, given Kerouac's spiritual development, is the Christian tradition, which provides a choice between the mysticism of affirmation and the mysticism of ascesis, between the 'Via Positiva' and the 'Via Negativa'. However, as Matthew Fox explains, the true mystic would always have understood that both these approaches to God's creation are necessary to mystical wisdom. The Via Positiva is about 'befriending creation': it affirms 'creation as blessing'; it involves 'a psychology of trust and expansion'; it knows holiness to be 'cosmic hospitality' and 'humility as earthiness''; it is based on a theology of incarnation.[43] The Via Negativa is about 'befriending darkness'; it involves a willingness to be 'emptied'; it embraces 'nothingness'; it teaches us to 'let pain be pain', so that we are purged of attachment to the self; it is based on a theology of the cross. Ultimately, one finds that the Via Positiva and the Via Negativa are complementary, so that whichever path one takes one finds that one has simultaneously taken the other. God is darkness as well as light.[44] Thus, we may say, at the very least, that Kerouac's final embrace of nothingness is spiritually legitimate.

In this context, we should make a special, final mention of his
quasi-fictional celebration of his brother, which he called, significantly,
Visions of Gerard (1963). A book steeped in the faith of his upbringing, perhaps overburdened with references to Catholic doctrine and
marred by a sentimental attitude to Catholic institutions, it is also
remarkable for Kerouac's ability to find new ways of affirming the
possibility of revelation. This possibility can arise only when one has
given up all certainties:

> Hearken, amigos, to the olden message: it's neither what you
> think it is, nor what you think it isn't, but an elder matter,
> uncompounded and clear – Pigs may rut in field, come running
> to the Soo-Call, full of sow-y glee; people may count themselves
> higher than pigs, and walk proudly down country roads;
> geniuses may look out of windows and count themselves higher
> than louts; tics in the pine needles may be inferior to the swan;
> but whether any of these and the stone know it, it's still the
> same truth: none of it is even there, it's a mind movie, *believe*
> this if you will and you'll be saved in the solvent
> solution of salvation and Gerard knew it well in his dying
> bed in his way, in his way. And who handed us down the
> knowledge here of the Diamond Light? Messengers unnumber-
> able [sic] from the Ethereal Awakened Diamond Light. And
> why? because is, is – and was, was – and will be, will be –
> t'will![45]

Serious as the subject matter is, Kerouac yet manages to mingle homely
and holy speech, to put spiritual ideas into worldly idiom. Moreover,
though the ultimate sanction for his assurance is Christian – the closing
phrases of this paragraph evoking the Lord's Prayer – he manages to
accommodate Buddhist insights and principles. His capacity for
paradox has not failed him.

For at the heart of this affirmation is the paradoxical figure of his
brother. Gerard is an innocent child with a saintly wisdom way beyond
the grasp of the adults who witness his torment. He is a boy who loves
both to play and to pray, who can engage in the usual games with his
younger sibling and yet who can enlighten the nuns about the nature
of salvation. Each 'vision' of Gerard is for Kerouac the manifestation
of the sacred in the profane. As such, he stands as both the challenge
of suffering and the answer to suffering. Intense pain pushes the young
invalid to the point of a despair which is only the prelude to spiritual
rapture. First we have the despair:

A stab of pain – 'Help me!' he involuntarily cries out loud –
'Nobody could know how much it hurts – O my Jesus you've
left me alone and you're hurting me – And you too, you were
hurted – Aw, Jesus – nothing to help me – nothing' ...[46]

Then we have the spiritual rapture: Kerouac is convinced that no
sooner has Gerard plumbed these depths than 'ecstasy unfolds inside
his mind like a flower ...'[47] Nor is his triumph solely an individual
matter: 'Unceasing compassion flows from Gerard to the world even
while he groans in the very middle of his extremity.'[48]

Such sombre sentiments may seem to take us a long way from the
bebop style of *On the Road*. But I hope to have shown that Kerouac's
'Beat' writing is a flexible medium, capable of articulating different
levels of experience at once. For Beat is a much more comprehensive
term than is commonly supposed. To ignore the spiritual connotation
is to do the movement an injustice: certainly it is to misread Kerouac.
We have demonstrated here his gradual realisation that, for him at
least, spirituality was best articulated in terms of a specific religious
practice – for him, the Catholic one. But even if one prefers not to
concur, one can still benefit from knowing about his spiritual quest.
The burden of his work is that those who are 'beat' by life are those
who are truly blessed, for it is they who are open to the 'beatific' vision.
It is up to the 'Beat' writer, inspired by the 'beat' of music, to articulate
that vision as powerfully as possible. As Sal Paradise is told: 'Go moan
for man.'

Notes

  1 Peter Townsend, *Jazz in American Culture* (Edinburgh: Edinburgh Univer-
    sity Press, 2000), p. 155.
  2 Jack Kerouac, *On the Road* (London: Penguin, 1957; 1972), p. 8.
  3 Jack Kerouac, *Mexico City Blues* (New York: Grove Press, 1959), p. 242.
  4 Kerouac, *Mexico City Blues*, p. 243.
  5 Kerouac, *Mexico City Blues*, p. 223.
  6 Gerard Nicosia, *Memory Babe: A Critical Biography of Jack Kerouac*
    (Berkeley: University of California Press, 1994), p. 461.
  7 Dennis McNally, *Desolate Angel: Jack Kerouac, the Beat Generation, and
    America* (Cambridge, MA: Da Capo Press, 2003), p. 39.
  8 Kerouac, *On the Road*, p. 281.
  9 Kerouac, *On the Road*, p. 281.
 10 Jack Kerouac, *Visions of Cody* (New York: McGraw-Hill, 1972), p. 295.
 11 Oswald Spengler, *The Decline of the West*, Vols I and II, trans. Charles
    Atkinson (New York: Alfred A. Knopf, 1926 and 1928).

12 Quoted in Barry Miles, *Jack Kerouac: King of the Beats: A Portrait* (London: Virgin Books, 2002), p. 149.

13 Jack Kerouac, 'About the Beat Generation', in Ann Charters (ed.), *The Portable Jack Kerouac* (New York: Viking Penguin, 1995), p. 559.

14 Kerouac, 'About the Beat Generation', p. 561.

15 Kerouac, 'About the Beat Generation', pp. 561–2.

16 John Lardas, *The Bop Apocalypse: The Religious Visions of Kerouac, Ginsberg, and Burroughs* (Illinois: Illinois University Press, 2001), pp. 64–5.

17 Jack Kerouac, 'The First Word', in *The Portable Jack Kerouac*, p. 486.

18 Quoted in Stephen Prothero, 'Introduction', in Carole Tonkinson (ed.), *Big Sky Mind: Buddhism and the Beat Generation* (New York: Riverhead Books, 1995), p. 6.

19 Jack Kerouac, *Satori in Paris* (New York: Grove Press, 1966), p 10.

20 Jack Kerouac, 'Lamb, No Lion', in *The Portable Jack Kerouac*, pp. 562–3.

21 Jack Kerouac, 'Beatific: The Origins of the Beat Generation', in *The Portable Jack Kerouac*, p. 566.

22 McNally, *Desolate Angel*, p. 9.

23 McNally, *Desolate Angel*, p. 9.

24 See Nicosia, *Memory Babe*, p. 179.

25 Carole Tonkinson, 'Jack Kerouac', in *Big Sky Mind: Buddhism and the Beat Generation* (New York: Riverhead Books, 1995), pp. 24–5.

26 Quoted in Tom Clark, *Jack Kerouac: A Biography* (London: Plexus, 1997), pp. 168–9.

27 Jack Kerouac, *Some of the Dharma* (New York: Viking Penguin, 1997), pp. 3, 63, 175.

28 Quoted in Nicosia, *Memory Babe*, p. 490.

29 Kerouac, *Mexico City Blues*, p. 211.

30 Jack Kerouac, *The Scripture of the Golden Eternity* (San Francisco: City Lights, 1960; 1994), p. 23.

31 Kerouac, *The Scripture of the Golden Eternity*, p. 25.

32 Kerouac, *The Scripture of the Golden Eternity*, p. 44.

33 Eric Chaline, *The Book of Zen: The Path to Inner Peace* (Gloucester, MA: Fair Winds Press, 2003), pp. 92–4.

34 Kerouac, *The Scripture of the Golden Eternity*, p. 46.

35 Kerouac, *Some of the Dharma*, p. 301.

36 Jack Kerouac, *The Dharma Bums* (London: Penguin, 1959; 2000). Further references to this edition are given after quotations in the text.

37 Quoted in Barry Miles, *Jack Kerouac: King of the Beats*, pp. 279–80.

38 Jack Kerouac, *Lonesome Traveler* (London: Penguin, 1960; 2000), p. 9.

39 Jack Kerouac, *Big Sur* (London: Flamingo, 1963; 2001), p. 157.

40 See Ursula King, *Christian Mystics: The Spiritual Heart of the Christian Tradition* (London: Batsford, 1998), pp. 142–6.

41 Quoted in McNally, *Desolate Angel*, p. 331.

42 Allen Ginsberg, 'Kerouac's Ethic', in *Deliberate Prose: Selected Essays 1952–1995* (London: HarperCollins, 2000), p. 370.

43 Matthew Fox, *Original Blessing: A Primer in Creation Spirituality* (Sante
    Fe: Bear & Co, 1983), pp. 134–9.
44 Fox, *Original Blessing*, pp. 132–72.
45 Jack Kerouac, *Visions of Gerard* (London: Penguin, 1963; 1991), p. 57.
46 Kerouac, *Visions of Gerard*, p. 68.
47 Kerouac, *Visions of Gerard*, p. 69.
48 Kerouac, *Visions of Gerard*, p. 70.

3 'Vision music': Bob Dylan via Jack Kerouac and Allen Ginsberg

In October 1975, Allen Ginsberg and the songwriter Bob Dylan visited the grave of Jack Kerouac. They had stopped off at the Edson Cemetery, Lowell, Massachusetts during the course of Dylan's tour of the east coast of the United States. He called the tour 'The Rolling Thunder Revue', this name being an allusion in general to the 'freewheeling', unplanned nature of the enterprise, and in particular to a Cherokee medicine man called Rolling Thunder, who had become involved. (There was also an unstated, presumably ironic reference to a famous bombing operation by the USA during the recently terminated Vietnam War.) The Rolling Thunder Revue was an ensemble entertainment featuring not only his friend Ginsberg, but also musical acquaintances such as Joan Baez, Rambling Jack Elliott, Joni Mitchell and Roger McGuinn.[1]

Ginsberg had known Kerouac since the 1940s, and they had been closely identified with each other and with the Beat movement of the 1950s. They only discovered their irreconcilable differences during the 1960s: while Kerouac became disenchanted with the mass counterculture which the minority subculture of the Beats had inspired, Ginsberg actually became a countercultural figurehead. Dylan, though he had not known Kerouac personally, had been impressed by his writing. Certainly, he was anxious to film this pilgrimage to the grave, for inclusion in his ambitious cinematic work, *Renaldo and Clara* (1977).

Ginsberg later reflected on the occasion, evoking its mood in his own idiosyncratic syntax:

His [Kerouac's] influence is world wide, not only in spirit, with beat planetary youth culture, but poetic, technical. It woke Bob Dylan to world minstrelry: 'How do you know Kerouac's

poetry?' I asked Mr. Dylan after we improvised songs and read
some *Mexico City Blues* choruses over Kerouac's gravestone
[in] Lowell's Edson Cemetery ... walking side by side under
high trees and shifting clouds as we disappeared down distant
aisles of gravestones. *Someone handed me* Mexico City Blues *in
St. Paul in 1959 and it blew my mind!* Why? I asked. Dylan
answered that it was the first poetry that spoke his own
language.[2]

It is possible that, with typical modesty, Ginsberg was exaggerating the
impact of Kerouac the poet on Dylan the songwriter at the expense of
his own influence. The truth surely lies between: Kerouac and Ginsberg
were equally influential on the young songwriter. As we proceed now
to align him with Kerouac and with Ginsberg respectively, we will
discover the tension which informs Dylan's remarkable achievement.
But whoever we identify as his mentor, the point is that we should have
no trouble in placing Dylan firmly within the Beat legacy.

'Trying to get to heaven before they close the door': Dylan and Kerouac

In the light of the above, we may legitimately compare the author of
On the Road and the creator of *Highway 61 Revisited* – to choose two
titles not entirely at random. After all, it is common knowledge that
Kerouac celebrates the road in his art, and that Dylan consistently
relies on the motif of the highway in his. Indeed, several commentators
on both writers have pondered the implications of this parallel. Here is
John Tytell, an authority on Jack Kerouac: 'Dylan participates in the
Beat affinity for the road, the symbol and attitude toward experience
that braves anything as long as movement is encouraged.'[3] Again,
Richard Brown, in an essay on Dylan's work, notes the parallel with
Kerouac's. In *On the Road*, he observes, the narrator Sal Paradise and
his friend Dean Moriarty 'cross and re-cross (east and west, north and
south) the spaces of the nation, linking up its list of place names in a
journey that becomes its own bohemian *zeitgeist* [sic] and *raison
d'etre*.' Similarly, Dylan's songs are 'typically full of roads, streets and
highways and of journeys to and from that give the impression of
perpetual motion from place to place, and from relationship to relationship as a condition of being'.[4]

   Such insights make perfect sense in their own right. But here I want
to emphasise, beyond the accumulation of travel imagery and the celebration of restless wandering, the deeper significance of the symbolism

of the road: that is, the nature of the spiritual quest. Though their backgrounds differ radically – working-class Catholic and middle-class Jew – the preoccupations of Kerouac and Dylan are uncannily close.

It is appropriate to acknowledge the kind of useful documentation that gives us some textual basis for our conjectures. It is particularly helpful to have such confirmations of continuity as the following, from a typically elaborate footnote in Michael Gray's exhaustive work, *Song and Dance Man III: The Art of Bob Dylan*:

> While the impact of Kerouac's work has been unquantifiably wide (like Dylan's), Dylan often refers to Kerouac titles, commonly recycling them into his own. Thus, *On the Road* (1957) – 'On the Road Again'; *The Subterraneans* (1958) – 'Subterranean Homesick Blues'; *Visions of Gerard* (1963) – 'Visions of Johanna'; *Desolation Angels* (1965) – 'Desolation Row'. This last Dylan song also recycles a phrase direct from the Kerouac book: 'in the perfect image of a priest'; the same book also yields the phrase 'housing project hill', which Dylan throws into the same album's 'Just like Tom Thumb's Blues'. (Kerouac's book was first published March 1965; the songs were recorded that August.)[5]

Such details are genuinely revealing: we may infer a substantial and coherent influence, the young songwriter's evocation of Kerouac being so consistent that one is reminded of the young T. S. Eliot's debt to Baudelaire, or even the mature Eliot's debt to Dante. Nor do the words 'influence' and 'debt' quite do the process justice: it is more a matter of registering and revivifying a whole way of thought.

* * * * *

If for the moment we confine ourselves to his youth and early adulthood, we could for convenience trace three stages in Dylan's relationship with the Beat movement. Firstly, there is Robert Zimmerman's early discovery of, and enthusiasm for, Beat writers such as Kerouac and Ginsberg in the mid- to late 1950s. Secondly, there is his realisation of the significance of Woody Guthrie, particularly for his own development as a songwriter. At this stage, Zimmerman – now known as Bob Dylan – does not so much repudiate the Beat cult of the visionary outsider as transmute it into terms of the collective idealism of the 'folk revival' scene of the early 1960s. Thirdly, there is his spontaneous

renewal of the Beat vision – already implicit even in the more adventurous of his 'folk' songs – in the mid-1960s. However, we will find
that, as always with Dylan's debts and relationships, the situation is far
from being as clear-cut as this three-stage progression would suggest.
But it is a model worth bearing in mind as we proceed.

In his recently published memoirs, Dylan reflects that as a youth he
had become aware that writers such as Kerouac, Ginsberg and Gregory
Corso had changed the cultural landscape. He refers to '[t]he *On the
Road*, *Howl* and *Gasoline* street ideologies that were signalling a new
type of human existence'.[6] It was such work that inspired his early
interest not only in literature but also in the possibility that a renewal
of post-war America was coming up from below – an idea that we have
already seen associated with Spengler's 'fellaheen'. Only those who are
'beat down', who have to live on the street, literally or metaphorically,
are granted the vision of an alternative culture.

However, by the time Robert Zimmerman had changed his name
and travelled from Minnesota to New York, there was another influence – one complementary to the 'street ideologies' mentioned above,
but much more focussed on rural communities, on political struggle
and on acoustic musical expression. This was the music of Woody
Guthrie. It is not sufficient to label Dylan as a 'Beat' without also doing
justice to his 'folk' context. Indeed, Dylan's early success as a songwriter came out of his apprenticeship in the Greenwich Village 'folk
revival' scene. Basing many of his melodies on traditional songs, and
inspired by the example of his songwriting hero, Guthrie, he produced
a music that had both deep roots and broad relevance, that sounded as
though it had been written long ago but which spoke to the contemporary condition.

So profound was the influence of Guthrie that for a while it made
the Beat vision seem incomplete, or even inadequate. Dylan recalls
reacting against what he then had come to see as the individualism and
irresponsibility of Kerouac's fictional protagonists, such as the wildly
hedonistic Dean Moriarty (loosely based on Neil Cassady), by contrast
with Guthrie's commitment to the collective struggle for social justice:

> Within the first few months that I was in New York I'd lost my
> interest in the 'hungry for kicks' hipster vision that Kerouac
> illustrates so well in his book *On the Road*. That book had
> been like a bible for me. Not anymore, though. I still loved the
> breathless, dynamic bop poetry phrases that flowed from Jack's
> pen, but now, that character Moriarty seemed out of place,

purposeless – seemed like a character who inspired idiocy. He goes through life bumping and grinding with a bull on top of him.[7]

It was as if Dylan were putting behind him his adolescence in deciding to follow Guthrie's example rather than try to live out a fantasy he had, rightly or wrongly, based on Kerouac.

In feeling that he had to make a choice, Dylan was only being sensitive to the conflict which characterised the New York scene at the time. David Boucher has provided a useful summary of the alternatives open to the young songwriter, stressing that it was the folk rather than the Beat scene that provided the appropriate language for him at this crucial moment in his career:

> The prime example in the context of the folk revival that
> enabled Bob Dylan to launch his career was the popularity
> of hootenannies, gatherings of folksingers in which audiences
> often join in. Initially, as Dylan's own route testifies, the
> beatniks were not reaching out to a mass disaffected audience.
> The message that the beatniks projected in talking of travel,
> freedom, and transcending experiential and experimental
> barriers, though radical and almost forbidden, was vague and
> suggestive in its vision, intensely personalized and escapist.
> Only the periphery of the 'silent generation' of apathetic
> college students of the 1950s turned to Beat, while gradually
> and accumulatively growing numbers turned to folk, with its
> emphasis on communal redemption and identifiable political ills
> with prescriptions for reform. The folk revival was constructive,
> whereas because the Beat movement was politically acute, in
> practice it seemed socially and personally destructive, and
> indeed was portrayed as such by the media that exploited the
> commercial potential of its subversiveness.[8]

It is significant that Boucher proceeds to identify the young Dylan's alternatives with the particular names of Guthrie and Kerouac:

> The folk revival offered constructive visions of communal
> defiance of social injustices. The road that the emerging
> politically conscious preferred was that of Woody Guthrie
> rather than Jack Kerouac. The folk inspiration was utopian

and naive, in that it called upon city dwellers to look to the country for the wholesome values that should guide their conduct.[9]

Less harshly, and with a wider historical framework, Greil Marcus characterises the folk revival as a movement that privileged 'the country over the city, labor over capital, sincerity over education, the unspoiled nobility of the common man and woman over the business-man and the politician, or the natural expressiveness of the folk over the self-interest of the artist'. When Dylan sang 'Blowin' in the Wind', he offered, in keeping with the expectations of the folk revivalists, a glimpse of 'a democratic oasis unsullied by commerce or greed'.[10]

As the movement spread, and as the youth of the United States and Europe began identifying with its message, jettisoning electric for acoustic guitars and modelling themselves on Dylan and his friend, Joan Baez, it seemed as though the sound and values of local, rural culture had permeated mainstream civilization, thus paradoxically become global. But the question inevitably arose: how far could the category of 'folk' extend without becoming something else? Dylan himself had his doubts early on. But his more immediate problem was that he had very soon become a victim of his own success. He began to resent the constrictions of the folk revival – not so much the received form as the expected vocabulary. As we know, he had long since discovered the Beats; and now the Beat ethos was becoming newly attractive, particularly as its emphasis on transcending the given society offered a welcome relief from the earnest engagement of the traditional music purists. It was hard both to 'dig' *Mexico City Blues* and to join enthusiastically in a group rendition of 'We Shall Overcome'.

However, mention of *Mexico City Blues* may remind us that Kerouac himself had defied the customary distinction between popular musical forms. For him, jazz was indistinguishable from blues, both being articulations of the vision of the 'fellaheen'. Similarly, while Dylan on his first album presented himself as a folk singer – even going so far as to recount the story of his arrival in Greenwich Village and his attempt to be accepted as such (in the song, 'Talking New York') – he gave over most of the album to blues classics (for example, 'Fixin' to Die', 'Highway 51' and 'See That My Grave is Kept Clean'). For he knew that the folk revival movement was entirely sympathetic to the tradition of rural, acoustic blues. Thus, he could indulge his own predilection without fear of censure. Early works associated with names such as Blind Lemon Jefferson were acceptably authentic to the folk purist. Moreover, having identified himself so strongly with the blues, as a dominant strain in the folk tradition, Dylan was effectively paving the way for his own subsequent use of electric instrumentation: after all, the rural, acoustic blues of the Mississippi Delta had developed in the 1940s into the urban, electric blues of Chicago and Detroit.

However, Kerouac's enthusiasm for 'blues truth' was not the only decisive factor. More important was Kerouac's habit in the late 1950s of reciting both poems and fictional extracts to the accompaniment of music. In pioneering the idea of literature as performance, he effectively legitmised the idea of popular song – itself a performance – as literature. In bringing together literary with musical expression, he opened up new possibilities of creativity. As we have seen, Bruce Cook regards the experiment of mixing poetry and jazz as a highly suggestive failure: the idea proved hugely influential, even if Kerouac's own practice was confused. Whatever our judgement about the use of jazz as accompaniment, we might say that it was Kerouac's bebop-inspired writing which impressed Dylan sufficiently to attempt to transform folk music in a manner parallel to the Beat writer's transformation of literature. Dylan's new form might be seen as a marriage of folk structure and Beat spirit.

Certainly, Dylan's success in effecting such a marriage was to earn him a place in the standard anthology of Beat writing, Ann Charters' *Portable Beat Reader* (1992). There he is represented not only by excerpts from his novel *Tarantula* (1966, published 1971), which might be read as a pastiche of the work of Kerouac's and Ginsberg's friend, William Burroughs, but also by three early songs usually identified with the folk revival: 'Blowin' in the Wind', 'The Times They Are A-Changin' and 'A Hard Rain's A-Gonna Fall'. In these songs from the period 1962–3, widely regarded as folk 'protest' at the time, the editor discerns 'a vivid and personal apocalyptic vision' which is characteristically Beat.[11] This is a legitimate insight, as even during his Guthrie phase Dylan always managed to turn out lines reminiscent of Ginsberg. For example, in 'Hard Rain', the 'blue-eyed son' who warns of imminent catastrophe has heard 'one person starve' and 'many people laughing', has heard 'the song of a poet who died in the gutter'.[12] These may be the commonplaces of Romanticism, but they betray a more recent debt, namely the opening line of 'Howl': 'I saw the best minds of my generation destroyed by madness, starving hysterical naked …'[13]

To return to Charters' choice of material and her comments upon it:

while it is good to see Dylan given his due, a doubt might arise. For, in identifying him as an essentially 'Beat' figure from the very beginning, she might be accused of effectively ignoring his folk credentials. In doing so, she perhaps fails to do justice to his actual development as an artist and also to his sheer skill as a songwriter – a skill just as evident in his reworking of folk conventions as in his elaboration of the Beat vision. A similar doubt might arise when reading the reflection on what Kerouac and Dylan have in common by Barry Miles in his biography of the former. Referring to Kerouac's 'theory of spontaneous composition', he asserts: 'His reliance on intuition and instinct to provide results automatically belied craft and tradition. ... The disregard for the rules was most evident in the sixties, particularly with the rock musicians, with Bob Dylan being a supreme example.'[14] It is surely misleading to argue that there is an absence of craft and tradition in either Kerouac's or Dylan's work. As we have seen in our discussion of Kerouac, he knew that the art of improvisation implied a received form within which to improvise. As for Dylan, nobody can accuse him of being ignorant of, or cavalier towards, the structure and legacy of popular song. He was not accorded almost instant respect by the folk revivalists for nothing.

With this proviso, then, we may yet acknowledge – and, indeed, affirm – the Beat connection. His biographer and friend, Robert Shelton, is surely entitled to claim that Dylan systematically 'put the beats [sic] and Woody Guthrie on his own highway.'[15] This is a legitimate, if cryptic, summation; but again we need to be careful. For it is more customary to date his true flowering as a Beat songwriter, not from the folk phase (despite Charters' chronologically restricted selection of material) but from his move through and beyond it. In this light, we might say that his rediscovery of Beat went with his rediscovery of beat. It would, then, be no coincidence that his music went electric at the same time as his language became, as far as the Greenwich Village purists were concerned, esoteric. He could be seen as abandoning 'the natural expressiveness of the folk', embodied in Guthrie, for 'the self-interest of the artist', embodied in Ginsberg. A crucial event was his appearance at the Newport Folk Festival in 1965, when he was backed by members of the Paul Butterfield Blues Band, playing new songs such as 'Maggie's Farm' in a driving rock'n'roll style. To the folk devotees, he seemed to be rejecting the acoustic authenticity of communitarian traditionalism – the songwriter, Pete Seeger, a longstanding friend of Woody Guthrie, being the most outspoken in his objections. But as we have already indicated, electrified performances by blues artists were nothing new: indeed, the blues singer, John Lee Hooker, had given one the year before at that very festival, without any objection being made.[16]

We might surmise that Kerouac would have sympathised with Dylan, had he taken an interest in such events, given his own taste for loud and lively bebop, and given his feeling for the blues. At any rate, we may say that, just as Kerouac saw blues and jazz as one, so Dylan seemed to be setting out to prove that blues, folk and rock'n'roll were one. Nor is it likely that Kerouac would have disapproved of Dylan's liking for rock'n'roll: we do know that the Beat writer was especially fond of the songs of Chuck Berry, and that he was known to have admitted that Dylan had talent.[17]

As always, however, we must avoid making Dylan's development seem too mechanical, or even predictable. His fourth album, *Another Side of Bob Dylan* (1964), is acoustic in format but incipiently Beat in ethos. There are two songs in particular which seem to be pivotal: 'Chimes of Freedom' and 'My Back Pages'. But before considering them, it is worth quoting from two interviews which Dylan undertook the following year. In April he was asked about 'protest' music, and he declared: 'I don't write finger pointing songs.' In December, when asked what kind of music he played, he declared 'I don't play folk rock. … I like to think of it more in terms of vision music.'[18] It is the nature of this 'vision music' which is our concern in this chapter.

Andy Gill has offered a most persuasive reading of 'Chimes', which is worth quoting at some length. Gill's reading is based on the interesting assumption that the earlier work, which the general public and the media labelled 'protest' and which Dylan himself seemed now to dismiss, was actually restrictive and divisive, despite the recurrent appeal within the lyrics to universal humanity. It offered a kind of vision – an ideal – but it was not visionary in the full sense. When Dylan had sung that the times were a-changing, he seemed to exclude more people than he included in his vision of a collective future. But now, in finally repudiating his role as spokesman of his generation, he spoke for all ages, types, colours and creeds. He had become a truly visionary artist:

> 'Chimes Of Freedom' is the song which first signals his move away from straight protest songs to more allusive 'chains of flashing images.' It's his own *Tempest*, a compelling account of a visionary epiphany experienced in an electric storm, rendered in a hyper-vivid poetic style heavily influenced by the French

Symbolist poet Arthur Rimbaud. As Dylan and his companion
dive into a doorway to avoid the thunderous downpour, a
church bell begins tolling, and the synaesthetic combination of
these two elemental forces – the sound and the fury – inspires
in him a vision of universal redemption.[19]

It is the universality of his vision that marks the change, according to
Gill:

> The song is Dylan's Sermon On The Mount: having spent the
> last couple of years supporting this or that specific cause, his
> chimes of freedom here toll for all of life's downtrodden and
> unjustly treated folk – unmarried mothers, refugees, outcasts,
> the disabled, conscientious objectors, the unfairly jailed and
> 'For the countless confused, accused, misused, strung-out ones
> and worse/And for every hung up person in the whole wide
> Universe.' It's a veritable army of underdogs and peaceniks in
> uplifting collusion, an anthem as generous and inclusive as 'The
> Times They Are A-Changin'' was divisive and exclusive.[20]

It is worth supplementing this account of the song by emphasising
how important the nineteenth-century poet Rimbaud was to the Beats
and to their songwriting successors, offering them a model of the
visionary writer. John Lardas observes that Kerouac in particular,
along with his friend Lucien Carr, 'understood Rimbaud as celebrating
the heightened sensitivity of the artist and calling for mental acuity
through experience in order to have access to the realm of the universal.'[21] They saw themselves as heirs to his idea of the artist's true vocation as that of *voyant*. Again, I note the recent broadcast of a radio
programme, entitled 'Like a Rolling Stone' (Radio 4, Saturday 1 April
2006). The promotion for the programme reads as follows: 'Arthur
Rimbaud's poems, dazzling products of a few youthful years, had a
huge impact on literature. His poetry lives on in many rock songs and
in the lives of those who sung them, like Bob Dylan, Jim Morrison and
Patti Smith. ... The writer and translator Jeremy Harding, who has
prepared a new English edition of Rimbaud's poems, explores the myth
of the gypsy troubadour and Rimbaud's surprising attachment to the
road home.'[22] Whether Dylan's discovery of the symbolist poet was due
to Ginsberg's influence it is hard to say, but he must have felt himself
to be building on a visionary tradition. Consider lines such as the
following: 'Through the mad mystic hammering of the wild ripping

hale / The sky cracked its poems in naked wonder.' Again, Gill would seem to be right that Dylan follows Rimbaud in deploying synaesthesia, the representing of one sense by another. Consider the refrain itself: 'And we gazed upon the chimes of freedom flashing' (p. 132).

To return to the chief thrust of Gill's argument, that Dylan in this song offers a 'vision of universal redemption' and avoids the espousal of a specific cause: it is worth emphasising that that would only bring it closer to the Beat ethos (though Gill does not make this inference). For if Kerouac and Ginsberg identified with the fellaheen, the dispossessed minority within the given civilisation, they did so because they saw in it the potential for a whole new culture: one in which spirituality and love would have overcome materialism and alienation.

We can pursue this theme in our second choice of song from *Another Side*. In 'My Back Pages', Dylan rejects 'lies that life is black and white', to which he sees his previous incarnation as having succumbed. By identifying himself with one half of an arbitrary equation, and defining himself against the other, he had not realised that he would 'become my enemy in the instant that I'd preach'. Having understood the error of his ways, he now hopes to have regained his visionary innocence. To the accompaniment of an acoustic guitar, associated with the very stance of 'finger pointing' which he is now in the act of transcending, he sings his refrain: 'I was so much older then, I'm younger than that now' (p. 139).

The articulation of the Beat vision in an exclusively folk format was short-lived, however. The opening track of *Bringing It All Back Home* (1965) is a harsh rockabilly song with irrepressibly inventive lyrics: it seems to owe more to Chuck Berry and Jack Kerouac than to Woody Guthrie. But as always, the situation is far from straightforward. Dylan's biographer and friend, Robert Shelton, has made a convincing case for the song's derivation from one of his musical mentor's more obscure compositions, 'Taking it Easy'. He asks us to compare Guthrie's 'Pa was in the cellar, mixing up the hops' with Dylan's 'Johnny's in the basement, mixing up the medicine'.[23] However, whatever context for 'Subterranean Homesick Blues' we find illuminating, the song undoubtedly represents Dylan's challenge to orthodoxy. For example, the verse that begins, 'Ah, get born, keep warm', offering a succinct summary of the prospects for the average youth in the United States at the time, is an extraordinary feat of linguistic dexterity matched by a sense of the absurd. It takes us beyond the self-conscious simplicity and sincerity of the folk revival.

According to Boucher, Dylan's Beat stance was bound to be seen as provocative, even though he himself was convinced that he was simply expanding the possibilities of popular expression:

> Besides the charge of commercialism against Bob Dylan, one equally applicable to Joan Baez, Peter, Paul, and Mary, the Clancy Brothers, the Kingston Trio, the Chad Mitchell Trio, Harry Belafonte, and the Weavers, Dylan's transition to a more poetic style of composition away from the popularist emphasis may have tapped into the latent hostility of the folkies toward the Beat poets. Dylan's adoption of the persona of poet, as well as his befriending of Ginsberg, would not have endeared him to the finger-pointers of Greenwich Village. Immediately prior to the infamous electric set at the 1965 Newport Folk Festival, Dylan was in London with Ginsberg, who appears in the D. A. Pennebaker film *Don't Look Back* (1967), lurking in the background of the opening sequences as Bob Dylan nonchalantly flips flash cards with key words from 'Subterranean Homesick Blues.' Even the title of the song betrays the Beat connection.[24]

Boucher is thinking in particular of Kerouac's novel, *The Subterraneans* (1953, published 1958). The key figures in Dylan's song – Johnny mixing his medicine, Maggie warning of imminent police harassment, the narrator standing 'on the pavement, thinking about the government' – belong in a literal and metaphorical 'basement'. This is the subterranean world, the darkness into which the fellaheen is always cast: 'Better jump down a manhole/ Light yourself a candle' (p. 164). But as those lines imply, it is only in that darkness that a new light might begin to be seen. 'Subterranean Homesick Blues' holds out little hope of this, but some other songs on *Bringing It All Back Home* certainly do.

One such is 'Mr Tambourine Man', which we will consider separately in due course. Another is 'Love Minus Zero', a hymn of praise to a woman who 'speaks like silence', who needs neither 'ideals' nor 'violence' – aware that they are often synonymous – and who 'knows too much to argue or to judge' (p. 167). The paradox of silence being a kind of speech, or of ideals being a kind of violence, evokes the spirit of Zen, beloved by the Beats. It was Kerouac who personally encouraged Ginsberg's interest in Buddhism, and it was Ginsberg who personally encouraged Dylan's. But be that as it may, Dylan could hardly avoid encountering Zen, given his fascination with the Beats.

Again, he clearly found himself in sympathy with the idea that there is another way of experiencing the world, beyond convention and abstraction. He might have represented this with a figure akin to the holy fools of Japanese Buddhism, but he chose a serene North American woman instead (loosely based on Sarah Lowndes, whom he was to marry the following year), in the context of a well-known but infinitely beguiling North American poem (one by Edgar Allan Poe). As Andy Gill comments in his summation of the whole song:

> [C]ritics dissect, rich girls presume, bridges tremble, statues crumble – but through it all, she remains untouched, unaffected, smiling with the knowing Zen-like calm of the Mona Lisa. By the song's conclusion, she occupies his thoughts as completely as the eponymous bird obsesses the hapless protagonist of Poe's *The Raven* – although the closing image of the bird with the broken wing tapping at the narrator's window could simply be an expression of her essential vulnerability despite that inner strength he so admires.[25]

It only remains to add, of course, that the coexistence of vulnerability and strength is in itself a delightful paradox with which Zen would be in sympathy. But even putting Zen aside, we can surely characterise 'Love Minus Zero' as a reaffirmation of Kerouac's 'beatific' vision. It celebrates a free spirituality, beyond the restraints of religious hierarchy. It celebrates 'communitas', a new way of living in harmony beyond the 'ideals or violence' of the dominant 'structure'.

In stating the case in such general terms, however, we should not forget that such a vision is rooted in what Dylan calls 'street ideologies'. He himself has already echoed these in 'Subterranean Homesick Blues', and they continue to inform his next album, *Highway 61 Revisited*. Highway 61 spans the whole length of the United States, from Dylan's birthplace, Minnesota in the far north, to New Orleans in the far south. The very title reminds us, firstly, of Woody Guthrie's 'This Land is Your Land', with its celebration of the open highway. It reminds us, secondly, of Kerouac's *On the Road*, and of the journey as metaphor for spiritual quest. It reminds us, thirdly, of the very tradition of popular song, as that famous route takes in most of the significant places associated with the development of the people's music – blues, jazz, country and rock'n'roll. Nor should we overlook, in this context, how important the symbol of the highway has been in so many classic songs in all of those genres – whether to suggest the travails of life's journey or the possibility of escape.

Especially important in the Beat context is the opening song, 'Like a Rolling Stone'. This offers an insight into the consumer society, represented by a privileged but ignorant young woman, from the perspective of 'street ideology'. The young woman, referred to significantly as a 'princess', has lived in a fairytale world: the song begins with 'Once upon a time', appropriately enough. She used to think it acceptable to laugh about all those who were 'hanging out': that is, the poor, the dispossessed, the fellaheen. At best, she 'threw the bums a dime', but most of the time she lived her life way out of their reach, on her 'steeple' with 'all the pretty people', exchanging 'precious gifts'. Complacent and arrogant, she was constantly being warned that she was 'bound to fall'.

Now, sure enough, the time has come for her to 'pawn' her 'diamond ring', and to learn 'how to live out on the street'. She must begin to understand and embrace the world of the fellaheen. She has to realise that 'the mystery tramp' is 'not selling any alibis': she must make a 'deal' with him. Perhaps he can teach her how to survive, now that she is 'invisible', with 'no secrets to conceal'. However, the burden of the song is not simply negative. Though its refrain demands to know 'How does it feel' to be 'like a complete unknown', its title, included in the refrain, emphasises the need to begin again, identifying with the fellaheen and its potential new culture rather than with the comfort, security and spiritual blankness of the given civilisation (pp. 191–2). Thus, by telling the truth the song opens up new possibilities of living. 'Like a Rolling Stone' may sound like an accusation; but it is ultimately an affirmation. A distinctively 'Beat' song, it reminds us that only those who have been 'beat' will attain the 'beatific' vision.

*****

We have been considering Dylan's lyrics in relation to the Beat assumption that it is the fellaheen – the worn down, the weary, the dispossessed – which has the spiritual future in its hands. This notion was, as we know, articulated most explicitly by Kerouac. As we shall see, there is also an affinity with Ginsberg. But it is important to pursue the Kerouac connection as far as possible here, because it has not been widely recognised. We must now consider, therefore, the parallel between Dylan's and Kerouac's spiritual development. For, while Ginsberg did not stray from Buddhism once he had embraced it, they both became dissatisfied with its 'non-theism' and made their way back to the traditional Judaeo-Christian theism within which they had been raised.

We saw in the previous chapter that Kerouac, even while espousing Buddhism, was particularly interested in how it might be reconciled with Christianity. This was, indeed, one of the main themes of his novel *The Dharma Bums*. He was never quite convinced by Snyder's exclusive devotion to Zen. Moreover, even though it was he who introduced Ginsberg to Buddhism, he continued to be haunted by the Catholicism of his childhood. It was as if he had two possible solutions to the perennial problem of pain – felt by him most acutely, not only because of his own physical ailments, but also because of the sense of loss occasioned by the early death of his brother Gerard. One solution was detachment from the desire which led to suffering: that was the Buddhist way. The other solution was dedication to the man who took it upon himself to suffer for the sins of humankind: that was the Christian way. We have seen how the novels *Big Sur* and *Visions of Gerard*, written under an increasing sense of the proximity of death, convey his shift of emphasis from the one to the other. In short, Kerouac chose to sit beneath the cross rather than the bodhi tree.

Dylan's work was from the outset steeped in the Bible. The so-called protest songs are full of allusions not only to the Judaic scriptures but also to what Christians call the New Testament. For example, 'The Times They Are A-Changin' ends with an invocation of Christ's promise: 'But many that are first shall be last; and the last shall be first' (Matthew 19:30). It is a powerfully effective allusion, for those who know their scripture. Nor should it strike us as unusual for Dylan to make it, regardless of any allegiance to a specific faith, whether Jewish or Christian. William Blake famously declared: 'The Old and New Testaments are the Great Code of Art.'[26] We could translate this, less peremptorily, by saying that all creative work in the West inevitably owes a debt to the Bible. But it is one thing to use the scriptures as a convenient cultural sourcebook; it is another to quote them with all the earnestness of a believer. Here we must make an important differentiation. Robert Zimmerman, brought up as an orthodox Jew, managed to familiarise himself with the Christian scriptures as well as the Judaic: hence the ease with which he quotes the words of Christ above. But if we are seeking for a parallel stage of development with Kerouac's, we are more likely to refer to what became known as his 'born-again' phase. Here his brief flirtation with Zen is forgotten as he affirms his faith in Jesus as the Messiah promised by prophets of Israel such as Isaiah. 'You Gotta Serve Somebody', he declares in a distinctly non-Zen idiom on his conversion album, *Slow Train Coming* (1979). Another song from the same album, 'Precious Angel', is dedicated to the woman who, we may infer, helped him come to believe in Jesus as the Christ. While she is a veritable agent of salvation, there are others who would distract him from his goal. The singer's 'so-called friends' tell him 'All is well' – perhaps suggesting pseudo-Zen complacency? – but he chooses to contemplate 'the darkness that will fall from on high'. Again, he addresses another woman, a shadow of the 'precious angel', who is 'drawing water for your husband, and suffering under the law'. In other words, she is spiritually oppressed, untouched by the grace of Christian salvation. As she draws the water, she is 'telling him about Buddha, and telling him about Mohammed in one breath', but she never refers to 'the Man who came and died a criminal's death' (p. 426). The spiritual eclecticism of the New Age is castigated here in the name of commitment to a definite faith and doctrine. What is commended is the strength and security of religion, not some vague sense of spirituality.

It is difficult not to be impressed by Dylan's conviction in such songs. However, it has to be admitted that his return to theism, like Kerouac's, has an air of desperation about it – though whether that disqualifies it is another matter, desperation being a legitimate response to some situations. One senses again and again in the songs on not only *Slow Train* but also *Saved* (1980) and *Shot of Love* (1981) a radical discontent with the ways of this world – to which belief in God, associated here with a desire for death, provides the balm. The same applies to what has been called the post-Christian songs, in which Dylan's theism is much more rooted in his Judaism – though the God addressed is more complex and elusive than the casual listener might suppose. We will be considering his use of Biblical symbolism in our discussion of his affinity with Ginsberg and Blake, but here it might be worth indicating how the theme of waiting for God continues to lend an intensity to the work produced almost twenty years after his 'born-again' phase.

The key album is *Time Out of Mind* (1997). A song with a deceptively simple title, 'Trying to Get to Heaven', manages to fuse spiritual yearning and cultural nostalgia in a subtly disquieting play of images. Intending to 'sleep down in the parlor / And relive my dreams', the singer ponders if 'everything is as hollow as it seems'. This hollowness at the heart of contemporary experience prompts the desire to retreat into a dream which is not only individual but also collective – the latter being the memory of how it was once possible for a significant minority to live authentically on the margins of civilisation. But now, in the era of globalisation, it is increasingly difficult to locate that small group of genuine outsiders, of free spirits: 'Some trains don't pull no gamblers / No midnight ramblers, like they did before.' In these dark days, the figure of the drifter, as honoured by Woody Guthrie, is as remote as the figure of the 'Dharma Bum', as honoured by Jack Kerouac. With their decline, the vision of a genuine alternative to conformist materialism seems to have vanished. We can no longer invoke the fellaheen; nor can we proclaim the values of 'communitas'. Materialist civilization has triumphed; 'structure' is impregnable. The only answer now is to try 'to get to heaven before they close the door'.[27]

The God who presides over this heaven is clearly not to be fooled with. The salvation he offers is available only to the few who make the necessary effort – as in Bunyan's *Pilgrim's Progress*, which narrates the arduous journey of the protagonist, Christian, to the heavenly city – and will not be available indefinitely. It is not so much that God is dead, as that God is planning to withdraw from his creation. In the words of the poet Geoffrey Hill, 'God / Is distant, difficult'.[28] He becomes even more distant and difficult in the song, 'Not Dark Yet'.

Very much in the spirit of the later Kerouac, Dylan's main preoccupation here is with death as a release. Tired of the false consolations of life – notably the unreliable love of an unnamed woman who has deserted him – the singer prepares to enter the darkness which is inevitable and which will be most welcome. He has no sense of spiritual identity, of inner life ('feel like my soul has turned into steel'); nor has he any sense of physical belonging ('not even room enough to be anywhere'). Such startling phrases build up to an apprehension of sheer negation: 'Every nerve in my body is so vacant and numb / I can't even remember what it was that I came here to get away from.' The convoluted syntax enacts the tortuous realisation. This in turn is placed in context with perfect simplicity by the almost casual remark: 'Don't even hear a murmur of a prayer / It's not dark yet, but it's getting there.'[29]

There is perhaps an interesting comparison to be made here with Thomas Hardy's poem, 'The Oxen', in which the poet expresses the desire to believe in the birth of Jesus as the son of God, an idea which he used to celebrate in kneeling before the nativity scene as a child. What if he were invited by someone to walk out with him on a Christmas Eve to do so again? 'I should go with him in the gloom, / Hoping it might be so.'[30] Hardy, an agnostic, puts a great deal of weight on that one word, 'hoping'. Dylan, a believer, allows free range to his doubt. As with Kerouac's later work, the implication of Dylan's song is that the only God worth taking seriously is the one who appears out of complete and utter darkness, when all hope has been abandoned.

Both Kerouac and Dylan might be categorised as modern artists in search of God. As such, they stand apart from what many people mistakenly assume to be the Beat ethos: that is, wild and irresponsible hedonism. Rather, their pursuit of the 'beatific' vision is serious and sustained. To use a metaphor, the conviction is that the raft of religion is needed in order to traverse the sea of spirituality. In that respect, they stand apart also from the spirit of the mass counterculture which the minority subculture of the Beats is credited with fostering. Neither Kerouac nor Dylan subscribed to the promise of infinite freedom of spirit held out by the 'love generation'. Where Ginsberg relished his role as guru to the hippies, Kerouac retreated – not only into alcoholism (the subject of much gossip, then and now) but also into Catholicism (scarcely mentioned, except as a sentimental error). Dylan too dissociated himself from psychedelia, from free love, from communes and other aspects of 'flower power', almost immediately after producing the 'hippest' three albums of the mid-sixties – *Bringing It All Back Home*, *Highway 61 Revisited* and *Blonde on Blonde*. In an apparent repudiation of the Beatles' *Sgt Pepper* album, which set the tone for 1967 with its ambitious orchestration, sound effects, and self-conscious lyrics, he produced *John Wesley Harding* (completed later that year, to be released in January 1968). That album contained austerely Biblical words set to simple, homely music performed by a group of four musicians (including Dylan). Nor should we overlook the significance of Dylan's absence from the Woodstock festival of 1969 – an event which for many seemed to sum up the values of the counterculture.

It is perhaps no coincidence that in the same year Kerouac made his definitive statement against the spirit of the age. In an article called 'After Me, the Deluge', he repudiated the idea that he was patron saint of the new youth movements such as the hippies and the 'Yippies' (Youth International Party). His tone is sarcastic, to say the least, as he pretends to play with the possibility that it might be good for his image to encourage this idea:

WHAT AM I THINKING ABOUT? I'm trying to figure out
where I am between the established politicians and the
radicals, between cops and hoods, tax collectors and vandals.
I'm not a Tax-Free, not a Hippie-Yippie – I must be a Bippie-
in-the-Middle. [But ...] No, I'd better go around and tell

everybody, or let others convince me, that I'm the great white
father and intellectual forebear who spawned a deluge of
alienated radicals, war protestors, dropouts, hippies and even
'beats,' and thereby I can make some money maybe and a 'new
Now-image' for myself (and God forbid I dare call myself the
intellectual forebear of modern spontaneous prose), but I've got
to figure out first how I could possibly spawn Jerry Rubin,
Mitchell Goodman, Abbie Hoffman, Allen Ginsberg and other
warm human beings from the ghettos, who say they suffered no
less than the Puerto Ricans in their barrios and the blacks in
their Big and Little Harlems, and all because I wrote a matter-
of-fact account of a true adventure on the road (hardly an
agitational propaganda account) featuring an ex-cowhand and
an ex-footballer driving across the continent north, northwest,
midwest and southland looking for lost fathers, odd jobs, good
times, and girls and winding up on the railroad. Yup, I'd better
convince myself that these thinkers were not on an entirely
different road.[31]

Kerouac is even prepared to disassociate himself from his earlier identification with the fellaheen, given that the radical politics of the
Yippies (famous, or notorious, for their antics at the Democratic
Convention in Chicago the year before) seems routinely to rely on a
false pose of solidarity with the wretched of the earth. Moreover, his
provocative summary of his novel *On the Road* deliberately under-
plays its spiritual significance, given what he sees as the pseudo-
spirituality of the hippies.

We might compare Kerouac's response at the time with Dylan's
retrospective reflection many years later. In *Chronicles* he offers the
following account of the counterculture, which might seem celebratory
at first reading but which really amounts to a devastating critique,
albeit modified by an acknowledgement of the wrongs which it
opposed:

In 1968 The Beatles were in India. America was wrapped up in
a blanket of rage. Students at universities were wrecking parked
cars, smashing windows. The war in Vietnam was sending the
country into a deep depression. The cities were in flames, the
bludgeons were coming down. Hard-hat union guys were
beating kids with baseball bats. The fictitious Don Juan, a
mysterious medicine man from Mexico, had become the new

consciousness craze, had brought in a new level of awareness or life force and was wielding it like a machete. Books about him were sailing off the shelves. Acid tests were in full swing, acid was giving people the right attitude. The new worldview was changing society and everything was moving fast – lickety-split. Strobes, black lights – freakouts, the wave of the future. Students trying to seize control of national universities, antiwar activists forcing bitter exchanges. Maoists, Marxists, Castroites – leftist kids who read Che Guevara instruction booklets were out to topple the economy. Kerouac had retired, and the organized press was stirring things up, fanning the flames of hysteria. If you saw the news, you'd think that the whole nation was on fire. It seemed like every day there was a new riot in another city, everything on the edge of danger and change – the jungles of America being cleared away. Things that had used to be in traditional black and white were now exploding in full, sunny color.[32]

The reference to Kerouac is surely significant: he represents the standard by which the above scene is being judged. If the young Dylan had during his folk period dismissed Kerouac's fictional characters, there can be little doubt of his consistent admiration for Kerouac himself. He represents Beat authenticity, as opposed to the chaotic, opportunistic superficiality of what followed in his wake.

The question arises of whether or not Dylan himself played a role in creating the spirit of the age. After all, it was he who had sung 'The Times They Are A-Changin''. But the Dylan of *Chronicles* feels himself able to endorse the scepticism regarding the outrageous claims of the sixties which he had felt at the time. He had known early on that something was going wrong:

Being born and raised in America, the country of freedom and independence, I had always cherished the values and ideals of equality and liberty. I was determined to raise my children with those ideals. A few years earlier Ronnie Gilbert, one of The Weavers, had introduced me at one of the Newport Folk Festivals saying, 'And here he is, take him, you know him, he's yours.' I had failed to sense the ominous forebodings in the introduction. Elvis had never even been introduced like that. 'Take him, he's yours!' What a crazy thing to say! Screw that. As far as I knew, I didn't belong to anybody then or now. I had a wife and children whom I loved more than anything else in the world. I was trying to provide for them, keep out of trouble, but the big bugs in the press kept promoting me as the mouthpiece, spokesman, or even conscience of a generation. That was funny. All I'd ever done was sing songs that were dead straight and expressed powerful new realities. I had very little in common with and knew even less about a generation that I was supposed to be the voice of. I'd left my hometown only ten years earlier, wasn't vociferating the opinions of anybody. My destiny lay down the road with whatever life invited, had nothing to do with representing any kind of civilization. Being true to yourself, that was the thing. I was more a cowpuncher than a Pied Piper.[33]

Once again, we have the image of the road: Kerouac is obliquely invoked. Indeed, the very celebration of the refusal to conform is reminiscent of Kerouac's own writing. Even the reference to being a 'cowpuncher' seems to echo the mention of the 'ex-cowhand' in the passage from 'After Me, the Deluge' quoted above. In both cases, the intention is to downplay one's own importance, and to query the idea that any one person should be credited with responsibility for the *Zeitgeist*. Kerouac and Dylan concur in finding that the beatific vision is best pursued in detachment from a mass movement, even if it invokes the name of 'Beat' in seeking credibility.

'To dance beneath the diamond sky': Dylan and Ginsberg

In comparing Kerouac and Dylan, we examined such themes as their identification with the dispossessed (the fellaheen) and their turn back to the Judaeo-Christian God (theism). More widely still, we raised general issues about the nature of the Beat legacy, confirming our initial hypothesis that it is a spiritual movement as much as a literary or cultural movement. At the very least, it will be clear from the material covered so far that if Kerouac and Dylan are representatively Beat, then 'Beat' means a lot more than drug-fuelled disaffection or even exuberant self-expression.

However, given that Dylan is the most important Beat songwriter, it would be misleading to confine our attention solely to his affinity with Kerouac, even though that affinity raises all sorts of issues about the continuity between the 1950s and 1960s. There are many sides to Bob Dylan, and we must not leave the impression that his art is solely

focused on death and darkness, as some of the lyrics quoted towards
the end of the last chapter would indicate. It will perhaps be by exploring his affinity with Ginsberg that we might redress the balance.
Having said that, nothing we can say is going to turn Dylan into a
countercultural guru with a tendency to public outrage, nor into a
devoted Tibetan Buddhist – both of which phrases would accurately
describe Ginsberg. Thus, we may say that Dylan and Ginsberg comple-
ment each other, deriving their poetic visions from a common source,
but with different emphases and interests.

We might gain some purchase on this connection by considering an
interview which Ginsberg gave in 1994. During the course of it he was
asked, 'Do you think that your poetry helped to make the work of
songwriters like Dylan possible?' He replied:

> Among others. I think that between Kerouac and myself and
> Burroughs, there was quite an impact. Dylan told me – I know
> Kerouac was a major inspiration for him as a poet. I think it's
> those chains of flashing images: 'the motorcycle black madonna
> two-wheel gypsy queen and her silver-studded phantom lover'
> come out of Kerouac's rhetoric.[34]

Ginsberg does not get the quotation quite right – the word 'lover' does
not figure in that line from 'Gates of Eden' – but his instinct is surely
correct that such phrasing does betray a strongly Beat influence. The
issue then is whether or not Kerouac's influence overshadowed that of
his own; and we must surely suspect that he is underplaying his own
importance in the above statement. Ginsberg it was whom Dylan
arranged to keep in touch with during the latter's 1965 tour of the UK,
making sure to feature him in the filmed sequence accompanying the
song 'Subterranean Homesick Blues', which formed the opening of
D. A. Pennebaker's hugely influential film on Dylan, *Don't Look Back*
(1967). Ginsberg it was whom Dylan invited to accompany him on
'The Rolling Thunder Revue' ten years later, as if to confirm that the
true spirit of the Beat movement, as opposed to the subsequent adul-
teration of it, lived on; we have already referred to the sequence, filmed
for *Renaldo and Clara* (1977), in which the two of them visit Kerouac's
grave.

In this light, we will try to trace Dylan's affinities with Ginsberg as
a visionary artist. Our chief concern is to clarify further the nature of
the 'beatific' vision, so we need not provide a point-by-point parallel
between the two: rather, we should see how they both relate to what
we have called the visionary tradition.

It should be clear by now that that tradition does not derive exclusively from the wisdom of the East. We have seen, for example, how Alan Watts invokes the name of Jesus in order to justify his hypothesis of a suppressed mystical undercurrent to Western religion. What we have not done is indicate how the Judaeo-Christian scriptures form part of the legacy inherited by Kerouac, Ginsberg and their peers. In order to bridge the gap between the Bible and the Beats, we will have to bring in at least one other representative of the visionary tradition. The obvious candidate is William Blake, whom we have referred to before. He was not only the first great English Romantic poet but also a major influence on the Beats – on Ginsberg in particular.

* * * * *

A Christian, but a highly unorthodox one, Blake set himself the task of revitalising the Christian myth; indeed, he was one of the first believers to conjecture that the story of Jesus really was a liberating myth, not a literal truth. Far from seeing the Bible as the last word – indeed, the ultimate Word – he felt able to rewrite it totally according to the dictates of his imagination, which he took to be a spiritual force. Thus, instead of setting out from the idea of an omniscient and omnipotent God who had created the cosmos and then created humanity, he saw humanity as the source of both cosmos and creator. That is, long before Hegel proposed, and Nietzsche confirmed, the 'death of God', Blake had comprehended that very principle within a new, radical Christianity.[35]

The God of the Jewish scriptures – what he, as a Christian, called the Old Testament – Blake identified with the abstract, inhuman deity of the eighteenth-century Enlightenment; he called him 'Urizen' (the product of 'your reason'). Moreover, according to his dramatic rewriting of the New Testament, that God – who had never existed in the first place, except as a human projection – could be said to have departed once and for all with the birth, death and resurrection of Jesus. For if Jesus showed us how to realise our own divinity, then we were now freed from the obligation to worship a deity distinct from ourselves. Moreover, if 'Empire' – the tyranny of Urizen – was 'against Art', then Jesus was the greatest of 'Artists'. When Blake famously declared the Bible to be 'the Great Code of Art', he immediately added: 'Art is the Tree of Life. God is Jesus.'[36] In other words, false religion was the dogma that enslaved; true religion was the story that liberated. But meanwhile, conventional Christianity went on clinging to its arid and abstract sky-father and preferring theological dogma to the infinite possibility of the sacred imagination.

Blake's particular genius was to remain faithful to the form of his 'Great Code' while turning its world, as far as the orthodox were concerned, upside down. *Songs of Innocence* (1789), with its comforting, apparently stable imagery of shepherd and lamb, father and child, forms the conventional prologue to this radical myth, which begins with *The Marriage of Heaven and Hell* (1793). Here he demonstrates that ostensibly stark opposites – heaven and hell, Eden and wilderness, good and evil, reason and desire – always turn out to be dialectical 'contraries', without which 'there is no progression'. Defying orthodoxy, Blake in the *Marriage* commends the wisdom of the 'devils', succinctly conveyed in the section called 'Proverbs of Hell'. For example: 'If the fool would persist in his folly he would become wise. ... What is now proved was once only imagined. ... The tygers of wrath are wiser than the horses of instruction. ... Exuberance is Beauty.' Humanity has suppressed this wisdom because it has forgotten that 'All deities reside in the human breast'. It is as if 'man has closed himself up, till he sees all things thro' narrow chinks of his cavern.' He has come to regard the very limits he has set himself as eternal and immutable. The alternative is stated boldly: 'If the doors of perception were cleansed every thing would appear to man as it is: infinite.' Such a cleansing would reveal that 'everything that lives is holy.'[37] Thus, in the poem 'London' from *Songs of Experience* (which was published to include the earlier *Innocence* volume in 1794) we learn that it is 'the mind-forg'd manacles' which keep humanity subject to state and church hierarchy.[38] If 'All deities reside in the human breast', then so do all oppressive doctrines.

In *The First Book of Urizen*, published the same year as *Experience*, the Book of Genesis is rewritten so that the creation of our cosmos turns out to have been simultaneous with the fall of humanity. For if the world we know is the result of Urizen's having separated himself out from a primal harmony known as eternity, and if Urizen, like all deities, is human in origin, an aspect of our own minds, then to find ourselves in this world of false laws and limits is effectively to have restricted our own vision. Letting reason take over from our other faculties, we have become alienated, or 'fallen'. We have constructed a false ideal, have come to believe in a tyrannous perfection by which to measure everything: 'One King, one God, one Law.'[39]

Against the dominance of 'your reason', it is the task of the imagination to provide a vision of freedom, in which all human beings may participate without surrendering to a sterile uniformity. In the famous 'Preface' to *Milton* (1810) the poet, in his capacity as tribal bard, declares that he 'will not cease from mental fight' until 'we have built Jerusalem / In England's green and pleasant land'.[40] The potentially infinite power of humanity is represented in his last major work *Jerusalem* (1804–20) by the figure of Albion, who is simultaneously England and the primal, universal man. He is woken from his long and heavy slumbers by Los, the artist, 'the Prophet of Eternity'. Albion realises that God, the cosmos and history are all products of his own mind. Having realised this, he is able to meet Jesus as an equal and as a friend. Jesus is, ultimately, Albion's waking self. Jesus's resurrected body may therefore be identified with that of a newly risen humanity, which has realised the power of imagination and love.[41]

* * * * *

In 1948, long before he had become an established poet, Ginsberg was lying on his bed in his apartment in Harlem, with a volume of Blake's poems open beside him. Twelve years later, at the height of his Beat fame, he looked back to that moment as decisive:

> Once, chancing to read Blake and dwelling on the words of 'Ah! Sunflower', I heard his voice and looked out of the window, realizing that *this* universe was the sunflower seeking eternity. The experience led me to know art as a time-machine to carry the secret revelation and transmit it unbroken from mind to mind.[42]

In the interests of balance, it should also be stated that Ginsberg's vision unsettled his mind, resulting in a short spell in the Columbia Psychiatric Institute in 1949; but even that ordeal provided him with visionary inspiration, which he was to put to good use in 'Howl', as we shall see. In 1969 Ginsberg recorded a selection of Blake's *Songs of Innocence and Experience*. In the liner notes, he explained why Blake meant so much to him, referring again to the revelation which he had had as a young man while reading that volume:

> Inspiration began 21 years, half my life ago, living in Harlem, in mind's outer ear I heard Blake's voice pronounce 'Ah! Sunflower' and 'The Sick Rose' (and 'A Little Girl Lost') and experienced an illumination of eternal consciousness, my own heart identical with the ancient heart of the universe.[43]

It is clear that the Blake vision – or auditory hallucination, to be exact – haunted Ginsberg throughout the most part of his poetic career. It gave him his faith in art as a medium between the profane and sacred realms – a faith substantiated by his interest in Spengler's idea of a correspondence between the microcosm and the macrocosm, between mundane experience and religious revelation.

Along with this ambitious ideal, however, it also reminded him of something rather more obvious: how close poetry is to song. In his liner notes, Ginsberg emphasises the musical quality of Blake's work, which he regards as inseparable from the visionary. That being so, he has no trouble in conceiving of a tradition which runs from Blake to Dylan. Having reminded us that 'The title *Songs of Innocence and of Experience* is literal; Blake used to sing them unaccompanied at his friends' houses', he proceeds to his typically audacious claim, made with the authority of one who knows that he too is the beneficiary of the legacy of inspiration:

> Ma Rainey, Pound, Dylan, Beatles, Ray Charles, Ed Sanders
> and other singers have returned language poesy to minstrelsy.
> As new generations understand and decipher poetical verses for
> gnostic-psychedelic and practical artistic messages, I hope that
> musical articulation of Blake's poetry will be heard by the Pop
> Rock Music Mass Media Electronic Illumination Democratic
> Ear and provide an eternal poesy standard by which to measure
> sublimity and sincerity in contemporary masters such as Bob
> Dylan, encouraging all souls to trust their own genius
> inspiration. For the soul of the planet is wakening, the time of
> dissolution of material forms is here, our generation's trapped
> in imperial satanic cities and nations, and only the prophetic
> priestly consciousness of the bard – Blake, Whitman or our
> own new selves – can steady our gaze into the fiery eyes of the
> tygers of the wrath to come.[44]

Thus, we have a visionary tradition which stretches back to the Bible, with its indictment of 'imperial satanic cities' such as Babylon, and comes right up to the present, in the persons of Ginsberg himself and his friend Bob Dylan. Popular song is as intrinsic to this tradition as is 'high' poetry. Blake showed the way.

We might also pause to note that those 'tygers of wrath' are an allusion to *The Marriage of Heaven and Hell*, from which we have already quoted – though we should not overlook the possibility of a reference to Blake's most famous song of experience, 'The Tyger'. Ginsberg would seem to be thinking in apocalyptic terms: that is, expecting catastrophe but hopeful of ultimate deliverance. In doing so, he is drawing on what Blake called 'the Great Code', and so would seem to regard himself as working within the same, broadly Biblical framework. That does not mean, of course, that Ginsberg is a believer, Jewish or otherwise – he was, as we know, much more sympathetic to the wisdom of the East – but it does mean that he was willing to adopt Blake's faith in the prophetic power of poetry. To put the case even more strongly, we may say that Ginsberg seemed to regard both Blake and himself – and, by association, Dylan also – as having an insight into the nature of apocalypse.

Let us clarify this term and its significance in this context. There are certain parts of the Bible which we call 'apocalyptic', from an ancient Greek word which means 'unveiling', because they offer to reveal the secret of the last days of history. Over the centuries, many poets have been inspired by these writings, notably Shakespeare, Milton and, above all, Blake. As for Ginsberg himself, we need only think of his most famous poem, 'Howl', which uses the long line and expansive rhetoric associated with Biblical verse. As for Dylan: we might say that he has worked mainly within the short lyric form associated with secular poetry and song, but he has never strayed far from the Biblical worldview which he acquired during his Jewish upbringing. There again, as we have seen, his commitment to the values of Judaism and Christianity has been variable, ranging from the tactical allusion of his early career, through the polemical commitment of the 'born-again' years, and so to a sombre theism. All in all, though, with whatever qualifications we might want to make, it seems appropriate to compare Ginsberg and Dylan in the context of 'the Great Code', and specifically in the context of apocalypse. Before doing so, however, we need some more Biblical background.

The most famous apocalyptic work of all is the Book of Revelation, which completes the Christian Bible. But the Judaic scriptures – the Old Testament of Christianity – also contain much apocalyptic material. For example, the Book of Isaiah includes a prophecy of the fall of the Babylonian empire, the oppressor of the Israelites. Since Revelation was written much later than Isaiah, at the time of the Roman persecution of the early Christians, 'Babylon' is used as a code word for Rome, which in turn is associated with all the forces opposed to Christ himself. We might take Revelation as representative of the apocalyptic genre.

It is written in the form of a vision: the author, known popularly as 'John the Divine', claims to have understood God's hidden plan to bring the present order of things to an end and establish his kingdom. He warns of imminent catastrophe – plague, famine, war, death – but he also promises 'a new heaven and a new earth'. At first, the forces of evil seem to be triumphing, with 'that old dragon, Satan' threatening to devour the male child born to the 'woman clothed with the sun'. But the boy is rescued, growing up to become the Messiah, the promised deliverer of his people. As such, he will subdue the dragon and all those who serve it: for example, the 'harlot' whose 'name is Mystery', living in luxury made possible by the toil of the oppressed; and the 'beast' whose 'mark' they are forced to wear. Looking forward, John promises the fall of Babylon and, after the final battle on the field of Armageddon, the establishment of God's city of Jerusalem. Thus, the apocalyptic vision is both negative (denouncing Babylon) and positive (announcing Jerusalem). But perhaps the most important thing about an apocalypse is that it should unsettle us: it should throw into doubt everything we have taken for granted. This is not a matter of specific symbols but of a general stance.[45] We can now assess Ginsberg and Dylan in relation to that stance.

* * * * *

Ginsberg first declaimed his long visionary poem, 'Howl', in San Francisco in 1955; it was published in a short volume published by City Lights Press, called *Howl and other poems,* the following year. At first, it seems to explore only the negative dimension of apocalypse, and that in its most extreme form: 'I saw the best minds of my generation destroyed by madness, starving hysterical naked' (p. 49). But when we come to consider its overall structure, we see that there is a definite movement towards spiritual affirmation. We have not only the castigation of Babylon – here closely identified with the materialism of the United States of America – but also the proclamation of a spiritual future. Ginsberg's three-part poem ends with a 'Footnote' which proclaims: 'Everything is holy! everybody's holy! everywhere is holy! everyday is in eternity! Everyman's an angel!' (p. 57). Significantly, this line is adapted from Blake rather than from the Bible itself. As we have seen, *The Marriage of Heaven and Hell* affirms that 'every thing that lives is holy'. Ginsberg, since having his Blake hallucination some years earlier, had read the Bible through the 'doors of perception' opened up to him by Blake. Though well-versed in scripture, Ginsberg always made sure to avoid identifying himself with any message of literal salvation and damnation.

Thus, when the 'best minds' are referred to, we are not to think of orthodox saints any more than of conventional intellectuals. Rather, they are 'angelheaded hipsters burning for the ancient heavenly connection to the starry dynamo in the machinery of night' (p. 49). Again, we need to remind ourselves of Kerouac's assumption that it is those with no investment in this civilization – the fellaheen – who will be granted the beatific vision, associated with an alternative culture. The 'angelheaded hipsters' are amongst them: their very desire for 'the ancient heavenly connection' is an indictment of our modern Babylon and a promise of a life beyond it. Both these senses of 'Beat' – 'beat down' and 'beatific' – are implied in a line near the end of Part I: 'the madman bum and angel beat in Time, unknown, yet putting down here what might be left to say in time come after death' (p. 54).

To prevent his rhetoric becoming too diffuse, Ginsberg in Part II of 'Howl' uses one dominant image, that of a terrible, devouring god. America, the new Babylon, is depicted as serving 'Moloch', whose demand for sacrificial victims is insatiable. As a matter of historical record, Moloch was a deity sacred to the Canaanites, not the Babylonians, but Ginsberg is only following the example of John the Divine in his creative play with time and place. The transposition works well, with the furnace which consumed the ancient god's victims being identified with the contemporary military-industrial complex of the United States – the large corporations profiting not only from the exploitation of industrial workers but also from the production and promotion around the globe of weapons of mass destruction. Hence we read: 'Moloch whose mind is pure machinery! Moloch whose blood is running money! Moloch whose fingers are ten armies!' Moreover, he makes it clear that all such barbarism is only made possible because people mentally assent to it. Hence we read: 'Moloch whose name is the Mind!' (pp. 54–5). This monster, while being manifested outside ourselves, has its source deep within ourselves. The inspiration here would seem to be Blake. It was he who declared that 'All deities reside in the human breast'. It was he who depicted the angry sky-father of the Old Testament as 'Urizen', the product of 'your reason' – like all tyrannical deities. It was he who coined that most astute phrase, 'the mind-forg'd manacles'.

The alternative to the deadly logic of Moloch is suggested in Part III by the poet's message of sympathy and solidarity to a friend of his. Ginsberg and he had met while both were detained in Columbia

Psychiatric Institute (here mysteriously confused with another location): 'Carl Solomon! I'm with you in Rockland where you're madder than I am' (p. 55). Here, of course, madness is not an accusation: Ginsberg is praising Solomon for his holy, visionary powers, which Babylon tries to classify and control as 'insanity'. The positive apocalypse is expressed in the poet's very expression of love for his friend, and in the affirmation of imagination. But we should note also the persistence of Biblical language, albeit dramatically updated, in and among the local references: 'I'm with you in Rockland where you will split the heavens of Long Island and resurrect your living human Jesus from the superhuman tomb' (p. 56).

'Howl', then, is all about the resurrection of the world through the resurrection of the mind, epitomised by 'angelheaded hipsters' who, though themselves 'destroyed by madness', find that their lunacy turns out to be 'holy' – pointing forward to a new life unimaginable to the inhabitants of Babylon. Following the Bible and Blake, we can call this Jerusalem, or we can simply refer to the closing line of the poem: 'Holy the supernatural extra brilliant intelligent kindness of the soul' (p. 56).

* * * * *

Ginsberg's 'Howl' uses extended and excessive language, as is appropriate for a poem originally written to make as dramatic an impact as possible at a poetry reading. Dylan's poems are also written for performance, but in his case the discipline of the song means that he often uses language in a highly compressed form. Sometimes we may not notice this. When, for example, in 'I Pity the Poor Immigrant', a song included on *John Wesley Harding* (1968), we are told that worldly visions 'in the final end / Must shatter like the glass', the word 'final' may seem redundant (p. 261). But Dylan is implying an important distinction: that between a temporary cessation and an ultimate fulfilment. He is, in fact, being very precise, and is trying to stress the second sense, that of apocalypse.

One of Dylan's most famous songs of ending is 'A Hard Rain's A-Gonna Fall' (1963). First drafted at the time of the Cuban missile crisis, when a nuclear war between the United States and the Soviet Union was certainly possible, it is full of foreboding: 'I heard the sound of a thunder, it roared out a warning, / Heard the roar of a wave that could drown the whole world' (p. 59). The language is clearly apocalyptic, but only intermittently derived from the Bible. However, it was followed shortly by the consistently scriptural vision of 'The Times

They Are A-Changin' (1963, released 1964). Referred to in our earlier discussion, this song is worth revisiting briefly here. Initially identified with the cause of civil rights for black Americans, this song survives for other occasions and causes because it is so firmly rooted in the Biblical tradition. Inspired by Isaiah 24:1 ('Behold, the Lord maketh the earth empty ... and turneth it upside down'), it uses the symbolism of flood ('accept it that soon / You'll be drenched to the bone') and warfare ('There's a battle outside / And it is raging'). Even-handed in its use of Judaic and Christian scripture, it ends with that invocation of the Gospels which we noted in the last chapter: 'But many that are first shall be last; and the last shall be first' (Matthew 19:30). Dylan declares: 'The order is rapidly fading / And the first one now shall later be last' (p. 91).

Such apocalyptic allusions proved very useful to the early Dylan in his denunciation of injustice and oppression in his contemporary America. But even after rejecting the title of 'protest singer' and eschewing 'finger pointing songs', he continued to draw on the Biblical language of imminent doom. 'All Along the Watchtower', another song from *John Wesley Harding* (1968), is based on the two different sets of writing which make up the Book of Isaiah. The first warns of the oppression of Israel by the Babylonians, but also of the eventual demise of the Babylonian empire itself: 'watch in the watchtower ... arise, ye princes, and anoint the shield' (Isaiah 21:5). The news of Babylon's fall will be brought by 'a couple of horsemen' seen riding in from the wilderness at the same time as a lion is heard calling (Isaiah 21:9). The second is written after that event, and concerns the attempt to rebuild Israel when the period of oppression is over. Though strangers 'shall be your ploughmen' (Isaiah 61:5), his sons 'shall not drink your wine' (Isaiah 62:8).

Dylan's song economically fuses the two historical moments to create an overwhelming sense of 'too much confusion': 'Businessmen, they drink my wine, ploughmen dig my earth', even while the 'princes' who are keeping watch see 'Two riders ... approaching' and hear a 'wildcat ... growl' (p. 252). The general effect is sinister and compelling: America is in the balance, and is being found wanting. It is left to the listener to decide whether the unstated news that the riders bring ('Babylon is fallen', in Isaiah) carries with it the positive promise of the divine kingdom. It is as if Dylan is despairing of the United States which, at the time the song was written, was waging a futile war of obliteration against the people of Vietnam. True, it is certainly not a 'protest' song; but it is nonetheless a devastatingly cryptic indictment of a decadent civilisation, which implies a distant hope of an alternative culture.

We know from our last chapter how sceptical Dylan was about any specific proposal for such an alternative culture. He never aligned himself with any countercultural movements in the late sixties or early seventies. Then, in 1979, he surprised many people by becoming what is called a 'born-again' Christian. But as the above evidence indicates, he had always worked within the Biblical idiom and had, unlike Ginsberg, frequently appealed to the justice of the father-God worshipped by both Jews and Christians. The difference now was that he seemed to be interpreting the symbolism of the scriptures entirely literally. In doing so, he alienated many of his early admirers, who did not take kindly to being warned, in song after song on *Slow Train Coming* (1979), that they might not find themselves 'saved' once the battle of Armageddon had been fought. In one particularly strident track, he demanded, in an echo of the Book of Revelation: 'When you gonna wake up and strengthen the things that remain?' (p. 432). However, even here we may note that the wish for an ultimate answer is, paradoxically, expressed in the form of a question. The 'things that remain' after hearing many of Dylan's 'fundamentalist' lyrics are not doctrines but feelings, yearnings, doubts. Thus, a song with a title of apocalyptic certainty, 'When He Returns', is actually an exploration of the very disquiet from which the apocalyptic vision springs: 'How long can I listen to the lies of prejudice? / How long can I stay drunk on fear out in the wilderness?' (p. 437). It is this capacity for self-doubt which characterises much of Dylan's subsequent work.

Most fascinating of all, perhaps, is the long and complex song which opens *Infidels* (1983). 'Jokerman' concerns, on the one hand, the human need to depict and explain divinity and, on the other, the difficulties and dangers of doing so. The paradox is focussed on the central figure. Who exactly is the character of the title? He may be Jesus ('Standing on the waters'): but then, his miraculous powers have their demonic aspect ('Manipulator of crowds'). For in the 'slippery world' of this song, nothing is certain. Where we look for a righteous Messiah who will destroy Babylon, we may only see a holy fool, dancing to 'the nightingale tune'. Meanwhile, we are told that a woman has just given birth to a 'prince', dressing him in 'scarlet'. What will he do? He will 'Take the motherless children off the street / And place them at the feet of a harlot'. To all this, the Jokerman does not 'show any response' (pp. 471–2). If he is the Christ, why does he not oppose the Antichrist whom Christian legend associates with the 'beast' of apocalypse? The song provides no answers to such questions. Rather, it subverts the symbolism of Revelation – for example, making the woman's offspring a satanic rather than a sacred prince, born to collude with the 'harlot' – in order, perhaps, that we might ponder our own collusion with the rule of Babylon. But then, as we have already noted, that is exactly what the apocalyptic genre is all about: it forces us to face ourselves and our situation in the light of the second coming, the time and nature of which it is granted to no man to know. Thus, Dylan's song, 'Jokerman', with the other lyrics we have discussed, may take its place alongside Ginsberg's 'Howl' in that great visionary tradition which goes all the way back to the Bible.

* * * * *

Having confirmed that Ginsbgerg and Dylan are visionary artists who feel themselves able, as appropriate, to draw on 'the Great Code', it yet remains to define Dylan's visionary art more exactly. My own instinct is that it is Dylan who benefits from any comparison with Ginsberg, because the sense of craft which informs Dylan's work makes its apocalyptic spirit that bit more intense and persuasive than Ginsberg's free-flowing utterance. The beatific vision seems to be served especially well by those who know how to deploy beat itself – measure, metre, music. Despite Ginsberg's acute understanding of Blake's skill as author of songs, much of the work for which he is famous lacks the focus and discipline which is required to produce anything comparable with the best of Blake or Dylan. As we shall see in our next chapter, Ginsberg became aware of this, and so made it his business to submit to the discipline of song – with some impressive results. But still, an overall comparison of his career with Dylan's would leave most people in no doubt as to who had the more substantial, consistent skill as songwriter. Having said that, it is not my intention to decide whether Dylan is a better poet than Ginsberg. It is my intention to make a claim for him as a great visionary songwriter who has certain advantages by virtue of his understanding of how poetry as performance can work economically: that is, intensively rather than extensively. We might substantiate this claim by looking in particular at his work of the mid-1960s.

When *Bringing It All Back Home* (1965), was released, it was hailed as marking Dylan's transition from 'folk' music to a new, more experimental form – referred to at the time by commentators, rather inadequately, as 'folk rock'. It was the year in which he repudiated the idea of 'finger pointing songs', associated with his earlier folk phase. With this new album, Dylan not only went electric musically but also seemed to have turned inward thematically, appearing to be less preoccupied with society than with the self. However, that did not mean that his words now amounted to nothing more than introverted rambling: rather, he explored the mysteries of the inner world in such a way as to provide a new perspective on the outer world. Indeed, he could hardly be said to have abandoned his accusatory stance: 'Subterranean Homesick Blues', 'Maggie's Farm', 'It's Alright Ma, I'm Only Bleeding' and 'Desolation Row' were, at the very least, scathing assessments of the materialism and commercialism of the USA. What was new, perhaps, was the attempt to go well below the surface of society and to summon up the spiritual and imaginative possibilities which it had suppressed. In taking this step, he was only following the example of the Beats, who in turn were following the example of Blake. That Dylan himself was conscious of this legacy early on is brought out by the response he gave to that question posed at a press conference in 1965, which we quoted earlier. When asked if his music should be called 'folk rock', he replied that he preferred the phrase 'vision music'.

Blake's famous declaration about the need to cleanse 'the doors of perception' influenced many songwriters of the sixties, most notably Jim Morrison, whose band, the Doors, took their name from Blake via Aldous Huxley, author of *The Doors of Perception*. When Dylan claimed to be producing 'vision music', we might surmise that he too had the great Romantic bard in mind. Blake famously aimed 'To see a world in a grain of sand / And a heaven in a wild flower / Hold infinity in the palm of your hand / And eternity in an hour'. In doing so, he would demonstrate the supremacy of imagination over reason, of spirituality over materialism. Dylan seems consciously to echo this in an interview given in 1976: 'I can see God in a daisy. I can see God at night in the wind and rain. I see creation just about everywhere. The highest form of song is prayer.'[46] But he seems to have been familiar with Blake a decade or more earlier, nowhere more evidently than on *Bringing It All Back Home*.

'Gates of Eden' is a song about our fallen world, as understood by contrast with the earthly paradise which, according to the Book of Genesis, we have lost. The Blakean twist of thought which Dylan adds is the proviso that paradise is by its very nature lost, since it is impossible for fallen humanity to conceive of it, except as the contrary state to the fallen world. The sacred may only be understood in dialectical relationship with the profane. Hence the litany of negatives which bring each verse to its climax: for example, there are 'no kings inside the Gates of Eden', and 'no truths outside the Gates of Eden'. Outside those gates, the world is populated by deluded souls: for example, the 'savage soldier' who 'sticks his head in sand and then complains', the 'paupers' who each wish 'for what the other has got', and the 'princess' and 'prince' who endlessly discuss 'what's real and what is not'. Moreover, the 'kingdoms of Experience' [sic] which rot in the wind are dominated by spiritual manipulators, such as the 'utopian monks' who sit 'sidesaddle on the Golden Calf' making false 'promises of paradise', and by material oppressors, such as the 'motorcycle black Madonna / Two-wheel gypsy queen' who causes the 'grey-flannel dwarf to scream' (p. 175).

That last description, as we have seen, is decidedly Beat in idiom, being worthy of a Kerouac or a Ginsberg; but then, the whole song is an interesting 'take' on the beatific vision. It presents beatitude simultaneously from the perspective of both the earthly paradise (the life of innocence) and the wilderness of this world (the life of experience). It is deeply indebted to Blake. Robert Shelton, too, has noted this debt:

> In 1793 Blake issued a series of pictorial emblems titled *The Gates of Paradise*. In 1818, he reworked many of plates and added a text called 'The Keys of the Gates'. The emblems traced man from cradle to grave, through various states of the soul's desire and mortal frustration. To Blake the grave was not a place of death, but of spiritual mystery, echoing the Bible, Spenser, Shakespeare, Milton, and Swedenborg. Is 'Gates of Eden' both a Blakean song of innocence and of experience?[47]

It is a rhetorical question, surely. Dylan is demonstrating that he can revisit the visionary landscape of Blake just as productively as can Ginsberg. Moreover, as Shelton intuits here, Dylan is fully aware of the dialectic which informs Blake's imagination – innocence and experience being 'contrary states', not opposed realms.

Another song from this period which manages to articulate the need for redemption from the depths of experience is one of the most striking achievements of the double-album, *Blonde on Blonde* (1966). 'Visions of Johanna' depicts life in the modern metropolis as alienated and fragmentary ('We sit here stranded, though we're all doing our best to deny it'), where even art offers no solace but rather a confirmation of disillusionment ('Mona Lisa must have had the highway blues – you can tell by the way she smiles'). While 'Louise and her lover' lie 'entwined' in a warehouse apartment, the solitary figure who stands by and who narrates such story as the song contains can only hope for his visions of Johanna to be fulfilled. We note that she is referred to also as 'Madonna' – a word which seems to be used here with its full spiritual association, unlike the ironic allusion in 'Gates of Eden' (pp. 223–4). Echoing Kerouac's *Visions of Gerard*, Dylan's song would seem to be about the hunger for beatific experience – the hope that the sacred realm might yet be glimpsed within the profane. Johanna, like Gerard, represents the salvation that comes out of suffering. But unlike Kerouac, Dylan depicts this possibility as tauntingly remote – a cause of suffering in itself. Thus, 'Visions of Johanna' is one of his major 'songs of experience', along with 'Gates of Eden'.

As we have acknowledged, the Blakean dialectic makes no sense unless we understand that innocence and experience imply each other: innocence is shadowed by experience, just as experience gestures towards innocence. Ultimately, Blake would see a renewed innocence, stronger and more coherent than pre-lapsarian innocence, emerging out of experience; but meanwhile the poet's task is to keep the dialectic of innocence and experience, sacred and profane, alive. We need, then, to remind ourselves of this possibility, by way of return to the key album, *Bringing It All Back Home*, in order to consider the song which, more than any other of Dylan's, celebrates the infinite potential of vision. I refer, of course, to 'Mr Tambourine Man' (pp. 172–3).

Unfortunately, the glib consensus over the years has been that its subject-matter is drugs. Besides the fact that Dylan himself has denied this hotly, it must be said that to interpret the figure of the tambourine man as a drug dealer is offensively reductive. To do so is to cut oneself off from the imaginative and spiritual potential of a great poem. In referring to the song as a poem, I am endorsing Ginsberg's judgement, bearing in mind that Dylan's is a poetry of performance rather than of the printed page. Relevant here is the fact that, though 'Mr Tambourine Man' is featured on the first album of Dylan's electric phase, the song itself is sung chiefly to the accompaniment of an acoustic guitar (as with the earlier work). It seems to invite us to ponder the lyrics in depth, all of which are articulated with precision by the singer-songwriter. If we pre-empt their meaning by simply 'ticking off' any possible allusions to drugs, we are hardly doing the song justice.

So, having decided to take this work of art seriously, we have to ask ourselves who we think the 'Tambourine Man' of the title really is. Here we could do worse than to consult the text that Dylan has previously drawn upon, namely the Bible. In the Judaic scriptures, the playing of a tambourine is frequently associated with spiritual ecstasy. Thus: 'Some of the people of Israel were playing music on small harps ... and on tambourines ... [King] David and the others were happy, and they danced for the Lord with all their might' (2 Samuel 6:5). Dylan's central symbol would seem, then, to be that of transcendence – or at least the desire for transcendence. In other words, the quest is for an apprehension of holiness, for a sense of the sacred. But his song is not conventionally religious, so perhaps it is indebted as much to Blake as to the Bible. That is, the aim is to cleanse 'the doors of perception', to experience 'Eternity in an hour', in defiance of the dead weight of conformist consumerism. Here again we note the 'Beat' connection, for the tambourine man is the bearer of the 'beatific' vision, even while the singer indicates a state of being 'beat'. Specifically, he asks him to 'play a song for me' at the moment when 'My weariness amazes me, I'm branded on my feet ...'.

The figure invoked, then is no more a religious teacher than he is a drug dealer: rather, he is the spirit of poetry or music. It is he who has the visionary power to transport the singer 'upon your magic swirling ship' and to 'cast your dancing spell my way'. In this light, we might be tempted to see him as the traditional figure of the Muse; but we need to bear in mind both that the Muse has always been thought of as feminine, and that the function of the Muse is to inspire poets rather than actually to create poetry. Though we might want to say that Dylan is the poet/singer seeking inspiration, his own song is an appeal to some superior force to create the ultimate 'song of songs'. Thus, the tambourine man is a personification of the power of poetry – poetry being understood, in traditional terms, as inseparable from music.

While the singer's initial request to the tambourine man is that he 'play a song for me' in order that he can be followed in the 'jingle jangle morning' – a morning brought alive by the sound of the tambourine – the figure addressed is more than a mere fellow-practitioner. He represents the force of art itself, which transcends time even while those who are touched by it necessarily remain in time. For if 'evening's empire has returned into sand' – the sand of an hourglass? the sand of the circus ring referred to later in the song? both simultaneously? – then we know that, so long as we live and breathe, we are part of the cycle of daily existence, during which evening and morning are endlessly repeated. The paradox is that, though time may appear to be the enemy of imagination – 'the ancient empty street's too dead for dreaming' – it is only in time that one may choose to surrender to the 'dancing spell'. In that moment, profane time is experienced as sacred time.

We can get closer to the heart of this paradox if we are open to the rich ambiguity of a line such as the following: 'And but for the sky there are no fences facing.' Now, the endless sky is an image of total freedom, but Dylan's song reminds us that, though we have a great more spiritual potential than our society allows for, we are all of us necessarily constrained by the need to articulate our yearning for eternity and infinity in time and space. Hence the singer advises the tambourine man that, if he hears 'vague traces of skipping reels of rhyme / To your tambourine in time,' he should remind himself that it is only 'a ragged clown' or 'shadow' in pursuit. Poetry itself – this very poem, which calls out for another poem ('play a song for me') – works through certain agreed principles, such as 'rhyme'. Even the 'tambourine' must be played 'in time'. The 'ragged clown' who follows 'behind', as a 'shadow', knows this, even as he celebrates the vision of eternity which he attributes to the elusive figure whom he invokes and pursues. As Blake tells us: 'Eternity is in love with the productions of time.'[48] Or, as Spengler suggests, the macrocosm is manifest in the microcosm. If the poet is he who can reveal eternity to us, he does so by means of the 'skipping reels of rhyme': in one aspect, they are what keep us where we are (as in the act of skipping); in another aspect, they are what makes possible the vision of eternity. The tambourine man would not exist in our imagination if some 'shadow' such as the singer of this song had not invoked him through the incantatory power of language.

So it is that the song concludes with the 'ragged clown' (he who is, we might say, 'beaten down' by time) knowing himself to be part of the 'dance' which the tambourine man creates (the 'beatific' vision, as it were). After the singer's situation has been described in a series of negatives ('there is no place I'm going to … I have no one to meet … my hands can't feel to grip'), we come to the moment of affirmation: 'Yes, to dance beneath the diamond sky with one hand waving free …' Here the sky represents eternity, but we are not intended to forget that the very image of eternal freedom is one that involves temporal movement.

After all, 'to dance beneath the diamond sky' is a moment of illumination that the singer hopes for rather than one he claims to have had. If he were ever to reach a state 'far from the twisted reach of crazy sorrow', he would have to be taken 'Down the foggy ruins of time, far past the frozen leaves, / The haunted frightened trees …' That is, the imagination would have to comprehend all the trials and tribulations of human experience. Even then, on the 'windy beach' he would be 'silhouetted by the sea' and 'circled by the circus sands'. Such images are deeply ambiguous. The sea might represent death just as much as dream, oblivion just as much as the infinite potential of the unconscious mind. The 'circus sands' might represent the absurd cycle of time – referring back to the image of 'evening's empire' returning 'into sand' – just as much as the play of art which produces vision.

The affirmation stands, however, by virtue of the paradoxical relationship between time and eternity, between rhyme and vision, which the song revisits. The singer is entitled to feel that 'memory and fate' – past and future – have been 'driven deep beneath the waves', and that he can 'forget about today until tomorrow'; but he knows that there is going to be a tomorrow, in which today will have become yesterday. Again, when he dances to the tune played by the tambourine man, he has 'one hand waving free': this is an image of constraint and abandonment simultaneously. But then, that is the very nature of imagination: it works through the dialectic between form and improvisation, between what one receives and what one gives.

It might be worth ending this account of the song with Dylan's response to another question which he was asked at about this time: did he think of himself primarily as a singer or as a poet? He replied that he thought of himself 'more as a song and dance man'.[49] No doubt intended to undermine the more pompous claims made on his behalf, such as 'spokesperson for a generation', his choice of words is nonetheless revealing. His song, 'Mr Tambourine Man', is a celebration of the power of the 'song' which is also a 'dance': one that releases us from the burden of time even as it follows the rhythm of time. Thus, perhaps ultimately the tambourine man represents that potential within ourselves to 'cleanse the doors of perception' and 'to hold infinity in the palm of your hand'. The 'ragged clown' will always be 'circled by the circus sands', but in his capacity as 'song and dance man' he will surely find a way to 'see a world in a grain of sand'. In the terms we have used from the outset, we might say that 'Mr Tambourine Man' is a classic example of the beatific vision: it pursues the possibility of spiritual freedom to the point of mystical transcendence, but remains faithful to the obligation of art to celebrate the profane world even as it makes manifest the sacred.

* * * * *

Would the real Bob Dylan please step forward? Is it the death-focussed writer who, with Kerouac, decides that only by adhering to the discipline of theistic worship may one 'get to heaven before they close the door'? Or is the broad-minded bard who, with Ginsberg, uses the language of apocalypse after the example of Blake, in order to 'dance beneath the diamond sky'?

The answer must, of course, be both. It is with Dylan more than anyone, perhaps, that the subtlety of the beatific vision is evinced. Were he to respond to such questions, he himself might justly invoke Emerson: 'A foolish consistency is the hobgoblin of little minds, adored by little statesmen and philosophers and divines. With consistency a great soul has simply nothing to do.'[50] But perhaps his most likely ally would be John Keats, a Romantic poet whom he has invoked in his lyrics more than once. In a famous letter, Keats formulated his idea of 'negative capability':

> [S]everal things dovetailed in my mind, & at once it struck me, what quality went to form a Man of Achievement especially in Literature which Shakespeare possessed so enormously – I mean NEGATIVE CAPABILITY, that is when man is capable of being in uncertainties, Mysteries, doubts, without any irritable reaching after fact & reason.[51]

We can pose the questions as starkly as we like: Dylan as conventionally religious writer, or Dylan as unconventionally spiritual writer? Dylan as orthodox theist, or Dylan as unorthodox mystic? But it would be reductive and misleading to insist on a final answer. As with all great artists, Dylan might justly reply that it is not his job to keep saying the same thing, but to be true to his art (without any 'irritable reaching after fact and reason'). After all, the Beats set out to do nothing more (nor less) than to convey a sense of 'religious reverence' through the power of their writing. Going further, though it may be heresy among Beat aficionados to say so, it strikes me that his work is sufficiently rich and powerful to merit placing him as high in the Beat canon as either Kerouac and Ginsberg. Indeed, there are those who would place him even higher, but here seems a good moment to draw our account of Dylan's significance to a diplomatic close.

Notes

1 See Sam Shepard, *The Rolling Thunder Logbook* (London: Sanctuary, 2004). For a less celebratory account, see Larry 'Ratso' Sloman, *On the Road with Bob Dylan* (London: Helter Skelter, 2002).

2 Allen Ginsberg, 'To America: Kerouac's *Pomes All Sizes*', in *Deliberate Prose: Selected Essays 1952–1995* (New York: HarperCollins, 2000), p. 374.

3 John Tytell, *Naked Angels: Kerouac, Ginsberg, Burroughs* (New York: Grove Press, 1976), p. 20.

4 Richard Brown, 'Highway 61 and Other States of Mind', in Neil Corcoran (ed.), *Do You, Mr Jones? Bob Dylan with the Poets and Professors* (London: Chatto & Windus, 2002), p. 200.

5 Michael Gray, *Song and Dance Man III: The Art of Bob Dylan* (London: Cassell, 2000), p. 83.

6 Bob Dylan, *Chronicles: Volume One* (New York: Simon & Schuster, 2004), p. 34.

7 Dylan, *Chronicles: Volume One*, pp. 57–8.

8 David Boucher, *Dylan & Cohen: Poets of Rock and Roll* (New York: Continuum, 2004), p. 30.

9 Boucher, *Dylan & Cohen*, p. 30.

10 Greil Marcus, *Invisible Republic: Bob Dylan's Basement Tapes* (London: Picador, 1997), p. 21.

11 Ann Charters (ed.), *The Portable Beat Reader* (New York: Viking Penguin, 1992), p. 370.

12 Bob Dylan, *Lyrics 1962–1985* (London: Jonathan Cape, 1987), p. 59. Further references to this edition are given after quotations in the text.

13 Allen Ginsberg, 'Howl', in *Selected Poems 1947–1995* (London and New York: Penguin, 1997), p. 49. Further references to this edition are given after quotations in the text.

14 Barry Miles, *Jack Kerouac: King of the Beats: A Portrait* (London: Virgin Books, 2002), pp. 194–5.

15 Robert Shelton, *No Direction Home: The Life and Music of Bob Dylan* (London: Penguin, 1987), p. 138.

16 Shelton, *No Direction Home*, pp. 301–3.

17 Dennis McNally, *Desolate Angel: Jack Kerouac, The Beat Generation, and America* (Cambridge, MA: Da Capo Press, 2003), pp. 235, 308.

18 Bob Dylan, *Bob Dylan In His Own Words*, ed. Barry Miles (London: Omnibus Press, 1978), pp. 48, 53.

19 Andy Gill, *Classic Bob Dylan 1962–69: My Back Pages* (London: Carlton, 1998), p. 58.

20 Gill, *Classic Bob Dylan*, p. 58.

21 John Lardas, *The Bop Apocalypse: The Religious Visions of Kerouac, Ginsberg, and Burroughs* (Illinois: Illinois University Press, 2001), p. 85.

22 *Radio Times* 1–7 April 2006, p. 121.

23 See Shelton, *No Direction Home*, p. 267.

24 Boucher, *Dylan & Cohen*, p. 55.

25 Gill, *Classic Bob Dylan*, p. 72.

26 William Blake, 'The Laocoon', in David V. Erdman and Harold Bloom (eds), *The Complete Poetry and Prose of William Blake* (New York: Doubleday, 1988), p. 274.

27 Bob Dylan, 'Trying to Get to Heaven', www.bobdylan.com/songs [accessed 1st November 2005].

28 Geoffrey Hill, 'Ovid in the Third Reich', *Collected Poems* (Harmondsworth: Penguin, 1985), p. 61

29 Bob Dylan, 'Not Dark Yet', www.bobdylan.com/songs [accessed 1st November 2005].

30 Thomas Hardy, 'The Oxen', in James Gibson (ed.), *The Complete Poems of Thomas Hardy* (London: Macmillan, 1976), p. 403.

31 Jack Kerouac, 'After Me, the Deluge', in Ann Charters (ed.), *The Portable Jack Kerouac* (New York: Viking Penguin, 1995), p. 573.

32 Dylan, *Chronicles: Volume One*, pp. 113–14.

33 Dylan, *Chronicles: Volume One*, p. 115.

34 Barry Alfonso, 'Elder Statesman, Unrepentant Rebel: A Chat with Ginsberg', in Holly George-Warren (ed.), *The Rolling Stone Book of the Beats: The Beat Generation and the Counterculture* (London: Bloomsbury, 1999), p. 254.

35 See Thomas J. J. Altizer, *The New Apocalypse: The Radical Christian Vision of William Blake* (Ann Arbor: Michigan State University Press, 1967).

36 Blake, 'The Laocoon', p. 274.

37 Blake, *The Marriage of Heaven and Hell*, in *Complete Poetry and Prose*, pp. 36–8, 39, 45.

38 Blake, 'London', *Complete Poetry and Prose*, p. 27.

39 Blake, *The First Book of Urizen* in *Complete Poetry and Prose*, p. 72.

40 Blake, *Milton*, in *Complete Poetry and Prose*, pp. 95–6.

41 See Blake, *Jerusalem*, in *Complete Poetry and Prose*, pp. 255–9.

42 Ginsberg, 'What Way I Write', *Deliberate Prose*, p. 255.

43 Ginsberg, 'Liner Notes to Blake Record', *Deliberate Prose*, p. 277.

44 Ginsberg, 'Liner Notes to Blake Record', pp. 278–9.

45 See Laurence Coupe, *Myth* (London: Routledge, 1997), pp. 74–89.

46 Blake, 'Auguries of Innocence', *Complete Poetry and Prose*, p. 490; Dylan, *Own Words*, p. 34.

47 Shelton, *No Direction Home*, p. 276.

48 Blake, *The Marriage of Heaven and Hell*, p. 36.

49 Dylan, *Own Words*, p. 73.

50 Ralph Waldo Emerson, 'Self-Reliance', *Essays* (London and Glasgow: Blackie & Son, 1940), p. 46.

51 John Keats, *Selected Letters*, ed. Frederick Page (London: Oxford University Press, 1954), p. 53. (Capitals are as in the original.)

4 'Mantra rock': the Beatles via Allen Ginsberg

Probably the first account of the British equivalent of what in the USA was to become known as the counterculture was Jeff Nuttall's *Bomb Culture*, written in 1967 and published the following year. Indeed, so quick off the mark was Nuttall that the book consists largely of hints and guesses about what seemed to be emerging from the streets, cafes, clubs, poetry readings, 'happenings', 'alternative' press, and, above all, popular music in mid-sixties Britain. Lacking the concept of a mass countercultural movement, Nuttall is content to use the word 'subcultures' as a way of indicating a pluralist, even fragmentary scene – the book's purpose being to find some pattern or potential in it all.

One formative occasion which Nuttall recounts is the visit of Allen Ginsberg to London in the summer of 1965. The main purpose of his visit was to participate in a poetry reading at the Albert Hall in June, along with his friend Lawrence Ferlinghetti and several 'underground' British poets such as Christopher Logue, Michael Horowitz and Adrian Mitchell. The reading was attended by 7,000 people: this was a record for a literary rather than a musical event, and it attracted a great deal of media attention. The American military disaster in Vietnam was a major referent, with many poets – including a drunken Ginsberg – featuring anti-war verse in their readings. The highlight was Mitchell's rousing rant, with its powerful refrain, 'Tell me lies about Vietnam'.[1] The feeling was that poetry was now as widely accepted as popular music itself, so long as it was offered as an oral performance rather than as words on the page. The process set going by Kerouac in the jazz clubs of New York and San Francisco, when he recited his work to the accompaniment of jazz, had come to fruition.

Nuttall himself, who had a reputation as an avant-garde poet and painter at the time, and who played a minor part in the Albert Hall 'happening', felt that there were more revelatory occasions. He was sceptical about the growing conviction that the barrier between high and low culture, between poetry and pop, was breaking down. When he met Ginsberg the previous month, he was struck by the American poet's enthusiasm, but had his doubts about its relation to the cultural reality of England. One of the first questions Ginsberg asked was: 'Did the young people read Blake?' Nuttall reflects:

> Rather in the same way that American reporters thought the Beatles were queer because of their haircuts, so Allen seemed to think that any long-haired British youth was steeped in Proust. The misunderstanding reached a hilarious peak when, stark naked, he encountered Lennon and McCartney (at that time very sharp little mods) at a party and demanded their embraces. It seems to indicate an insight beyond error, that now two years later both the Beatles and their fans would enjoy Proust very much indeed.[2]

There is surely some ambivalence evident here: the purpose of Nuttall's anecdote seems to be to make Ginbserg's expectations appear foolish; but then he goes on to concede the possibility that they might be being realised by the time of writing. However, the idea of either the Beatles or their fans immersing themselves in *A La Recherche du Temps Perdu* is improbable. The question is whether Nuttall's hyperbolic quip carries a degree of truth. Did the Beatles' development represent the triumph of the Beat ideal of an adventurous art rooted in popular culture?

The connection between the Beatles' vision and Ginsberg's is worth considering – especially as Kerouac was by this time becoming disenchanted with the spreading of his own word among the young and naïve. Perhaps a bit more information about that first meeting, when two of the Beatles were invited to Ginsberg's thirty-ninth birthday party on 3 June 1965, might help. Here is the account by Barry Miles, one of the organisers of the Albert Hall poetry event, who knew both Ginsberg and the Beatles, and who was a central figure of the British underground:

> At the party Allen got completely drunk and stripped off his clothes, putting his baggy underpants on his head and hanging a hotel 'Do not disturb' notice round his cock. It was at this moment that two of the Beatles arrived: John with [his wife]

Cynthia, and George with [his girlfriend] Patti. John and
George quickly checked that no photographers were present.
Allen kissed John on the cheek, and John told him that he used
to draw a magazine at art school called the *Daily Howl*; they
were friendly enough and accepted drinks, but then made
quickly for the door. I asked John why he was leaving so soon.
'You don't do that in front of the birds!' he hissed in my ear.[3]

On the one hand, this account would seem to substantiate Nuttall's
dismissal of the Beatles as 'sharp little mods' – even though it corrects
the detail about which Beatles were actually present. On the other
hand, and more importantly, it contradicts Nuttall's assumption that
they had very little awareness of the cultural scene lying beyond the
three-minute pop songs that they were so efficient at producing. Here
is the rest of Miles's anecdote:

> However, the next year, hearing that Allen was in the audience
> at the Beatles concert at the Portland Coliseum on their 1966
> American tour, John called out a greeting to him from the stage
> between numbers. Of course John himself was to appear naked
> on an album sleeve four years later. When *Two Virgins* came
> out, I couldn't resist reminding him of his meeting with Allen,
> and his revised attitude towards nudity. 'That wasn't my
> problem with Allen,' John snapped at me. 'The trouble with
> Allen was that he always got up real close, and touched you,
> and shouted in yer ear!' Then he laughed. Allen was always
> ahead of his time.[4]

In what follows, I do not intend to argue that the Beatles were fully
aware of Ginsberg's importance and, indeed, deeply influenced by him.
Rather, I want to consider the Beatles' vision as a Beat vision, which
has parallels with Ginsberg's – particularly insofar as it emerges as a
'beatific' vision. Thus, I am not interested, for example, in tracing
allusions to 'Howl' on *Sgt Pepper's Lonely Hearts Club Band*: rather,
I am interested in assessing whether the Beatles realise the Beat ideal
in their own distinctive way, in broad sympathy with Ginsberg's
trajectory.

Perhaps we could take our cue from Adrian Mitchell, who reflected
on the Beatles' development as artists in a BBC radio talk, transcribed
in the pages of the *Listener* magazine in October 1968. Though he
specifically mentions Ginsberg, he avoids any implication of imitation.

His point is that both the poet and the pop group have displayed aesthetic daring:

> When Allen Ginsberg was last over here, he gave a reading of Blake and Ginsberg at the Roundhouse, Chalk Farm, at a time when all honest chalk farmers were in bed dreaming of the sprouting pink, blue and white lengths of chalk which decorate the dusty fields around the blackboard forest. Between poems Ginsberg talked about fear. He said that 10 or 15 years ago he had been full of fear, but that he'd worked at cutting down his terror ration and had changed until he was hardly afraid of anything. I sat in the audience and felt the lump of fear which I always carry diminish. The Beatles appear to be moving, zigzag, in the Ginsberg direction. They've already shown some courage in a traditionally cowardly trade – for in pop music the aim is to be loved by everyone, villains included. Maybe it was foolhardiness when they filmed their own *Magical Mystery Tour*. It contained some images – policemen holding hands on top of a concrete bunker or shelter while The Beatles played below in Disney masks – which were way beyond the heads of most of the critics. The progress of their songs from 'Please please me' (instantly likeable and who, at that time, could ask for anything more) to 'Penny Lane' (poetry) and 'A day in the life' and 'I am the walrus' (adventurous poetry) has been an exciting voyage to follow. ... Snipers from the press will keep trying to shoot them down and keep missing, because The Beatles have more to offer than the press. Most people, without envy, wish them good luck on their journey. More than that, many people hope that their courage increases, and not just for the sake of their art. There are obviously more important issues.[5]

Mitchell's ultimate insight is that the Beatles' bravery is more than aesthetic, but certainly not less. As with Ginsberg, a willingness to break down barriers in art complements the challenge to social and cultural assumptions. Mitchell even goes so far as to claim that, so long as the Beatles are producing original, provocative work, it becomes less and less likely that racist propaganda will flourish in England. In retrospect such an assertion may seem naïve; but it is important to recognise how profound was the impact of the Beatles' music at the time.

Ginsberg himself never had any doubts about the political relevance of his writing. The apocalyptic vision of 'Howl', with its equivalence between Moloch and the American military-industrial complex, is the most obvious example. But throughout the 1960s Ginsberg only became more and more radical as a poet. The key text is 'Wichita Vortex Sutra', which is his account of the impact of the Vietnam War on the collective consciousness of the United States. It is typical of Ginsberg to use a religious form of writing, the Buddhist 'sutra' (discourse, sermon), in order to engage with the material world. For him problems in the profane realm are only solved by way of realisation of the sacred dimension of existence. Vietnam is a symptom of what he calls 'Lacklove', that hatred of self and others which is born of repressed emotions: 'All we do is for this frightened thing / we call Love, want and lack – / fear that we aren't the one whose body could be / beloved of all the brides of Kansas City, / kissed all over by every boy of Wichita – / O but how many in their solitude weep aloud like me …' His remedy is to invoke the agents of spiritual revelation, in whichever culture they originate, whether from East or from West: 'Shivananda who touches the breast and says OM / Srimata Krishanji of Brinadban who says take for your guru / William Blake, the invisible father of English visions … / Sacred Heart my Christ acceptable.' The poet, inspired by their presence is able to 'lift my voice aloud, / make mantra of American language now, / I hear declare the end of the War!'[6]

One implication here is that the world of warfare is 'maya', an illusionary construct which belies the sacred reality in which we are all invited to participate. To defeat it, one must draw on the power of the holy Word, in this case, the Hindu 'Om': in effect, mantra overcomes maya. Bear in mind that in 1968 Ginsberg chanted 'Om' tirelessly in an effort to defuse the violence that occurred when the Youth International Party marched in protest against the Vietnam War to coincide with the Democratic Party convention in Chicago. For him, the chant was simultaneously a religious, an aesthetic and a political act.

More generally, we may say that Ginsberg's historical sense is inseparable from his spiritual vision and his poetic gift. As with the earlier 'Sunflower Sutra' – inspired by Blake's 'Ah! Sunflower' – the idea of 'Wichita Vortex Sutra' is to discover and celebrate the sacred dimension of profane space and time through the power of poetry. Commonplace reality becomes illuminated. It would be misleading to call this realism, despite its fidelity to experience, since the reality is transformed in the process. Blake it was who advised cleansing 'the doors of perception', so that the world might appear 'as it really is, infinite'. Blake it was who declared: 'To generalize is to be an idiot. To particularize is the alone distinction of merit ...'[7] No less than for Blake, Ginsberg's aim is to charge 'minute particulars' with visionary intensity.[8] Hence the poet's excitement at seeing even that choked, begrimed plant, 'the gray Sunflower poised against the sunset'.[9] But for Ginsberg it is a fine distinction between this kind of heightened realism and surrealism proper. For example, the opening line of the ambiguously titled 'The Lion for Real' (1958) reads: 'I came home and found a lion in my living room ...' The starving creature threatens to eat the poet, but departs, leaving him imaginatively obsessed rather than physically consumed: 'Your starved and ancient Presence O Lord I wait in my room at your Mercy.'[10] It is obvious by now that the lion's origin is Biblical – Ginsberg evokes the Lion of the Tribe of Judah, the Messiah who will establish his kingdom at the end of history – and that he represents divine inspiration. Thus, realism and surrealism imply the same sacred conclusion. Ginsberg is rarely zany in the secular sense – even given titles like 'Television Was a Baby Crawling Toward the Death Chamber' – but always willing to play the holy fool.

We have already mentioned, in connection with Blake and Dylan, Ginsberg's orientation towards song. This is implicit in his idea of art as spontaneous utterance. But his reputation is as a master of the long, liturgical line derived from the Bible, and his forays into song have been overlooked. It is important to bear in mind, though, that the Psalms themselves were composed as words for music. Thus it might be worth looking briefly at his psalm-like utterances. His vision had always been straightforward – essentially, love conquers all – but as he developed he gained more and more courage to let his soul 'clap its hands and sing', as Yeats would have it. Or, to revert to the Blake connection, we might say that Ginsberg's development was the counterpoint to his master's, who moved from simple (though not simplistic) lyrics to elaborate prophecies; Ginsberg moved from the former to the latter.

If anything, Ginsberg's songs were simpler than the lyrics of the pop composers who were consciously expanding the possibilities of their art. As pop became self-consciously poetic, his poetry became artlessly direct. But then, Ginsberg had never been ashamed to stand naked, whether literally or metaphorically. Consider 'Gospel Noble Truths' (1975). It begins: 'Born in this world / You got to suffer/ Everything changes / You got no soul.' This is sound Buddhist doctrine, expressed with stark beauty. It only gets starker, and it ends as follows: 'Die when you die / Die when you die / Lie down you lie down / Die when you die.'[11] Whether Ginsberg ever managed to produce a song comparable in scope and subtlety to those of Dylan and the Beatles is debatable. There again, he was not setting up in competition with them: he was trying to revivify poetry. Hence his willingness to risk mockery for his seeming naivete.

The gift to be so effectively simple can only come from having simultaneously nurtured both craft and spontaneity – if that does not sound too paradoxical. Early on, Ginsberg put his faith in the inspiration of the moment. In 1959, he declared his belief in Kerouac's idea that if 'mind is shapely' then 'art is shapely':

> I really don't know what I'm doing when I sit down to write. I figure it out as I go along and revise as little as possible. … While writing, my feeling for the subject can deepen, I begin to improvise and build up a rhythm. I cry if I write something beautiful. Sometimes this appears to be divine inspiration – I get the feeling, it's an ecstatic lucidity, that the world can be entered and prophesied to buy a single soul, alone.[12]

Ginsberg's own phrase for this faith in the flow of the mind and in the art that can capture and convey it, compelling the attention of the world, is 'Spontaneous Bop Prosody' [sic] – a phrase he coined the year before in a celebration of Kerouac's prose style.[13] The allusion to bop is telling: if we take this to cover blues and jazz at the very least (as Kerouac seemed to allow), we may take Ginsberg to be celebrating the same potential for authentic utterance in popular song as well as in poetry. It is a skill which is easily misunderstood, however: it might appear to involve abandoning all notions of order; but of course it relies on the mind being 'shapely', as a result of meditation and other mental disciplines.

For our present purposes, it is worth noting that when Ginsberg develops these thoughts in an essay of the mid-sixties, his argument happily moves between 'high' and 'low' art. Lamenting that poetry has become reified as text, rather than celebrated as performance, he looks to popular music for hope of rejuvenation, which he sees as confirming, not contradicting, the insights of that great poet of elitist experimentation, Ezra Pound:

> But young minstrels have now arisen in the airwaves whose poetic forms outwardly resemble antique verse including

regular stanzas refrains and rhymes: Dylan and Donovan and
some fragments of the Rolling Stones because they *think* not
only in words but also in music simultaneously have out of the
necessities of their own space-age media and electric machinery
tunes evolved a natural use of a personal realistic imaginative
rhymed verse. Principle of composition here is, however, unlike
antique literary form, primarily spontaneous and improvised
(in the studio if need be at the last minute), and prophetic in
character in that tune and language are invoked shamanistically
on the spot from the unconscious. This new ear is not dead
because it's not only for eye-page, it's connected with a voice
improvising, with hesitancies aloud, a living musician's ear.
The old library poets had lost their voices; natural voice was
rediscovered; and now natural song for physical voice. Oddly
this fits Pound's paradigm tracing the degeneration of poesy
from the Greek dance-foot chorus thru minstrel song thru
1900 abstract voiceless page.[14]

Having Pound on his side, he can now proceed to his affirmation of the
life-changing power of popular song. It is a power that is potentially
spiritual:

So now returned to song and song forms we may yet anticipate
inspired creators like Shiva Krishna Chaitanya Mirabai and
Ramakrishna who not only composed verse in ecstatic fits, but
also chanted their verse in melody, and lifted themselves off the
floor raised their arms and danced in time to manifest divine
presence. Mantra repetition – a form of prayer in which a short
magic formula containing various god names is chanted
hypnotically – has entered Western consciousness and a new
mantra rock is formulated in the Byrds and Beatles.[15]

The Beatles as saviours of poetry, and the Beatles' art as 'mantra rock':
these are intriguing thoughts, which we might bear in mind as we
proceed.

Given the above pronouncement, made in the mid-sixties, it was
with some conviction that Ginsberg was able to claim twenty years
later that he had always appreciated the Beatles' significance. In 1984
he wrote:

I remember the precise moment, the precise night I went to this
place in New York called the Dom and they turned on 'I Want

to Hold Your Hand', and I heard that high, yodelling alto sound of the OOOH that went right through my skull, and I realized it was going to go through the skull of Western civilization. I began dancing in public the first time in my life complete delight and abandon [sic], no self-conscious wallflower anxieties. It was joyful rhythm, generosity, the openness, youthfulness and communality of their voices. They were four guys who were a gang, and they loved and appreciated each other. I remember realizing that night at the Dom that black dancing had been brought back to the white West, [that] people were going to return to their bodies [and] that Americans were going to shake their ass. The Beatles changed masculine American consciousness, they introduced a new note of complete masculinity allied with complete tenderness and vulnerability. And when that note was accepted in America, it did more than anything or anyone to prepare us for some kind of open-minded, open-hearted relationship with each other – and the rest of the world.[16]

Ginsberg here is manifestly welcoming the Beatles into the countercultural fold. Their music resists the aridity of Western dualism, and in particular North American puritanism; it involves a new, expanded sense of self; it demonstrates a capacity for connection, both social and planetary. It is, in short, 'Beat'; and it is 'Beat' from the start, not just in its later, experimental phase.

Lest we are in any doubt that the Beatles are consistently seen by Ginsberg as labouring in the same vineyard as himself, we should take note of his 'Definition of the Beat Generation' (1981), from which we quoted briefly in the Introduction. There he lists the various meanings of the term 'Beat': first, the beat of jazz; second, the state of being 'exhausted' and 'rejected by society'; third, 'beatific'; fourth, the literary movement itself. The list might seem complete, but he then adds another dimension: the effects of the movement within the wider culture. Amongst these are the 'spread of ecological consciousness', the opposition to the 'military-industrial machine civilisation' and the attention to 'what Kerouac called, after Spengler, "Second Religiousness" developing within an advanced civilisation'. But in the present context, the most important one is this: the 'evolution of rhythm and blues into rock'n'roll into high art form, as evidenced by the Beatles, Bob Dylan, and other popular musicians influenced in the late 1950s and '60s by beat [sic] generation poets' and writers' works.'[17]

Of the four Beatles, it was John Lennon who best epitomised for Ginsberg the new consciousness, which he and Kerouac had anticipated. Yet Ginsberg insisted that Lennon, like the Beats, was drawing on the past even while he spoke for the future. Reflecting in 1973 on the work produced by Lennon with his partner Yoko Ono, both in the later Beatles years and after the group's demise, he repudiated the idea that Lennon's verse was simplistic: 'On the contrary, it's an ancient perfectly subtle, humble, artful simplicity: the condensation of common, social language into hard strong personal verse.' He concluded:

> To sum up, Lennon/Ono is a conscious poet coherently
> adapting traditional poetic song devices to new consciousness
> new technology electronic mass ear education: one brilliant
> development of modern poetry, completely realized. If
> Lennon/Ono disappear tomorrow to heaven, they'd take an
> immortal laurel crown (traditional poetic gift of the muses)
> to the pearly gates, great work finished.[18]

The spirit which Ginsberg had responded to when he first heard 'I Want to Hold Your Hand' was for him brought to perfection by Lennon, in a process best understood as a concentration of sound and word rather than an elaboration of ideas and images.

As we have seen, Ginsberg became increasingly intrigued by the power of song, which enabled him to balance spontaneity and craft in pursuit of further intensity. Interestingly, his last major work, written two years before his death, was a composition designed to be narrated to the accompaniment of the guitar – and not just any guitar, the guitarist being none other than Lennon's former songwriting partner, Paul McCartney. 'The Ballad of the Skeletons' is one of his most incisive indictments of globalising materialism: 'Said the Buddha skeleton / Compassion is wealth / Said the Corporate skeleton / It's bad for your health.' Again: 'Said the Ecologic Skeleton / Keep Skies blue / Said the Multinational Skeleton / What's it worth to you.'[19] Ginsberg may be running the risk of appearing naïve, but his performance of the poem with McCartney seemed very much in keeping with the Beat ideal.[20] That said, nobody present could have thought that Ginsberg was trying to attempt anything comparable to what McCartney himself had achieved. The Beat poet had embraced the music of the Beatles, but they had produced a distinctive body of work that went further musically than he could ever have done. The important question, which we must now address, is how far was the Beatles' achievement indebted to the Beat vision, which we understand here to be a 'beatific' vision? In order to do so, we need to give an account of both the context and the content of their work.

*****

In June 1965, John Lennon was interviewed on television by the journalist and broadcaster Kenneth Allsop on the occasion of the publication of Lennon's second book, *A Spaniard in the Works*. After he had read two extracts from the volume, he was asked whether he would rather have been published on the strength of his writing talent than on the strength of his fame as a member of the Beatles. Lennon replied: 'If I hadn't been a Beatle, I wouldn't have thought of having this stuff published. I would have been crawling round broke, and just writing it and throwing it away.' He paused briefly, then added: 'I might have been a Beat poet!'[21]

The connection between the words 'Beat' and 'Beatle' is problematical. The standard interpretation of the group's name is that it was created in honour of their hero Buddy Holly's group, the Crickets: by punning on the name of an insect, they were paying Holly & co oblique homage. However, Lennon's own whimsical account, written before their success, is wilfully evasive. Even at this early stage, he is enjoying a joke at the expense of those solemnly seeking a hidden meaning:

> Many people ask what are Beatles? Why Beatles? Ugh, Beatles, how did the name arrive? So we will tell you. It came in a vision – a man appeared on a flaming pie and said unto them, 'From this day on you are Beatles with an 'A'. Thank you, Mister Man, they said, thanking him.[22]

Flaming pies aside, we may say that the transition from 'Beetles' to 'Beatles' must have been meant to suggest that Lennon's group was at the very least a 'beat' group. The question, then, is how far may we consider the 'Beatles' as 'Beats'?

Again, it is Lennon who provides the possibility of a link. As he was proudly to tell Ginsberg, he had, in his final year at Quarry Bank School, more than once produced in his exercise book a collection of poems, stories and drawings which he called 'The Daily Howl', to be circulated amongst his friends.[23] That would have been the academic

year of 1956–7, so there can be little doubt that the publication of
Allen Ginsberg's *Howl and other poems* in 1956 must have had an
influence. It may be true that Lennon did not familiarise himself with
the whole of 'Howl' until the mid-1970s, when he heard Ginsberg
reading it on the radio.[24] But it is highly probable that a teenager who
was attracted to the bohemian lifestyle, and who was shortly to attend
art college, would have been receptive to the resonance of 'Beat'
writing.

Moreover, his friendship with Stuart Sutcliffe, 'the fifth Beatle',
would have ensured that he was kept in touch with cultural innovations and aesthetic developments in his student days. Bill Harry, an
authority on the Beatles, has refuted the idea that they began as 'uncul-
tured young lads' who 'knew nothing about art and culture':

> Nothing could be further from the truth in Stuart and John's
> case. Stuart was a dedicated artist and knew far more about
> painting than his new friends at Hamburg [where he went on to
> study]. At Liverpool College of Art, their group of friends
> continually discussed the Beat Generation, San Francisco poets
> and the Angry Young Men, and watched films by Jean Cocteau,
> Salvador Dali and Luis Bunuel at the college film shows ...[25]

It was the trip to Hamburg that enabled Sutcliffe to persuade Lennon
to abandon his teddy boy image and to adopt the more 'arty' style
encouraged by his new girlfriend, Astrid Kirchherr: hair combed
forward, clothes dark, jackets collarless. But we need not imagine that
Lennon was resistant to the change. Moreover, he seemed sympathetic
to the bohemian scene in Hamburg. It was he who, intrigued by Kirchherr, Klaus Vormann and other German fans of the group, dubbed
them the 'Exis' – because they reminded him of the French Existential-
ists, whom he admired.

If Lennon was able to recognise 'Exis', he surely would have known
of 'Beats', whose fame had spread far more widely. Certainly, Harry is
convinced that one of the books both Lennon and Sutcliffe read avidly
was Kerouac's *On the Road*.[26] Moreover, the term 'beatnik', coined in
the States to describe the hangers-on around the Beat movement of
writers, soon became well established in England. It referred to any
youth who was thought to be idle, scruffy, disaffected and pretentious;
and rumour had it that there was a collection of such creatures in most
of the major cities, particularly in the vicinity of universities and art
colleges. Predictably, the two friends were drawn to that kind of milieu.

In 1959, a reporter from the *Sunday People*, researching the topic of bohemian life in Liverpool, took a photograph of the untidy workroom in the flat rented by Lennon and Sutcliffe. The headline read: 'This is the Beatnik Horror.'[27] The future Beatle was already being associated with the Beat phenomenon. For the record, we may also note that less than a year later, the Silver Beetles, as they were known – comprising Lennon, McCartney, Harrison and Pete Best (the last of these to be eventually replaced by Ringo Starr) – became friends with one Royston Ellis, a pop music journalist who was gaining a reputation as a Beat-style poet. Not long after that came the change of name to 'Beatles'.[28]

Here, however, we need to recognise the distinct way in which the Beatles exemplified an English 'pop' equivalent of the Beat vision. The conventional wisdom is that it was thanks to Dylan that the group realised that song lyrics could go way beyond 'moon-june' cliché. The Beatles, we are frequently told, realised their potential by way of a mutual influence: that is, if they demonstrated to Dylan the possibilities of electrified music, thus encouraging him to forge in the mid-1960s what became known as 'folk rock', it was he who simultaneously demonstrated to them the possibilities of 'poetic' pop. According to this version of history, the Beatles became serious songwriters at about the same time Dylan became a 'rock' star. However, we have already read Ginsberg's reflections on his response to the power of the early Beatles music, which suggests that one of the most important of Beat writers had already recognised them as congenial artists. So it would hardly do them justice simply to survey the middle to late years of the Beatles, awarding points for the proximity of particular songs to Dylan's kind of work. While it would no doubt be an amusing exercise to note the 'Dylanesque' qualities of this or that performance – 'I'm A Loser', 'You've Got to Hide Your Love Away' or 'Norwegian Wood', for example – it would not help us in our present task.

More generally, it is worth taking note of Ray Coleman's reflections on the context and significance of Lennon's achievement in the mid-1960s, both as lyricist and as literary writer (author of *In His Own Write* and *A Spaniard in the Works*): 'There was an Englishness to his work that ran in sharp contrast to the stream-of-consciousness poetry of the American beat [sic] poets of the day, like Allen Ginsberg.'[29] Granted the misrepresentation of the Beat aesthetic – 'stream-of-consciousness poetry' does not do justice to the principle of 'Spontaneous Bop Prosody' – Coleman does have a point. He would seem to have in mind the wealth of material already available to Lennon, growing up in England in the 1950s: the legacy of music hall, the rise of 'skiffle' (the peculiarly English adaptation of the American folk blues of Leadbelly and others, chiefly associated with the name of Lonnie Donegan), children's fantasy (Lewis Carroll and Edward Lear in particular), and radio shows such as *The Goons* (written by, and featuring, one of the Beatles' heroes, the eccentric Spike Milligan). Lennon did not need Dylan to show him how to develop a more adventurous kind of popular song – any more than he needed to have studied 'Howl' in depth to realise that he could benefit from its expansion of aesthetic possibilities.

Perhaps the safest inference to make is that, if we take the overall achievement of the Beatles throughout the 1960s, there can be little doubt that their evolution was towards an art which is the equivalent of – rather than merely the product of – the Beat phenomenon. We might even say that Lennon's own work comes particularly close, if we think of his reliance on spontaneity and free association in writing lyrics. The title of 'I Am the Walrus' may invoke Carroll's 'The Walrus and the Carpenter'; and the English strain of surrealism that stems from writers such as him and Edward Lear is suggested by lines such as 'Elementary penguin singing Hare Krishna ...' But many lines in the song are reminiscent of the typical Ginsberg cadence: for example, 'pornographic priestess boy you been a naughty girl you let your knickers down ...'[30] There again, it would be misleading to focus on the lyrics to the exclusion of the music. We need to bear in mind the visceral impact on Ginsberg of the sheer sound of the early Beatles, regardless of the rudimentary nature of the lyrics at that stage. Ian MacDonald's account of their significance endorses that response:

> Like Irving Berlin and Noel Coward, Lennon and McCartney were not only unable to read music, but firmly declined to learn. Writing, to begin with, mainly on guitars, they brought unpredictable twists to their tunes by shifting chord-positions in unusual and often random ways, and pushing their lines in unexpected directions by harmonising as they went along in fourths and fifths rather than in conventional thirds. In short, they had no preconceptions about the next chord, an openness which they consciously exploited and which played a major role in some of their most commercially successful songs (eg, I WANT TO HOLD YOUR HAND).[31]

However, we might want to part company with MacDonald when he goes on to claim that such achievements were chiefly expressive of the

consumer ideology of the post-war years: 'The mass shift to individu-
alistic materialism came into full swing as the Beatles appeared, and the
records they made in their early career reflect its mood with unselfcon-
scious elation: "good time" music, simple in feeling and with the accent
on physical excitement.'[32] MacDonald seems to be using the word
'materialism' in its sense of dedication to commercial values, rather
than in its philosophical sense. We might agree that the success of songs
such as 'She Loves You' and 'I Want to Hold Your Hand' was an
important aspect of a newly secular hedonism; but, if we are to bear in
mind Ginsberg's response to such songs, we cannot confine the spiritual dimension of their work to the 'flower power' period represented
by such albums as *Revolver* and *Sgt Pepper*.

Let us address this question of continuity explicitly, before we
proceed any further. According to MacDonald, when the Beatles joined
'the Consciousness War' on the side of the hippies against a society
based only on self-interest, they effectively broke with their earlier
function. They now gave voice to 'the countercultural revolt against
acquisitive selfishness – and, in particular, the hippies' unfashionable
perception that we can change the world only by changing ourselves'.[33]
However, I would suggest that it might be more accurate, rather than
make a neat distinction between the Beatles of 'secular materialism'
and the Beatles of 'idealistic spirituality' (to coin the complementary
phrase), to see the later Beatles as realising the potential of the early
Beatles. If the group came to exemplify something akin to the Beat
vision, it did so by following through lyrically the radical potential of
the sound which they so boldly created in the beginning – and which a
major Beat poet responded to with such excitement.

*****

I have suggested that it is misleading to divide up the Beatles' career
into early hedonism and later hippiedom. To my mind, it is much
more interesting and productive to follow Ginsberg's lead and see their
work as forming a visionary unity. Obviously, one has to take account
of the growing sophistication of the lyrics. Obviously, too, it would be
naïve to think that each of the three main songwriters – Lennon,
McCartney, Harrison – was in consistent accord with the others.
(As the Beatles headed for the famous moment of disbandment in
1970, antagonisms came to the surface.) However, it is surely worth
suspending disbelief in order to enter into the spirit of the Beatles'
extraordinary achievement.

We could do worse than to rely on the guidance of the musicologist Wilfrid Mellers. True, his *Twilight of the Gods: The Beatles in Retrospect* (1973) was initially mocked for its pretentiousness, given its implicit equivalence between Wagner and the songwriting team of Lennon and McCartney and its insistence on treating Beatles songs as if they were comparable to classical compositions. I would suggest, however, that its general thesis has stood up well to long-term scrutiny. Let us begin by noting his unstinting praise for the early work up to and including the film album, *A Hard Day's Night* (1964). For Mellers, these songs are songs of innocence: '[This] music is more open, whiter, fresher, tenderer than the age-old black blues, for its Anglo-Irish affiliations lead it towards innocence rather than ecstasy, pleasure rather than pain, whole-ness rather than blueness.'[34] But nothing is simple where the Beatles are concerned, and if anyone is qualified to find subtlety, it is Mellers. Observing that 'the ambivalence of the Negro blues ... is not entirely alien to Beatle music, even in their early days', he goes on to offer the following assessment:

> Blue rawness and 'reality' temper their innocence; whilst their innocence transmutes aggression. It's this synthesis of qualities – American black and Anglo-Irish white – that makes the physical beat, which is their music's most *immediately* recognisable quality, a stimulus rather than a narcotic; and this again is what makes the happiness not mindlessly euphoric, but for real. The irony, or comedy, that often springs from this fusion is also pertinent here; the objectivity their songs achieve reconciles individual with corporate identity and this helps to explain their tremendous impact on a whole generation. They were simply and sensuously affirmative; babes newborn, rejecting the past, yet singing for *dear life*.[35]

With Blake evidently in mind (though without much explicit mention of him), Mellers cannot speak of innocence without also speaking of experience: 'because Beatle happiness was true, it had latent within it the awareness of pain and the negative emotions.' He suggests that this becomes evident in 'the deepening range of the songs that conclude their first period. Interestingly enough, these are associated with their first film, entitled *A Hard Day's Night*.'[36]

Mellers' appreciation of the title song of the album accompanying the film is persuasive:

[It] is another number about Love, identified with Home; but a more 'experienced' quality is evident in the verses, which use less youthfully abstract jargon, more down to earth fact. John has been 'working like a dog' to get money to buy his girl *things*. He should now, after his hard day, be 'sleeping like a log', but knows he won't be, because the things she'll do when he gets home will make him 'feel alright'. So there's again a division between innocence (the ecstasy of being 'held tight') and experience (things, making money, the tedium of work, suggested by the long repeated notes in the tune's first phrase). Both poetically and musically, however, this is subtler, because more equivocal, than in any previous song. Indeed one might say that the song sees innocence and experience as interdependent; the freedom couldn't be so lovely were it not for the tedium.[37]

I quote this specific analysis because it gives substance to Mellers' overview of the Beatles development. Unlike MacDonald, he assumes a coherence of vision, so that the early work makes sense as part of an emergent dialectic. One recalls Blake's declaration in *The Marriage of Heaven and Hell*: 'Without contraries is no progression.'[38]

It is when he comes to the *Sgt Pepper* album, which he sees as marking 'the climacteric point' in the Beatles' career, 'their definite breach with the pop music industry' and the creation of 'their own self-justifying aesthetic world', that he feels able to make his case and offer his overview:

The pattern of their young lives seems clear. In their boyhood they discovered a lost Eden, creating a danced music of which the euphoria was valid because newborn. Their first period ends with their hard day's night's discovery of human relationships and responsibilities; and this 'second period' is consummated in *Sgt. Pepper's Lonely Hearts Club Band*. If Pepper, however, is the apotheosis of the second period, he also initiates the third: much in the same way as *A Hard Day's Night* had one foot in the first period, the other in the second. For whereas many songs in *Pepper* are concerned with the young mind and senses in relationship to the external world, others follow *Tomorrow never knows* (from *Revolver*) in re-entering the world of dream. This preoccupation with the life 'within you' is no longer child-like and innocent, for it absorbs the experience of the Beatles' middle years.[39]

Thus, the Beatles' work forms a dialectical progression, analogous to Blake's, involving three overlapping periods: first, that of innocence and dream; second, that of experience and social reality; third, that which sees a renewal of the first period in the light of the second, involving a search within oneself for an answer to the dilemma posed by external pressures. As for that third period: though Mellers does not make the comparison, one cannot help thinking of the 'beatific' vision which, for Kerouac and Ginsberg, is only possible given pain and loss. The authenticity of that vision will depend upon the depth of understanding occasioned by the entry into experience. Indeed, if Mellers' scheme has a fault, it is that it makes it appear as though the second period is somehow incomplete; whereas it is surely the case that it contains its own revelation, often more satisfactory than that of the third, where the art and the vision become more evasive. The crucial albums of the second period are *Revolver* (1966) and *Sgt Pepper's Lonely Hearts Club Band* (1967); the crucial single is 'Penny Lane' / 'Strawberry Fields Forever' (1967).

Turning to *Revolver*, there is surely very little risk involved in claiming 'Eleanor Rigby' to be a lyrical achievement which stands up well next to any Beat poem. Certainly, it shares the Beat worldview – though with an interesting variation. On the one hand, the spinster who 'picks up the rice in the church where a wedding has been', and who has to live in a 'dream' in order to sustain herself against a world which marginalises and demeans her, may have something of Kerouac's fellaheen about her. Eleanor stands for the ignored, the neglected, the rejected – those who do not seem to matter. On the other hand, Eleanor has little hope of spiritual revelation, and little hope of escaping the dead weight of her given world. The lost soul who wears 'a face that she keeps in the jar by the door' may be viewed in a surrealist perspective, but her life is firmly rooted in the all-too-familiar community of Father Mackenzie, 'darning his socks in the night when there's nobody there'. Even if the song does not hold out the possibility of an alternative vision, however, the compassion it articulates for those like Eleanor, whose lives are choked by convention and habit, gives it a Beat-like intensity. Moreover, it invites us to see through the empty rituals of a society which has no time for people like Eleanor. The song's refrain embraces the plight of 'all the lonely people'; its conclusion, as Father Mackenzie walks away from her grave after the burial, is that 'No one was saved'. When we are asked rhetorically, 'What does he care?', we are to infer that the merely conventional religion which the priest represents cannot satisfy the hunger for spiritual nourishment felt by people like Eleanor – nor does it even provide solace for him (p. 111). To encompass all these ideas in the space of a short song is a remarkable achievement. This is an art which is as powerful as any Beat poem but, extending no further than a page of text and performed audaciously to the accompaniment of a string quartet, may be said to extend the possibilities of the beatific vision.

Complementing McCartney's account of a lost soul in a wilderness of indifference is Lennon's apprehension of the healing emptiness which lies beyond all the hopes and dreams of this world. 'Tomorrow Never Knows' not only subverts the whole idea of a future in which the ambitions of the ego might be realised: with its extraordinary sound, suggestive of Eastern religious ritual and liturgy, it places its listener in the centre of 'The Void' (the song's original title). It was inspired by Lennon's reading of Timothy Leary's version of *The Tibetan Book of the Dead*. On page 14 of *The Psychedelic Experience*, he came across the statement, 'Whenever in doubt, turn off your mind, relax, float downstream'.[40] This becomes the first line of 'Tomorrow Never Knows', which is then embellished by encouragement to 'surrender to the void' – a state beyond both 'living' and 'dying'. The only valid path is to 'play the game existence to the end', knowing that that is also 'the beginning' (p. 124). Again, it is the sheer economy of expression (which is by no means dispersed by the ritualistic repetition of phrases) that strikes the listener: what Kerouac and Ginsberg were after in their dedication to Buddhism is distilled here. It is not that we need credit Lennon with vast scholarship in Eastern wisdom, but we may allow him his intuition and insight, which do seem to be informed by research that extends beyond merely browsing in Leary's book. Moreover, if 'Eleanor Rigby' casts a compassionate light on a painful life that can only be relieved by death and oblivion, 'Tomorrow Never Knows' conveys an overwhelming sense of release into what, at the time of composition, was all too glibly referred in fashionable circles as 'cosmic bliss'. We might prefer to call it the beatific vision.

That vision is inseparable from the feeling of identity with the fellaheen that we have witnessed in 'Eleanor Rigby'. *Sgt Pepper* is the most extensive confirmation of this insight. If we bear in mind that 'Penny Lane' and 'Strawberry Fields Forever' were intended to be part of the sequence of songs on that album, whose theme originally was to be the memory of a Liverpool childhood, then we have a very impressive achievement indeed. It is a cause for regret that they did not get included, but the reason was commercial not aesthetic: the group's manager, Brian Epstein, insisted that they be released separately as a double-sided single in order to satisfy the pop market, which demanded a new Beatles product prior to the release of *Sgt Pepper*. Let us turn to Mellers' account of the first of those two songs. Though he may make rather too much of the Beatles' experimentation with psychedelic drugs, which he sees as the common origin of both 'Penny Lane' and 'Strawberry Fields', his instinct is surely right that the predominant impulse of 'Penny Lane' is a yearning to discover a paradisal dimension to mundane experience:

> [Both songs] relate the LSD experience to childhood memory and a *new* Eden discovered within the mind; both, if they can hardly 'justify' the drug experience, demonstrate its relevance to the Beatles' development. Penny Lane is a real place, a bus roundabout in Liverpool, and the barber, the banker, the fireman, the children who figure in it are at once revocations of the Beatles' own childhood and mythic figures from a children's comic. It really is 'very strange' that the banker 'never wears a mac in the pouring rain'; and the fireman who likes to keep his `clean machine' clean is at once real and surreal: as indeed is the whole streetscape 'in my ears and in my eyes, there beneath the blue suburban skies'. There's a deeply mysterious poetry of the commonplace here ...[41]

Putting this into the terms used by Eliade, we would say that the song enacts the dialectic of the sacred and the profane: an ordinary area of a city in the North of England becomes the focus of a beatific revelation. In the moment of the song's duration, eternity is now and infinity is here. We might add that the poetry of the commonplace in 'Penny Lane' is beautifully enriched by the subversion of what we take to be reality, rendering the mundane world mysterious. The key moment here is that of 'the pretty nurse' selling poppies: 'though she feels as if she's in a play / She is anyway' (p. 127).

As for 'Strawberry Fields Forever', we should note that, as with Penny Lane, Strawberry Field (spelt without an 's') was a real place: a Salvation Army children's home near to the house where Lennon lived for most of his childhood, with his Aunt Mimi. He spent many happy hours there playing in the grounds; he would also make a point of attending the annual summer fete. But unlike McCartney's song, the impulse is not to place specific memories in a visionary framework, but to explore the very nature of vision itself. True, there are vague recollections of childhood activities: 'No one I think is in my tree', for example, suggests the games which Lennon might have enjoyed in the grounds; but one has to infer such experiences. In 'Penny Lane' the sights, smells and sounds of the area are all evoked, if thoroughly defamiliarised. In 'Strawberry Fields Forever', the knowledge imparted is more abstract: we learn that 'Living is easy with eyes closed', and that 'Nothing is real' (p. 127). If McCartney conjures up a fascinating microcosm, Lennon takes us to the edge of the macrocosm, beyond which lies the void. Either way, there is an assumption of a correspondence between the two realms, such as we find espoused by Spengler.

The unsettling sound of the music is what carries the meaning – but even a musicologist such as Mellers finds it hard to state quite how. We can perhaps cast some light on the song's series of cryptic utterances, however, by seeing it as a challenge to our normal mode of perception. If an habitual error is closing the eyes and 'Misunderstanding all you see', then the question of what is real becomes problematical. At first hearing, Lennon seems to pronounce the world illusory, but on reflection he is more probably articulating a tenet of both Hinduism and Buddhism, that it is our 'common sense' interpretation of the world which is illusory. Whether we call it 'maya' or 'samsara', that is what is implied in this context by the statement, 'Nothing is real' – particularly in the context of 'Misunderstanding all you see'. Of course, I may be crediting Lennon with more wisdom than he had, but the fact remains that the song itself insists on this direction of thought. As with 'Penny Lane', we are intrigued by the exploration of the borderland between illusion and reality. Again, as with that song, the implicit invitation is to regain one's sense of innocence and one's capacity for vision, which are taken to be synonymous. Ian MacDonald detects 'an eerie longing for a wild childhood of hide-and-seek and tree-climbing: the visionary strawberry fields of his imagination'. If he is right, then 'Strawberry Fields Forever' is much closer in spirit to 'Penny Lane' than at first appears: 'for the true subject of English psychedelia was neither love nor drugs, but nostalgia for the innocent vision of the child.'[42] Here we are reminded of the Blakean context which Mellers has insisted upon. The first-period songs celebrate innocence but begin to encounter experience; the second-period songs comprehend experience but gesture towards a visionary dimension of experience; the third-period songs recover the power of innocence and dream, with a new intensity derived from that dimension. 'Penny Lane' and 'Strawberry Fields' are, then, neatly poised between the second and the third.

* * * * *

Even though those outstanding songs did not finally form part of *Sgt Pepper*, the album still seems to the casual listener to form an artistic unity; and it is remarkable for both its musical and its lyrical innovation. The full title is worth dwelling on. Sgt Pepper himself emerges from the collective memory of the Beatles, perhaps in particular from Lennon's recollection of the Salvation Army band which used to play at Strawberry Field. The band now belongs to the 'lonely hearts club': we are in the world of Eleanor Rigby and all the other lost souls seeking love. By 'love', I refer to something broader and deeper than adolescent infatuation, the standard theme of 'pop'. When the Beatles will sing, shortly after the release of this album, 'All You Need Is Love', they imply that what matters once basic material needs have been fulfilled, is spiritual identity. Love in this sense is the force that facilitates mystic union – the realisation of the One. The tension which sustains the album, then, is that between loneliness and love, between alienation and integration, between loss and restoration.

At this stage, it might seem appropriate to claim that *Pepper* can withstand comparison with a work written by any Beat. However, it would be misleading to do so without acknowledging its affinity with earlier literary achievement. For, looking further back, we might even think of it as the Beatles' equivalent of a long poem published forty-five years before: one which has widely been regarded as the most important of the twentieth century. I refer, of course, to T. S. Eliot's *The Waste Land* (1922). Mention of that work might seem to take us away from our focus on the Beatles as Beat songwriters, but a brief digression in order to take account of Eliot might prove illuminating.

Even as we digress, it has to be conceded that the more usual comparison made is that between *The Waste Land* and 'Howl'. For example, John Tytell uses the two texts as markers of a major shift in sensibility, from Eliot's impersonal modernism to Ginsberg's subjective neo-Romanticism:

> The objective camera eye of 'The Waste Land' [was] replaced
> by the 'I' of the personal 'Howl'; the difference can be felt
> simply by listening to the sound of Eliot reading his work –
> dry, unemotional, ironic, distant – and comparing that to
> Ginsberg's impassioned, arousing rhapsody of voice. The Beats'
> denial of the artistic mask had extraordinary implications for
> the nature of language in literary art and the quality of

experience to be expressed. Prematurely conscious of the
potentials for lying on a national scale, the Beats raised the
standard of honesty no matter what the artistic consequences.
Art is created by the polar tensions of spontaneity and artifice,
improvisation and contrivance, and the Beats passionately
embraced the extremes of uncontained release and denounced
superimposed and confining forms.[43]

We must qualify this assessment, of course, by reminding ourselves that
the Beats at their best managed to work within the tension between
craft and spontaneity, between expertise and expression, between what
Eliot himself called 'tradition' and 'the individual talent'. Indeed, we
have had occasion before to query those commentators who have
assumed that the Beat aim was to break all aesthetic rules. The work
of Kerouac and Ginsberg which we have discussed could hardly be
characterised as 'uncontained release'. However, it remains true that
their writings are nearer to Romanticism than to modernism, based as
they are on the assumption that the writer has unique access to the
beatific vision, and has his or her own special way of communicating
it. That is, they favour sincerity over artifice, and they do not believe
in wearing an aesthetic mask. But then where do we place the Beatles
in this scheme?

What is remarkable about their work of this period is not that they
push further in the direction of expressivity, but that if anything they
pull back in the opposite direction, towards impersonality – albeit that
of popular culture rather than elitist poetry. According to the literary
critic, Richard Poirier, writing soon after the album's release, the
Beatles in *Sgt Pepper* manage to balance artifice and spontaneity by
way of their capacity for taking pleasure in the paraphernalia of
Englishness. This is evident in their relish for the legacy of music hall
and other popular forms of entertainment, as well as in their acute
sense of the dramatic:

This historical feeling for music, including their own musical
creations, explains I think the Beatles' fascination with the
invented aspects of everything around them, the participatory
tenderness and joy with which they respond to styles and
artifact, the maturity with which they have come to see the
coloring of the human and social landscape of contemporary
England. ... Not everyone their age is capable of seeing the odd
wonder of a meter maid – after all, a meter maid's a meter

maid; fewer still would be moved to a song of praise like
'Lovely Rita' ('When it gets dark I tow your heart away'); and
only a Beatle could be expected, when seeing her with a bag
across her shoulder, to have the historically enlivened vision
that 'made her look a little like a military man.'[44]

Poirier is aware that he may be over-interpreting such an apparently
trivial song from the album. But he wishes to assert that what he finds
in *Sgt Pepper* is more than a simple awareness by young Liverpudlians
of 'the residual social and cultural evidences from World War II and
even from the First World War'. As he explains:

> In response to these and other traces of the past … the Beatles
> display an absolutely unique kind of involvement. It isn't simply
> that they have an instinctive nostalgia for period styles, as in
> 'She's Leaving Home' or 'When I'm Sixty-Four', or that they
> absorb the past through the media of the popular arts, through
> music, cinema, theatrical conventions, bands like Sgt. Pepper's
> or music-hall performers. … No, the Beatles have the
> distinction in their work both of *knowing* that this is how they
> see and feel things and of enjoying the knowledge. It could be
> said that they know what Beckett and Borges know but without
> any loss of simple enthusiasm or innocent expectation, and
> without any patronization of those who do not know. In the
> loving phrases of 'Penny Lane', 'A pretty nurse is selling
> poppies from a tray, / And though she feels as if she's in a play,
> / She is anyway.'[45]

This quotation clinches his argument so well that one might almost
regret that 'Penny Lane' and its accompanying song, 'Strawberry Fields
Forever', did not make it onto the completed album – even though the
album certainly gives the impression of forming a unity.

Mention of such literary luminaries as Beckett and Borges may serve
to remind us of the comparison to which Poirier's exposition is building, and which I have already announced: that between *Sgt Pepper* and
The Waste Land. Why, we may ask, is Poirier interested in Eliot rather
than Ginsberg? The clue may lie – though, again, he does not spell this
out – in what he has said about the love of artifice. Eliot's great poem
is remarkable for the number of different styles which it parodies (from
Jacobean drama to music hall ditties) and for its wealth of allusions
(Dante, Shakespeare, Baudelaire and at least thirty other writers). In

this respect, it might not anticipate 'Howl', but it certainly anticipates *Sgt Pepper*. Both Eliot's poem and the Beatles' album display a relish for keeping alive the cultural past in the cultural present – the only place, after all, in which it will live or die:

> They have placed themselves within a musical, social and historical environment more monumental in its surroundings and more significantly populated than was the environment of any of their early songs. Listening to the *Sgt. Pepper* album one thinks not simply of the history of popular music but of the history of this century. It doesn't matter that some of the songs were composed before it occurred to the Beatles to use the motif of *Sgt. Pepper*, with its historical overtones; the songs emanated from some inwardly felt coherence that awaited a merely explicit design, and they would ask to be heard together even without the design.[46]

Poirier then goes on to suggest what that design is. He notes two aspects of it which anticipate the claim to which he is building up, namely the parallel between the Beatles' and Eliot's art. There is the sense of many lives being acted out in a social drama, sometimes blurring into one another; and there is the subversion of linear time, so that past and present become indistinguishable.

Here Poirier does not make explicit the Eliot connection, but those familiar with *The Waste Land* will catch his drift:

> Under the aegis of an old-time concert given by the type of music-hall band with which Lennon's father, Alfred, claims to have been associated, the songs, directly or by chance images, offer something like a review of contemporary English life, saved from folksong generality by having each song resemble a dramatic monologue. The review begins with the 'Sgt. Pepper' theme song, followed immediately by 'A Little Help from My Friends': Ringo, helped by the other Beatles, will ... try not to sing out of 'key', try, that is, to fit into a style still heard in England but very much out of date. Between this and the reprise of 'Sgt. Pepper', which would be the natural end of the album, are ten songs, and while some are period pieces, about hangovers from the past, as is the band itself, no effort is made at any sort of historical chronology. Their arrangement is apparently haphazard, suggesting how the

hippie and the historically pretentious, the genteel and the mod,
the impoverished and the exotic, the Indian influence
and the influence of technology are inextricably entangled
into what is England.[47]

As with Eliot, one aim is to query our conventional sense of self, so that
we are more aware of human life as the acting out of a series of roles.
As with Eliot, another aim is to invoke the past in the service of the
present. The sense of where we have come from is indispensable in
deciding what are our current possibilities. The album ends with a
sense of 'release', Poirier suggests, which is all the more powerful for
being so hard-won:

> Right after the reprise of the 'Sgt. Pepper' song, with no inter-
> val and picking up the beat of the 'Sgt. Pepper' theme, an
> 'extra' song, perhaps the most brilliant ever written by Lennon
> and McCartney, breaks out of the theatrical frame and enters 'a
> day in the life', into the way we live now. It projects a degree of
> loneliness not to be managed within the conventions of Sgt.
> Pepper's Lonely Hearts Club Band. Released from the controls
> of Sgt. Pepper, the song exposes the horrors of more contempo-
> rary and less benign controls, and it is from these that the song
> proposes the necessity of still further release.[48]

Rather than an afterthought, or an ironic comment on the performance
of Sgt Pepper and his band, the final song of the album has a sense of
inevitability, according to Poirier. The whole work of art has implied
the desire for release which the song articulates. (Whether or not 'A
Day in the Life' was recorded last of all need not concern us: we are
talking here about the imaginative logic of the complete album.)

At this point, talk of 'release' might seem more suggestive of Ginsberg than of Eliot. As previously, one could have wished that Poirier
had included some account of the poem's Beat affinities, but perhaps
that is too much to expect from an otherwise exhaustive and
compelling case for taking the Beatles' art seriously. If I might interpose
my own interests, then, I would suggest that when Poirier does come
to the point of making the comparison between *Sgt Pepper* and *The
Waste Land*, he does so in a context which might allow us to comprehend 'Howl'. Ginsberg's poem, we will recall, takes us through a
demonic vision of contemporary life to a beatific vision, the latter being
articulated through the seemingly endless repetition of the word 'holy'.

Eliot's poem has a similar, if less extensive and more equivocal, post-script to its own demonic vision: the repetition three times of a Sanskrit word, 'Shantih', which might be defined as the mystical peace which comes when one has attuned oneself to Brahman, the Godhead. Poirier ingeniously proposes an equivalence between Eliot's closing refrain and that of 'A Day in the Life'. The fact that this involves a drug reference might encourage us in trying to accommodate a Beat poem in our comparison, though that would have to be our own gloss on Poirier's commentary. Moreover, it would have to be understood, as with Dylan's 'Mr Tambourine Man', that the drug reference can take us only so far. Perhaps we should simply let Poirier speak for himself. The song, he tells us, conveys 'the necessity of further release' as follows:

> It does so in musical sounds meant to convey a 'trip' out,
> sounds of ascending-airplane velocity and crescendo that occur
> right after the first 'I'd love to turn you on', at midpoint in the
> song, and after the final, plaintive repetition of the line at the
> end, when the airplane sounds give way to a sustained
> orchestral chord that drifts softly and slowly toward infinity
> and silence. It is, as I've suggested, a song of wasteland, and the
> concluding 'I'd love to turn you on' has as much propriety to
> the fragmented life that precedes it in the song and in the whole
> work as does the 'Shantih, Shantih, Shantih' to the fragments of
> Eliot's poem. Eliot can be remembered here for still other
> reasons: not only because he pays conspicuous respect to the
> music hall but because his poems, like the Beatles' songs, work
> for a kaleidoscopic effect, for fragmented patterns of sound that
> can bring historic masses into juxtaposition only to let them be
> fractured by other emerging and equally evocative fragments.[49]

In the light of this ambitious but credible reading of the album's conclusion, I would suggest that the Beatles' achievement in *Sgt Pepper* stands poised between that of Eliot and that of Ginsberg. To confirm the Eliot connection, we may say that its sense of life as an endless drama, in which lost souls wander in a rootless world, reminds us of *The Waste Land*. Consider Billy Shears, the singer in the band, who is afraid that his audience will 'walk out' on him; consider the girl who is 'leaving home' and 'meeting a man from the motor trade' in a desperate attempt to have 'fun'; consider the disaffected, churlish persona of 'Good Morning Good Morning', whose only comment on his tedious existence is that he has 'nothing to say but it's OK'. Again,

as with Eliot's poem, the alienation of such lives is consistently juxta-
posed with the tantalising sense of a healing unity, which is ultimately
spiritual in nature. In *Sgt Pepper*, this sense is articulated in George
Harrison's centrally placed song, a kind of sutra chanted to the accompaniment of sitar and tabla. 'Within You Without You' declares: 'When
you've seen beyond yourself, then you may find peace of mind is
waiting there / And the time will come when you see we're all one, and
life flows on within you and without you' (p. 137). But that, of course,
is what distinguishes the album from Eliot's poem, in which the sense
of spirit comes in scattered fragments only – even the closing allusion
to the Upanishads consisting of that one word, 'Shantih', repeated
thrice. Thus, the fact that the Beatles allow for a more extensive affirmation of spiritual meaning suggests their second affinity – that with
Ginsberg, whose poetry (as opposed to his songs) could hardly be
accused of terseness. We are reminded much more of 'Spontaneous Bop
Prosody' than of modernist restraint. Where Eliot's sense of sacred
meaning comes through in cryptic, tight-lipped allusion, the Beatles are
able where appropriate to articulate a heartfelt yearning to discover
sacred potential within the sphere of the profane. Thus, though 'Within
You Without You' has usually been disregarded as a concession to
Harrison's fascination with Indian music, it is central not only to *Sgt
Pepper* but to the Beatles' overall vision. It proposes a way out of the
waste land: a way that is affirmed by the closing chord of 'A Day in
the Life'.

Ian MacDonald's commentary on those two songs might prove
helpful here. He defends the first with some vigour:

> Harrison's WITHIN YOU WITHOUT YOU finishes with a
> spasm of embarrassed laughter added by its composer during
> the final day of work on it (the last day of recording for
> *Sergeant Pepper* as a whole). His wryness was prescient: this
> ambitious essay in cross-cultural fusion and meditative
> philosophy has been dismissed with a yawn by almost every
> commentator since it first appeared. Bored by the track's lack
> of harmonic interest, critics have focused on the lyric,
> attacking it as didactic and dated. Apart from its offence to the
> Me Generation in pointing out how small we are, the trouble
> with WITHIN YOU WITHOUT YOU for most of its detractors
> lies in the song's air of superiority and sanctimonious finger-
> wagging at those 'who gain the world and lose their soul' ('Are
> you one of them?'). Yet, seeing the world from the metaphysical

perspective of Indian philosophy, it was only natural that
Harrison should find himself wailing that people could save the
world 'if they only knew'. As for the accusatory finger – bad
manners in times of relativism and making-do – this is a token
of what was then felt to be a revolution in progress: an inner
revolution against materialism. For better or worse, it is
impossible to conduct a revolution without picking a side and
pointing out the drawbacks of its rivals. ... As such, WITHIN
YOU WITHOUT YOU is the conscience of *Sergeant Pepper's
Lonely Hearts Club Band*: the necessary sermon that comes
with the community singing. Described by those with no grasp
of the ethos of 1967 as a blot on a classic LP, WITHIN YOU
WITHOUT YOU is central to the outlook that shaped *Sergeant
Pepper* – a view justifiable then, as it is justifiable now.[50]

MacDonald's commentary on the latter song suggests that he has
intuited its reliance on the first. Making allowance for a rather reductive formulation of the wisdom that is being articulated, this does seem
to capture the spirit of the music:

The message is that life is a dream and we have the power, as
dreamers, to make it beautiful. In this perspective, the two
rising orchestral *glissandi* [scalar runs made by a sliding of the
fingers on string instruments] may be seen as symbolising
simultaneously the moment of awakening from sleep and a
spiritual ascent from fragmentation to wholeness achieved in
the final E major chord. ... Though clouded with sorrow and
sarcasm, A DAY IN THE LIFE is as much an expression of
mystic-psychedelic optimism as the rest of *Sergeant Pepper's
Lonely Hearts Club Band*. The fact that it achieves its transcendent goal via a potentially disillusioning confrontation with the
'real' world is precisely what makes it so moving.[51]

MacDonald insists, persuasively, that the 'sorrow and sarcasm' are ultimately put in their place, and that the final, affirmative chord is devoid
of irony. Thus, we might infer that the meaning expressed in 'Within
You Without You' is fully realised in the transcendent moment of
sound which closes 'A Day in the Life'.

At the risk of retracting from this endorsement, it is perhaps worth
repeating, by way of balance, Poirier's insight. The Beatles' relish for
received forms of cultural expression, and for artifice itself, is what

makes *Sgt Pepper* such a rich achievement. One might say that they display their spontaneity best in the ease and assurance with which they incorporate the culture they inherit. It is as if they are paradoxically rendering the Beat vision both more aesthetic and more accessible. 'Howl' is undoubtedly a work of inspiration; but perhaps it does not quite achieve the visionary coherence of *Sgt Pepper*.

* * * * *

As we proceed to the work composed after *Sgt Pepper*, we should perhaps remind ourselves of how Mellers characterises third-period Beatles. At this stage, he says, the songs are clearly 're-entering the world of dream'. He adds: 'This preoccupation with the life "within you" is no longer child-like and innocent, for it absorbs the experience of the Beatles' middle years.'[52] In seeking to illustrate this phase, he settles on two complementary songs included in the film for television which they made in late 1967, *Magical Mystery Tour*: 'The Fool on the Hill' and 'I Am the Walrus', the former by Paul McCartney, the latter by John Lennon.

Predictably, perhaps, Mellers immediately invokes Blake: 'The Fool is an astonishing invention, who justifies the implicit parallel with Blake's holy innocent.'[53] From Blake to the Beats is not such a large step; and I would suggest, encouraged by Mellers' comment, that the song depicts a man who has attained the beatific vision, implicit in the 'foolish grin' which those who are ignorant of the sacred dimension of profane life find contemptible. As a 'man of a thousand voices' who has his 'head in a cloud', he assumes archetypal significance: he has gone beyond ego to attain identity with the divine. Hence he is able to embrace the world and all its woes with equanimity: he 'sees the sun going down' and 'the world spinning round', but 'he never gives an answer' because he knows the inadequacy of words in the face of the ineffable, sacred Word. His silence honours the Word; the chatter of the worldly crowds who despise him makes them the real fools, as the final stanza indicates (p. 150).

But it is never sufficient to honour holiness without taking into account the shadowy side of humanity. To celebrate 'the Fool' as 'holy innocent' does not do justice to the spiritual complexity of our experience, no matter how ethereal our understanding. Lennon's 'I Am the Walrus' redresses the balance. True, it confirms the other song's insight that our everyday egoic existence is meaningless, emphasising the interchangeability of social identities: 'I am he as you are he and you are me and we are all together ...' But the sneering tone renders this insight disquieting rather than reassuring. More generally, we may say that it speaks from the contrary position. Whereas the Fool has ascended the hill, has climbed the mount of spiritual wisdom, and remains aloof from the world, the Walrus dwells in the waters below, sneering at the absurdities of profane experience. We have already commented briefly on the song's verbal technique: specifically, English-style surrealism ('Elementary penguin singing Hare Krishna ...'); more generally, 'Spontaneous Bop Prosody' ('pornographic priestess boy you been a naughty girl you let your knickers down ...'). It is much more obviously a Beat work of art, in the standard usage of 'Beat', than is 'The Fool on the Hill'. But both songs make sense mainly in relation to the beatific vision: the one positively, the other negatively. Mellers' commentary would substantiate this view. Taking his cue from the refrain of 'I'm crying' in 'Walrus', he remarks: '[T]he naughty things that bubble up from the depths and make us "cry" in a false related melisma are inseparable from the Fool's foolish positives; and the Walrus's sub- or unconscious also promotes fertility ("I am the eggman") in upward rising sequences, and seems to be part of the fool-child's mythical English world.'[54] Returning to his dominant theme of the Beatles' spiritual sense being inseparable from their nostalgia for paradise, Mellers concludes:

> The two songs together incarnate – give aural flesh to – a
> psychological truth. Rebirth means regression, which cannot be
> partial; to relax our minds and 'float downstream' is to accept
> whatever flotsam and jetsam the subconscious throws up.
> Newness entails wholeness, and etymologically to be whole is
> to be hale, which is to be holy: so the Fool couldn't be holy
> without the Walrus's obscenities.[55]

What Mellers does not reflect upon is that this is probably the last occasion on which Lennon and McCartney worked in a complementary manner. *Magical Mystery Tour* not only heralds the Beatles' third period, but it also brings to a close the idea of a unified vision. From now on, the three main songwriters of the group will pursue their differing routes to revelation. That said, those routes only have bearings given the idea of a shared commitment to revelation.

We get a sharp sense of differing emphases of attention on their final album *Let It Be* (1970). It is the title track which is the key. 'Let It Be' (1969) is one of the last songs recorded by the group, during the course of its disintegration and open hostility amongst the members. In it McCartney evokes his Roman Catholic past and his memory of the comfort offered to his childhood self by his mother, whose name was indeed Mary, in the opening line: 'When I find myself in times of trouble / Mother Mary comes to me / Speaking words of wisdom, let it be.' The specific woman, McCartney's mother, is implicitly identified with the figure revered as Holy Mary, the Mother of God, by Catholics the world over. Thus, not only does the song meet the troublesome present with the assurances of the past, but it also fuses the mundane dimension of a Liverpool council house childhood with the sacred dimension of the Christian cosmos. Moreover, the refrain, 'let it be', distils the wisdom of the East into three simple words: one should let trouble be, because it is transient and illusory; one should allow the 'it' of absolute reality to manifest itself without the intervention of the 'I'; one should wait patiently for things to take their course, aware of the limited nature of one's partial perception of events. That is not a bad achievement for a song which Lennon dismissed as sanctimonious nonsense. Nor should we overlook the sheer power of exhortation in the lyrics, endorsed by the swelling music: when the 'broken hearted people ... agree' / There will be an answer, let it be' (p. 215). The effect is very close to gospel music, so strong is its affirmation of faith. Indeed, it might not be going too far to categorise the song as a contemporary hymn, so effective is its sound and so memorable are its words. Perhaps Lennon's vitriolic response, indicated most clearly by his prefacing the track on the *Let It Be* album with an imitation of a small boy announcing in a nervous, high-pitched voice, 'Now we'd like to do Hark the Angels Come', was a begrudging compliment to its stature.[56]

But what are we to infer about Lennon himself from his sarcasm in the face of McCartney's reaffirmation of the beatific vision? Was it simply a case of 'the Walrus' playing his role as counterpoint to 'the Fool'? Or was it more significant, suggesting his disillusionment with the spiritual pretensions of 'second-period' Beatles songs, including his own? Lennon was certainly becoming impatient with his role as a Beatle at this time. But it is it is hard to believe that he would repudi- ate outstanding achievements of his own, such as 'Strawberry Fields Forever'. Though it bore witness specifically to his exploration of Eastern wisdom in the mid-sixties, it successfully survived that moment as a challenge to its listeners to wake up to the illusory nature of their habitual and conventional perception of the world. If this were to happen, the song suggested, they would apprehend the 'void' beyond, behind and beneath our everyday lives. The Lennon of 'third-period' Beatles does not seem to have repudiated that perspective: witness the poetic mysticism of 'Across the Universe' (recorded 1968), from the very same album as included McCartney's 'Let It Be'. When Lennon sings 'Nothing's going to change my world', however, he was perhaps providing the epitaph to the kind of 'laid-back' spirituality with which the Beatles had become associated. It is, of course, possible to interpret that line, not as expressing a kind of self-satisfied serenity, but as implying that waking up to the nothingness underlying what we call reality will indeed change one's worldview. This equation of the sacred with emptiness or nothingness is reminiscent of Buddhist thinking – which in turn reminds us of Lennon's Beat credentials. But what is also happening in this moment of the Beatles' disbandment is that he begins to take his scepticism about the normal perception of the world as far as it can go, and in a manner that avoids any hint of quietism.

Less than six months after he had reluctantly played on the title track of what was to be the Beatles' final album, he was recording 'Come Together', the song which introduced the penultimate album, *Abbey Road*. (The confusion between recording times and release times is clarified by Ian MacDonald in *Revolution in the Head*.) Its refrain, 'One thing I can tell you is you've got to be free', may suggest a late flowering of beatnik-style bohemianism, as characterised and castigated by Alan Watts, but the sentiment is miles away from the position held by a deeply disillusioned Kerouac in the final years of his life – 1969, the year of 'Come Together', being also the year of Kerouac's death. It is the refrain of all the pseudo-Dharma Bums who claimed him as their spiritual mentor, but whom he despised.

Gary Lachman situates the song in the context of the growing unravelling of the hippie promise, as the imperative of 'doing one's own thing' became more and more sinister:

> [Lennon] had agreed to pen a tune for Timothy Leary's ludicrous California gubernatorial campaign. The song's title, 'Come Together', is a grab bag of double entendre; among other things it is the name of one of the hexagrams of the *I Ching*. But the idea of a peaceful gathering of people symbolized by the hexagram was belied by the changing atmosphere of the counterculture. Not too long after, Leary himself would be telling his followers that to kill a short-haired, robot cop was a sacred act. A late entry in Lennon's war against reason, epitomized in the Lewis Carroll-like 'I Am The Walrus',

'Come Together's' 'Toe jam football', 'spinal cracker', and other
jabberwockery [create] a weird sense of unspecified menace, the
shadows closing around the Age of Aquarius.[57]

One might supplement this insight by inferring that, in this song,
Lennon wants to reaffirm what he now understands to be the Beat
vision, but without any specifically religious connotations. If Zen is
present here, it is only in the resemblance between the central figure –
'old flat top', who 'Got to be a joker he just do what he please' – and
the Zen lunatics of old. But this is a cultural parallel, rather flippantly
made, with no spiritual dimension. Lachman sees this disillusionment
with that dimension, which grew in the final year of the Beatles' career
– the final year of the 1960s, after all – fully realised in Lennon's first
solo album, *Plastic Ono Band* (1970):

> Lennon's interest in spirituality bottomed out. An intellectual
> impulse buyer, by the time of his first solo album in 1970, he
> had finished with mysticism altogether, his interests taken up
> with trendy radical politics and a growing heroin habit. In [the
> song] 'God', his consciousness flushed out to a bare minimum
> by his latest obsession, Arthur Janov's Primal Scream Therapy,
> Lennon renounced the whole pantheon of mystic sixties
> ideology. Lennon didn't believe in magic, *I Ching*, tarot,
> Buddha, Jesus – even the Beatles didn't survive his austere
> renunciation.[58]

However, it was not possible consistently to repudiate such a rich
legacy, and Lachman notes a certain ambivalence even in Lennon's
hard-line philosophical materialism:

> By the end of the sixties Krishna Consciousness was just
> another scam and in 'I Found Out' Lennon turned his back on
> his old guru. But Lennon himself seemed unable to drop the
> Eastern trip entirely. One of his first solo hits after the break-up
> of the Beatles was a tune called 'Instant Karma', whose chorus
> has echoes of Aleister Crowley's suggestive one-liner, 'Every
> man and every woman is a star.'[59]

Perhaps more significant than the passing debt to Crowley, a pseudo-
mystic who dabbled in the occult and perpetrated a dubious doctrine
of spiritual anarchism, is the invocation of a Hindu-Buddhist principle.

'Karma' is the law by which all actions – or, indeed, intentions – have spiritual consequences. In this respect, the key line in that song is: 'Better recognise your brother – everyone you meet.' It is as if for Lennon the law survives the religious discourse in which it was originally formulated. This is in keeping with his move to a vague, irreligious sense of oneness, evident in songs such as 'Give Peace a Chance'. It is echoed too on the title song of his solo work, *Imagine* (1971), in which we are invited to imagine that there is 'no need for greed or hunger' because there are 'no possessions', 'no countries' and 'no religion'.[60]

But between the songs 'Give Peace a Chance' and 'Imagine' lies the trauma of the 'primal scream' album, *Plastic Ono Band* (1970). The song 'God' is almost wholly negative, with its opening insistence that 'God is a concept by which we measure our pain', and its subsequent catalogue of non-belief, alluded to above by Lachman: 'I don't believe in magic ... Bible ... Jesus ... Buddha ... mantra ... Gita', all the way to 'Zimmerman' (Dylan) and, finally, 'Beatles'. However, there is a sense of relief in the return to reality and authentic existence: 'The dream is over ... / I was the Walrus / But now I'm John.'[61] Why seeing through mystification should also mean seeing through mysticism – and with it, the whole wealth of spiritual wisdom which both the Beats and the Beatles uncovered – is not made clear. But Lennon's instinct is perhaps legitimate insofar as the beatific vision of Kerouac, Ginsberg and Snyder was at that time being trivialised and debased by the 'plastic hippies' who had learnt how to intersperse their stoned ramblings with Hindu and Buddhist terminology.

Lennon's reaction against the hedonistic excesses of the counter-culture – including his own drug addiction – could even be seen as a reaffirmation of the original Beat impulse. Certainly, he was in agreement with Kerouac that the attempt to widen out the Beat rebellion into a mass movement was not universally liberating. As he reflected in an interview given the following year:

> At the time [of the Beatles' success] it was thought that the workers had broken through, but ... it's the same people who have power; the class system didn't change one little bit. Of course there are a lot of people walking round with long hair now and some trendy middle-class kids in pretty clothes. But nothing changed except that we all dressed up a bit, leaving the same bastards running everything.[62]

Were he alive, Jack Kerouac, a working-class Catholic from Lowell, Massachusetts who came to despise and disown the hippies, 'Yippies' and other factions, would surely have concurred.

Moreover, there is much in *Plastic Ono Band* that places the post-Beatles Lennon firmly within the Beat tradition. One song in particular, perhaps, might have gained Kerouac's approval, dedicated as he was to 'blues truth': this is 'Isolation'. Disillusioned with the camaraderie of the 'love generation' and with the idea of the Beatles as an harmonious group (even in the literal sense), Lennon states the case as clearly as he can. Reflecting on the popular view of himself and Yoko, he replies: 'People say we've got it made / Don't they know we're so afraid?' Pushing this sense of human vulnerability further, and admonishing his listeners for their complicity in a civilisation based on callous indifference to one's fellow-men, he seeks out a reason for the amount of pain people cause one another: each of us is 'just a human, a victim of the insane'. Nor is Lennon content to broaden the issue out to include the socio-psychological dimension. As in his former incarnation as Beatle, he has to extend the song's scope to cosmic proportions, devoting the final verse to an acknowledgement that we do well to be 'afraid of the sun', given that the world will in time be consumed by it.[63] In doing so, in taking the fear as far as it can go, the song achieves a paradoxical serenity. Mellers offers a striking insight here, which would substantiate my suggestion of the 'blues truth' embodied in the song:

> The final stanza ... sees our fear against the world's impermanence and the sun's eternity, re-establishing the music's blue gravity which, whatever the words say, withstands terror. In this powerful song Lennon has done something which the Beatles in their togetherness couldn't have done. He has created an English 1970 equivalent for the Negro blues, which is an urban folk art of the solitary heart. In this his achievement as an Englishman is collateral with Dylan's as a white American.[64]

In reminding us so forcefully of our alienation and of our need for connection, the song complements the spiritual affirmation of earlier work. Again, if Zen is about seeing what is there, without preconception and without false ideals, 'Isolation' is a truly Zen work of art. Its very simplicity and directness owes much to that aesthetic tradition – as does the beautifully simple poise of another song from the same album, 'Love' ('Love is real, real is love ... / Love is living, living love').[65]

Lennon's distinctive post-Beatles statement is not paralleled by anything McCartney produced. The latter crafted some engaging music in his immediate post-Beatles days ('Another Day', 'Maybe I'm Amazed', and so forth): but he was demonstrating his flair within the medium of popular song rather than trying to convey a message. Predictably, Lennon was scathing about his former songwriting partner's achievement. In 'How Do You Sleep?' on the album, *Imagine* (1971), he sneers: 'The sound you make is muzac to my ears / You must have learnt something after all these years.'[66]

Lennon's admiration for George Harrison, however, seemed to increase in proportion to his denigration of McCartney. This may seem curious, given the direction the youngest member of the band was now taking. While Lennon could be seen to be perpetuating the Beat Zen spirit in seeking to do away with all illusions and promoting a stance of stark clarity, Harrison was embracing traditional theism, in the form of dedication to the Hindu god, Krishna. We clarified the issue of theism in our Introduction. Here we might remind ourselves: insofar as Hinduism adheres to terms such as 'Godhead' (Brahman) and 'god' (Brahma), it is theistic; Buddhism is by contrast non-theistic since, though it posits an absolute reality (Buddha-nature, or Buddha-mind), it does not speak of this as 'Godhead'.

Now, if Harrison embraced theism, what are we to make of Lennon's position on *Plastic Ono Band*? As we have said, the urge to be free of illusions – including that of conventional religion – may be reminiscent of Zen. Hence the position would be one of non-theism. But when Lennon declares that 'God is a concept by which we measure our pain', or when he tells members of the working class that the bourgeois state keeps them 'doped with religion and sex and TV', he comes close to a purely secular atheism, of the sort we associate with Marxism.[67] This makes it all the more remarkable that Lennon should have resumed his friendship with Harrison in the year that saw the release of the former's *Plastic Ono Band* and the latter's *All Things Must Pass*.

All Things Must Pass consists mainly of what we might call love songs to God. It is a devotional, mystical work – the seeming antithesis of Lennon's album. Yet perhaps they have more in common than is at first obvious – apart from the fact that they were both produced by the eccentric Phil Spector. For each album is a reaction against the spirit of the age – a spirit which both songwriters had done much to encourage previously. To put the matter bluntly, if Lennon reacted against the hippie philosophy itself by adopting a radical, materialist politics, Harrison sought to redeem the hippie philosophy by purging it of its more decadent, self-indulgent tendencies and reaffirming the authentic religious tradition which lay behind it. Each album is telling its listeners that they have lost their way. One album says: wake up to material reality, which is the only reality there is. The other album says: surrender to the absolute reality of the Godhead.

Harrison's spiritual journey began early, with his discovery of Indian culture and in particular the music of Ravi Shankar, whom he met in the mid-1960s. In his autobiography, Shankar recalled his meeting with him: 'His quest was beautiful, although at the time it was more like a child's; he wasn't fully matured back then. Nevertheless, his interest in and curiosity for our traditions, mostly in the fields of religion, philosophy and music, was quite genuine.'[68] Shankar came to admire the Beatles' music through his friendship with Harrison, whom he coached on the sitar. As the above quotation indicates, he approved wholeheartedly of Harrison's turn to the East, because he felt it was sincere. But he disapproved of the wider youth culture for which they had become iconic, as he felt that it – unlike their music itself – was degenerate:

> With many groups, such as The Beatles, I never had any
> disturbing feelings about rock music, but gradually what I was
> to hear later was different. The loud and pounding sound of
> hard rock [and] acid rock ... with the ear-splitting amplification
> of shrieking voices and the metallic reel sound, created a feeling
> of violence. The kids would get into a violent sexual frenzy,
> with musicians and listeners both high on drugs. I expected that
> 'this too shall pass', since everything seems to come and go in
> pop music (as in life), but I am appalled that this has not been
> the case.[69]

The cavalier attitude to Eastern wisdom was also a source of concern for Shankar. Again, though, we must realise that he is clearly excluding Harrison from the following stricture:

> Then there was the shallowness of the hotch-potch of ideas.
> I felt offended and shocked to see India being regarded so
> superficially and its great culture being exploited. Yoga,
> tantra, mantra, kundalini, ganja, hashish, Kama Sutra – they
> all became part of a cocktail that everyone seemed to be
> lapping up! This was bugging me, especially upon the opening
> of my school. Of all the hundreds of kids who were enrolling at

Kinnara in LA, I found only one or two of them genuinely
interested in the music and working hard at it. Most of them
were doing it simply because it was the fad or the vogue.[70]

It was against this world that Harrison was reacting during the break-
up of the Beatles – the period in which he composed most of the material on *All Things Must Pass*.

The most famous track on the album, and Shankar's favourite, is
'My Sweet Lord'. If one is any doubt about Harrison's embrace of
theism, one should listen to that. It is a song to God – a hymn – and it
is brimming with devotion. It is the melody which carries the conviction, rather than any particular part of the lyric. Harrison's desperate
plea – 'Really want to see you, lord / But it takes so long, my lord' – is
sustained by an insistent rhythm that builds to a feeling of ecstatic
surrender. Boldly, Harrison chooses to convey this mood by chanting
first 'Hallelujah' and then 'Hare Krishna'.[71] Far from evincing shallow
eclecticism, this affirmation of the affinity between the Christian and
Hindu paths is in keeping with the conviction of a 'perennial philosophy', a mystical wisdom underlying apparently divergent doctrines. To
equate Jesus and Krishna is to confirm the validity of cross-cultural
theism. Harrison is committed to Hinduism, but is simultaneously
honouring the Christian path. He may do this, because the essence of
Hindu mysticism is that the Godhead is universal, with each specific
god offering a focus for devotion. Thus, all avatars are to be revered:
Jesus as well as Krishna.

This rich, ecstatic theism is just as valid a reaction as Lennon's
austere atheism against what Shankar called 'the hotch-potch of ideas'
or 'cocktail' of passing interests which characterised the scene of the
late sixties. Harrison seems to indicate his awareness of the dangers of
faddish superficiality and hedonistic opportunism in his song, 'Beware
of Darkness': 'Take care, beware of soft shoe shufflers / Dancing down
the sidewalks, / As each unconscious sufferer / Wanders aimlessly, /
Beware of MAYA ...'[72] Against this, in the title song of the album
Harrison commends the wisdom of the ancients, with its stress on the
transience and insubstantiality of temporal existence: 'All things must
pass / None of life's strings can last.'[73] Harrison has made a bold
attempt to validate the beatific vision – not in repudiation of the hippie
'love generation' but in a spirit of friendly encouragement. Mysticism
should not be sought as a momentary, sensational experience, but as
part of a spiritual quest; and spirituality is best nourished by keeping
in touch with its religious roots. In this respect, Harrison's work

parallels that of his friend Bob Dylan, with its Judaeo-Christian emphasis. Nor should we conclude without acknowledging that Lennon himself regained his Zen poise after the hiatus of primal therapy. 'Imagine' suggests such a poise, even while it seems to espouse a secular atheism. If it tells us to imagine that there is 'no heaven' and 'only sky' above us, and if it advises 'living for today', it thereby echoes the wisdom of Zen, which is all about embracing reality without being distracted by metaphysical speculations. Zen is the religion of no religion. As Alan Watts has it: 'This is IT.' Thus, Lennon's way may not be Harrison's, but they each offer a valid perspective on the nature of beatitude, the focus of the Beat vision. Their respective struggles only make those perspectives the more intriguing. As for Ginsberg: the fact that he remained at ease with both Lennon's atheism and Harrison's theism may be taken by his detractors as confirmation of his shallow eclecticism or by his admirers as testimony to his artistic magnanimity. Either way, he is undeniably the Beat writer who not only recognised what the Beatles were about but also welcomed the friendly challenge of their music and their vision. Like them, he was interested in what follows from discovering that life is 'within you', being realised fully by cleansing the 'doors of perception', whilst simultaneously realising that the 'I' of habitual perception is illusory. Hence spiritual liberation consists in getting beyond the ego, and identifying with the whole of which one is only a very small part: life, in that sense, is 'without you'. It is not necessary to decide here whether it is Ginsberg or the Beatles who articulate this paradox the more persuasively. It is sufficient to recognise that they are speaking the same language, and to appreciate why the poet should respond so enthusiastically to their 'mantra rock'.

Notes

1 See Laurence Coupe, 'Tell Me Lies about Vietnam: English Poetry and the American War', in Alf Louvre and Jeffrey Walsh (eds), *Tell Me Lies About Vietnam* (Milton Keynes: Open University Press, 1988), pp. 167–80. For the record, the author now considers that he was far too dismissive of the British underground poetry scene.
2 Jeff Nuttall, *Bomb Culture* (London: MacGibbon & Kee, 1968), p. 239.
3 Barry Miles, *In the Sixties* (London: Pimlico, 2003), pp. 55–6.
4 Miles, *In the Sixties*, p. 56.
5 Adrian Mitchell, 'Beatles', in Elizabeth Thomson and David Gutnam (eds), *The Lennon Companion* (London: Sidgwick & Jackson, 1987), pp. 151–2.
6 Allen Ginsberg, 'Wichita Vortex Sutra', in *Selected Poems 1947–1995* (London and New York: Penguin, 1997), pp. 169, 171.

7 William Blake, 'Annotations to the Works of Sir Joshua Reynolds', in David V. Erdman and Harold Bloom (eds), *The Complete Poetry and Prose of William Blake* (New York: Doubleday, 1988), p. 641.

8 Blake, 'Chapter 3', Jerusalem, in *The Complete Poetry and Prose of William Blake*, p. 205.

9 Ginsberg, 'Sunflower Sutra', *Selected Poems*, p. 60.

10 Ginsberg, 'The Lion for Real', *Selected Poems*, p. 75.

11 Ginsberg, 'Gospel Noble Truths', *Selected Poems*, p. 289.

12 Allen Ginsberg, 'Poetics: Mind Is Shapely, Art Is Shapely', in *Deliberate Prose: Selected Essays 1952–1995* (New York: HarperCollins, 2000), p. 254.

13 Ginsberg, 'The Dharma Bums Review', in *Deliberate Prose*, p. 346.

14 Ginsberg, 'Some Metamorphoses of Personal Prosody', in *Deliberate Prose*, p. 258.

15 Ginsberg, 'Some Metamorphoses of Personal Prosody', p. 259.

16 Ginsberg, 'Beatles Essay', in *Deliberate Prose*, p. 456.

17 Ginsberg, 'A Definition of the Beat Generation', in *Deliberate Prose*, pp. 236–8, 239.

18 Ginsberg, 'Lennon/Ono and Poetic Tradition', in *Deliberate Prose*, p. 455.

19 Ginsberg, 'The Ballad of the Skeletons', in *Selected Poems*, pp. 402, 403.

20 See *No More to Say & Nothing to Weep For': An Elegy for Allen Ginsberg* directed by Colin Still, Channel 4 Television, 1998.

21 *Tonight*, BBC television, 18 June 1965.

22 John Lennon, 'Being a Short Diversion on the Dubious Origins of Beatles', in *Mersey Beat*, 6 July 1961, p. 1.

23 See Bill Harry, *The John Lennon Encyclopedia* (London: Virgin, 2000), pp. 179–81.

24 See Barry Miles, *Allen Ginsberg: A Biography* (London: Virgin, 2002), p. 469.

25 Harry, *Lennon Encyclopedia*, p. 456.

26 Harry, *Lennon Encyclopedia*, p. 874.

27 See Ray Coleman, *John Lennon* (London: Warner Books, 1992), p. 93.

28 See Steve Turner, *A Hard Day's Write: The Stories Behind Every Beatles Song* (London: Seven Oaks, 2005), p. 101.

29 Coleman, *John Lennon*, p. 130.

30 The Beatles, *The Beatles Illustrated Lyrics*, ed. Alan Aldridge (London: Macmillan, 1990), p. 148. Further references to this edition are given after quotations in the text.

31 Ian MacDonald, *Revolution in the Head: The Beatles' Records and the Sixties* (London: Pimlico, 1995), pp. 9–10.

32 MacDonald, *Revolution in the Head*, p. 27.

33 MacDonald, *Revolution in the Head*, p. 34.

34 Wilfrid Mellers, *Twilight of the Gods: The Beatles in Retrospect* (London: Faber & Faber, 1973), p. 42.

35 Mellers, *Twilight of the Gods*, p. 42.

36 Mellers, *Twilight of the Gods*, p. 42.

37 Mellers, *Twilight of the Gods*, p. 43.

38 Blake, *The Marriage of Heaven and Hell*, in *Complete Poetry and Prose*, p. 34.
39 Mellers, *Twilight of the Gods*, p. 101.
40 Miles, *In the Sixties*, p. 113.
41 Mellers, *Twilight of the Gods*, p. 82.
42 MacDonald, *Revolution in the Head*, pp. 172, 173.
43 John Tytell, *Naked Angels: Kerouac, Ginsberg, Burroughs* (New York: Grove Press, 1976), pp. 16–17.
44 Richard Poirier, 'Learning from the Beatles', in Jonathan Eisen (ed.), *The Age of Rock: Sounds of the American Cultural Revolution* (New York: Random House, 1969), pp. 172–3.
45 Poirier, 'Learning from the Beatles', p. 173.
46 Poirier, 'Learning from the Beatles', p. 177.
47 Poirier, 'Learning from the Beatles', pp. 177–8.
48 Poirier, 'Learning from the Beatles', p. 178.
49 Poirier, 'Learning from the Beatles', p. 178.
50 MacDonald, *Revolution in the Head*, pp. 193–4.
51 MacDonald, *Revolution in the Head*, p. 182.
52 Mellers, *Twilight of the Gods*, p. 101.
53 Mellers, *Twilight of the Gods*, p. 108.
54 Mellers, *Twilight of the Gods*, p. 111.
55 Mellers, *Twilight of the Gods*, p. 111.
56 See MacDonald, *Revolution in the Head*, p. 270.
57 Gary Valentine Lachman, *Turn Off Your Mind: The Mystic Sixties and the Dark Side of the Age of Aquarius* (London: Sidgwick & Jackson, 2001), p. 293.
58 Lachman, *Turn Off Your Mind*, p. 293.
59 Lachman, *Turn Off Your Mind*, pp. 293–4.
60 John Lennon, 'Imagine', www.lennon.net/music/imagine [accessed 1 December 2005].
61 John Lennon, 'God', www.lennon.net/music/onoband [accessed 1 December 2005].
62 John Lennon, *John Lennon In His Own Words*, ed. Barry Miles (London: Omnibus Press, 1980), p. 94.
63 John Lennon, 'Isolation', www.lennon.net/music/onoband [accessed 1 December 2005].
64 Mellers, *Twilight of the Gods*, p. 163.
65 John Lennon, 'Love', www.lennon.net/music/onoband [accessed 1st December 2005].
66 John Lennon, 'How Do You Sleep?', www.lennon.net/music/imagine [accessed 1 December 2005].
67 John Lennon, 'Working Class Hero', www.lennon.net/music/onoband [accessed 1 December 2005].
68 Ravi Shankar, *Raga Mala: The Autobiography of Ravi Shankar*, ed. George Harrison (New York: Welcome Rain Publishers, 1997), p. 193.
69 Shankar, *Raga Mala*, p. 200.
70 Shankar, *Raga Mala*, p. 203.

71 George Harrison, 'My Sweet Lord', www.georgeharrison.com [accessed 1 December 2005].
72 George Harrison, 'All Things Must Pass', www.georgeharrison.com [accessed 1 December 2005].
73 George Harrison, 'All Things Must Pass', www.georgeharrison.com [accessed 1 December 2005].

5 'Eco-Zen', or 'a heaven in a wild flower': from Gary Snyder to Nick Drake

In his celebrated critique of the Beats, made in the days before his canonisation by the counterculture, Alan Watts exempted one writer in particular from the charge of misappropriating Buddhism. That was the poet Gary Snyder:

> Whatever may be said of Kerouac himself and of a few other characters in the story, it would be difficult indeed to fit Snyder into any stereotype of the Bohemian underworld. He has spent a year of Zen study in Kyoto, and has recently (1959) returned for another session, perhaps for two years this time.[1]

Snyder, that is, represented Zen proper, not what Watts then saw as the affectation – or 'fuss' – of the Beat cult of Zen. Certainly, Snyder has ever since had the reputation of being a serious, committed Buddhist who has managed to infuse his poetry with religious knowledge and spiritual insight. Kerouac, as we know, became early on disillusioned with Zen, and finally moved away from Buddhism and back to Christianity. Ginsberg, having flirted with both Hinduism and Zen throughout the sixties, finally became a Tibetan Buddhist in the early seventies. But Snyder has stayed true to Zen for over half a century.

This dedication has resulted in some beautifully precise evocations of nature, very much in the spirit of Zen haiku, though not confined to that particular format. For example: 'Down valley a smoke haze / Three days heat, after five days rain / Pitch glows on the fir-cones / Across rocks and meadows / Swarms of new flies.'[2] What is particularly interesting about Snyder's dedication to Zen, however, is that it has gone hand in hand with ecological activism. More than any other Beat, he has demonstrated that spirituality may be complemented by political engagement – though not of the conventional, philosophically materialist kind. Where a Marxist, say, would want to refer all political issues to the conflict which takes place in a purely human context, Snyder has always seen the defence of nature itself as crucial to the maintenance of our human integrity and dignity.

Thus, in 'Front Lines' he speaks for the land – with which both the Native Americans and the creatures who inhabit it have existed in harmony – against the rapacious logic of 'development': 'A bulldozer grinding and slobbering / Sideslipping and belching on top of / The skinned-up bodies of still-live bushes / In the pay of a man / From town.' This outrage against the environment is seen for what it is in the context of the earth's beauty and intrinsic value: 'Behind is a forest that goes to the Arctic / And a desert that still belongs to the Piute / And here we must draw / Our line.'[3] Such a stance might accurately be described, to adopt a phrase used by Alan Watts in another context, as 'Eco-Zen'. This was the title of one of a series of lectures which Watts gave in the late sixties, entitled *The Philosophies of Asia*, in which he explained to his North American audience the necessity of breaking out of the illusion of being an isolated individual set over against a hostile nature. To find out who you are you have to wake up to your identity with the environment, with the whole. That is what Zen is all about. Ecological awareness is the same as mystical awareness: all is One. The most obvious, practical consequence of this awareness for Americans would be the realisation that 'using technology as a method of fighting the world will succeed only in destroying the world, as we are doing.' They would then stop 'turning everything into a junk heap'.[4]

As Snyder says, then: 'here we must draw / Our line.' Patrick D. Murphy, one of his most astute commentators, has read this poem as an intervention rather than simply an indictment. It is a call to action:

> In 'Front Lines' the individual working the bulldozer is not treated as the 'enemy.' Here, rather, Snyder's wrath is reserved for the man from the city, who is engineering this destruction without having any direct contact with the environment that he is having razed for financial gain. Snyder demands of himself and readers that they take a stand, here and now, against further devastation of the natural world. For Snyder, defense of the forests is both a planetary issue, in relation to the decimation of the rain forests and their potential impact on the greenhouse effect, and a local one. His area of California

borders the Tahoe National Forest, and that part of the country
has been badly damaged in the past by both hydraulic gold
mining and clear-cutting of forests. The poem, then, reflects not
only a general political stance but also a specific one speaking
to the local defense of nature in which he and his neighbors
have been engaged.[5]

Snyder's Buddhism is emphatically not a form of quietism; it is not a
rationale for passivity.

Another commentator on his work, David Landis Barnhill, has
inferred from his fusion of Zen and ecology that Snyder's concern is to
extend the implications of the vow which all Buddhists take: 'I take
refuge in the Buddha, I take refuge in the dharma, I take refuge in the
sangha.' We know the first two of those terms, but might not be familiar with the third. 'Sangha' is the collective noun for those engaged in
practising the dharma and seeking to follow the path of the Buddha,
with a view to waking up to their Buddha-nature. Snyder's whole
endeavour – as poet, as essayist, as activist – effectively interprets
'sangha' in the widest possible sense. For example, in the poem 'O
Waters' Snyder invokes 'great / earth / sangha'. As Barnhill explains:

> Traditionally, *sangha* refers to the community of monks, people
> who have devoted their lives to spiritual practice separated
> from normal society. Snyder has clearly departed from that
> notion here: the *sangha* is the ecosphere of the planet. In this
> one image is suggested two fundamental characteristics of his
> thought: a creative extension of both Buddhism and ecology by
> seeing each in terms of the other, and an overriding concern
> with community.[6]

For every Buddhist, this recognition of the interconnectedness of all
beings is a suitable subject for contemplation. For Snyder, it becomes
also a suitable inspiration for intervention on behalf of all other beings.

We have just quoted from Snyder's ecologically polemical poetry;
but we have also previously indicated, in relation to Watts, his willingness to challenge institutional Buddhism itself, where he suspects it
may collude with corrupt, environmentally irresponsible regimes. We
referred in particular to his poem 'Mother Earth: Her Whales' and to
his essay, 'Buddhism and the Possibilities of a Planetary Culture'.
Perhaps here it might be appropriate to state explicitly that, in advo-
cating a 'planetary culture' – one in which humanity would know and

love its place in the great web of interbeing – against the assaults of an irresponsible, destructive, soulless 'civilisation', Snyder represents the 'counterculture' at its most principled and uncompromising.[7]

Snyder's dedication to the cause of ecology goes hand in hand not only with his Buddhism but also with his absorption in the legacy of mythology. An early volume of poetry is entitled *Myths and Texts* (1960). According to Murphy, Snyder's dual premiss is that espoused in his undergraduate thesis, written nearly ten years earlier: that myth is a 'reality lived' and that reality is 'a myth lived'. As Murphy explains: 'Myth, then, places people in a cultural and physical matrix, providing them with a coherent sense of presence in place and time.'[8] For Snyder, the mythopoeic poet – constantly revitalising that body of stories which tell us where we are and who we are – has a crucial function: 'The poet would not only be creating private mythologies for his readers, but moving toward the formation of a new social mythology.'[9]

There is, of course, the body of Judaeo-Christian mythology to draw upon; but Snyder sees this as something to be corrected, even countered, so that the pre-Biblical mythology of the ancient world, and also the native mythology of North America, might be given its due. The epigraph to *Myths and Texts* is a passage from the Christian New Testament, which gives us an indication of the kind of high-handed attitude to pagan myth and ritual which he opposes: 'the temple of the Goddess Diana should be despised, and her magnificence should be destroyed, whom all Asia and all the world worshippeth' (Acts 19:27). Again, in the course of the sequence which opens the volume, entitled 'Logging', we are reminded of the aggressive stance taken by the Hebrews against the supposed idolatry of the fertility myths and rituals which were flourishing at the time they were seeking their own promised land: 'But ye shall destroy their altars, break their images, and cut down their groves' (Exodus 34:13).[10]

'Logging 1' might be taken as representative. Here Snyder invokes the goddess worship which was suppressed by Judaeo-Christianity: he refers to the origin of the 'May Queen' in fertility ritual, and he mentions by name Venus (the Roman version of Aphrodite, a deity associated with fertility) and Io (mother of Dionysus, a god associated both with fertility and ecstasy). Not only that: he simultaneously invokes Native American mythology: 'The year spins / Pleiades sing to their rest/ at San Francisco / dream dream ...'[11] Murphy surmises: 'the myth pertaining to the setting of the Pleiades has to do with beliefs of Native peoples who lived in what is now the San Francisco area, while the invocation to "dream / dream" places the dreamer in that city as

well. The invocation suggests the sensory realm of the collective unconscious, the locus for mythic vision.'[12]

The myths and rituals of the American Indians are frequent refer-
ents in this volume, and in Snyder's work generally. For him they make
perfect sense in the context of ecology and also in the context of
Buddhist thinking. 'Logging 12' refers to the Sioux chief, Crazy Horse,
who was a leading figure in the resistance to white settlement on American Indian land – tragically being defeated and murdered by General
Custer in 1877.[13] Quoting from the poem, Murphy reflects:

> [I]t becomes clear that the mythic vision of native and ancient
> peoples is not merely of historical interest or a dream time
> psychic salve, but an opening into an alternative culture by
> which humans, in league with 'the four-legged people, the
> creeping people, / The standing people and the flying people,'
> could live in this world at this time.[14]

If we are alert to what is being described in the lines quoted by
Murphy, we recognise that this alternative culture includes shamanism.
In Native American lore, the shaman is the tribal 'medicine man', at the
very least; at the height of his powers, he is the visionary who mediates
between the tribe and the gods. He has the capacity to enter sacred
time and sacred place on behalf of his community, ensuring that it does
not lose touch with the realm of spirit. From American Indian shamanism to Zen is not such a large step for Snyder. Each is a standing refu-
tation of the values of Western civilisation.

As we have had a good deal to say about Zen in this book, and as
we will be returning to the subject shortly, it might be appropriate to
end our account of Snyder by stressing that, of all the Beats, it is Snyder
who has most consistently realised Kerouac's intimation in *On the
Road* that 'the earth is an Indian thing'. An important strain in a
genuinely North American counterculture must be an identity with,
and defence of, the Native American way of life – intimately connected
as it has been to the environment. Snyder's interest in that way of life
has been as consistent as his adherence to Zen. The poem we quoted
earlier, 'Front Lines', comes from a volume entitled *Turtle Island*
(1974). If we absorb the full weight of this title, we can only confirm
that Snyder's interest in ecology is simultaneously an interest in
mythology. He offers the following definition in the introduction to the
volume – a statement sufficiently important for him to merit repetition
in a later volume of polemical prose:

Turtle Island – the old-new name for the continent, based on many creation myths of the people who have been living here for millennia, and reapplied by some of them to 'North America' in recent years. Also, an idea found worldwide, of the earth, of cosmos even, sustained by a great turtle or serpent-of-eternity. ... The poems speak of place, and the energy pathways that sustain life. Each living being is a swirl in the flow, a formal turbulence, a 'song'. The land, the planet itself, is also a living being – at another pace. Anglos, black people, Chicanos, and others beached up on these shores all share such views at the deepest levels of their old cultural traditions. Hark again to those roots, to see our ancient solidarity, and then to the work of being together on Turtle Island.[15]

From Zen to ecology via mythology and shamanism: Snyder's work extends the possibilities of 'Beat'. Essentially, he makes us realise how deeply the beatific vision is concerned with nature, and with the relationship between spirituality and nature. Blake had declared that one could see 'a heaven in a wild flower'; the Beats concurred with this. But, as with Blake himself, they were capable of constantly shifting emphasis: between the idea that the natural world is sacred in itself and the idea that its sacredness is only visible once human beings have cleansed the 'doors of perception'. Snyder would seem to adhere more or less constantly to the former emphasis; Kerouac and Ginsberg would seem to veer towards the latter (though neither of them are notable for consistency, it has to be admitted).

In what follows, we shall be exploring the dialectic between nature and vision, as exemplified by a small group of songwriters who are clearly indebted to the Beat movement. Given that we have previously discussed Dylan in connection with Kerouac and Ginsberg, and the Beatles in connection with Ginsberg, it might be illuminating now to situate these songwriters in the context which Snyder has provided. The intention is not to provide a taxonomy of parallel themes, but simply to take our cue from his 'green' Buddhism – or what we are calling 'Eco-Zen' – and see where it leads us. In order not to apply the term too mechanically, it will be best to keep in mind, by way of a gloss upon it, Blake's desire to see 'a heaven in a wild flower'.

*   *   *   *   *

Our first songwriter is Jim Morrison, who certainly shares Snyder's fascination with Native American culture, and who also addresses the plight of the earth. Thus, in discussing him, we will probably be staying quite close to Snyder's worldview. With others, we will necessarily stray away from it. But that is all to the good. The Beat vision is about making revealing connections.

Morrison was an icon of what became known as West Coast Rock, being the founder and singer-songwriter of the Californian band, the Doors, which flourished in the late sixties. The source of that name was, of course, Blake: 'If the doors of perception were cleansed, everything would appear to man as it is: infinite.'[16] It is likely that Morrison also had in mind a short work by Aldous Huxley, entitled *The Doors of Perception*, in which he gave an account of his experimentation with the psychedelic drug, mescalin.[17] It is Blake who is the primary source, however, as evinced by the frequent allusions to the rest of his work in the body of Morrison's lyrics. For example, certain lines from 'End of the Night' (1966) – 'Some are born to sweet delight / Some are born to endless night' – are directly quoted from Blake's 'Auguries of Innocence'.[18] Blake, as we know, was an inspiration to the Beat movement generally, offering a model of revelatory art. He, if anyone, had attained the beatific vision.

Mention should also be made of another role model, whom we have referred to in our account of Dylan. That is Arthur Rimbaud, the Symbolist poet. On 15 May 1871 Rimbaud wrote a letter to his friend Paul Demeny: 'The poet makes himself a *visionary* by a long immense and reasoned *derangement* of all the senses ... For he comes to the *unknown*!'[19] Wallace Fowlie has well documented the influence which the writer of those words had on the singer-songwriter of the Doors.[20] Morrison clearly saw himself as a visionary, and was certainly prepared to undergo a derangement of the senses in acting out the role. Moreover, he followed Rimbaud in seeking both to write and to live mythically, in defiance of convention.

Thus we may place Morrison in a visionary tradition, running from Blake through Rimbaud. Just as important in the present context is Morrison's absorption in shamanism. This seems to have begun in his childhood, when he believed himself to have been possessed by the spirit of a dead American Indian whose body the Morrison family saw by the roadside shortly after he had been killed in a motor accident.[21] The shamanic desire to pass over from profane time and space into sacred time and space is stated most dramatically in the key line from an early song: 'Break on through to the other side.'[22] Shamanism is implicit, though, in the whole endeavour of the Doors, for whom a rock concert was a 'ceremony'. Describing the impact and import of the group in 1967, Jim Morrison invoked the power of ritual. He saw America in need of rebirth: that is, redemption from the narrow, bureaucratic rationality that led to Vietnam and to global pollution. The only way to counter the warfare state of North America was to recover the wisdom of archaic ceremony:

> First you have to have the period of disorder, chaos, returning to a primeval disaster region. Out of that you purify the elements and find a new seed of life, which transforms all life and all matter and the personality until finally, hopefully, you emerge and marry all those dualisms and opposites. Then you're not talking about evil and good anymore but something unified and pure. Our music and personalities are still in a state of chaos and disorder with maybe an incipient element of purity kind of starting.[23]

Conceiving of his art as a 'purification ritual' which might take himself and his audience through disorder and chaos to 'some cleaner, freer realm', Morrison may seem in the above quotation to be identifying himself solely with the medieval alchemist. But always, the most important authority for him is the figure of the shaman – archaic in authority, but still much needed now. Speaking of that figure in the past tense, aware that their wisdom has been largely excluded from most people's worldview, he explains that the shaman achieved 'a sensuous panic, deliberately evoked through drugs, chants, dancing'. Shamans were 'professional hysterics' who 'were once esteemed'. Indeed: 'They mediated between man and spirit-world. Their mental travels formed the crux of the religious life of the tribe.'[24] Taking Morrison's point, we may add that the important thing about the shaman is that, in contrast to a conventional priest, he is not instructed in a body of doctrine; rather, he acquires his own powers. There is no fixed scheme or formula for him to hold onto: he has to trust to inspiration and vision. Only by transcending all definitions, whether of spirit or of self, can transformation take place. Orthodox beliefs and systems have to be left behind, and one must proceed by the sheer force of imagination. Only thus may temporality and totality coincide, and time be turned into eternity.

According to Suzi Gablik, we have recently witnessed a revival of interest in shamanism – and, indeed, a concerted effort to restore the power of the shaman in the modern world. Art has been the focus: she describes a process in which 'the artist as shaman' becomes 'a conductor of forces', who is able 'to bring art back in touch with its sacred sources'. That is, 'through his own personal self-transformation, he develops not only new forms of art, but new forms of living'. For Gablik, the new shaman is a 'mystical, priestly, and political figure' who has become a 'visionary and a healer'.[25] She might almost have been describing Jim Morrison.

Wallace Fowlie, reflecting on Oliver Stone's attempt in his film, *The Doors*, to do justice to the power of Morrison's persona, points out how the songwriter's shamanic role is informed by a general immersion in world mythology, particularly the ancient Greek myth of Dionysus. For it was he who represented the embrace of chaos and ecstasy, with the possibility of rebirth into a new kind of existence, beyond the conventional self:

> [Stone attempted to] demonstrate how the singer-poet, in the space of a few years, was changed into a legend. The legend which the film depicts has been accepted by a generation too young to have known Jim as the singer-performer in the concerts of the Doors. For Stone himself, Jim was a god, a Dionysian figure who in ancient Greek myth was a seducer of women and a companion of satyrs. More pagan than Christian, Jim incarnated the Indian spirit who in his function of shaman has to intoxicate himself. By dancing he was able to put himself into a trance. In the most successful concerts, the audience was riveted to the lead singer who, to many, resembled a cherub rocker, with his black ringlets of hair.[26]

Fowlie observes that Morrison seems to have seen the ritual of the typical Doors concert – or even of the recorded performance, as heard in the right frame of mind in one's home – as being intimately related to the need to ensure that mythology is acted out:

> Jim's persona had everything to do with the principle of Dionysus, the dark, self-defeating eroticism. In speaking once of his typical audience and trying to explain his movements on the stage and his singing, Jim said: 'I can take their trip for them.' Was he conscious of uttering the sacred formula of the sacrificed god, Dionysus or the Fisher King, the one whose death would restore health and fertility to the community? I believe Jim was conscious of the myth and of how it applied to his performances and to the demons that were gradually taking him over.[27]

If mythology is the focus, then particular attention should be paid to Morrison's monumental song, 'The End' (1966), which is a powerful invocation of fertility myth and ritual, about which he had learnt through his reading of the classic study of the origins of magic and religion, James Frazer's *The Golden Bough*.[28] In this light, we are struck by the way the song brings ancient symbolism alive in the present. The setting is 'a Roman wilderness of pain': that is, the contemporary United States, well into its era of decline and fall. We are told that 'all the children are insane': the hippies and other young dropouts have been driven mad by the militarism and materialism of that civilisation. The picture becomes more mythically promising when we hear that this land is 'waiting for the summer rain' and 'desperately in need of some stranger's hand'. We may infer that this refers to the need for a new god to replace the old (as in a variety of fertility myths), or for Sir Perceval to replace the ailing Fisher King (as in the Grail legend), to ensure that the life of the earth – and so the life of the human community which depends upon it – is renewed. But of course, it also re-enforces the need for America to be redeemed from its military-industrial sins. Hence, if the 'stranger' is the wandering Dionysus, bringing the threat of disorder to whichever community he visits, but ultimately granting the gifts of fertility, ecstasy and transcendence, then it will be the 'insane' children with whom he will communicate, encouraging dissent from the edicts of the powers that be.[29]

In his poem, 'An American Prayer', which Morrison would often recite at Doors concerts in the late sixties, he explicitly advocates a newly mythic awareness and challenges the logic of modern rationality, which for him inevitably culminates in war. He calls for us to 'reinvent the gods, all the myths of the ages', in order to counter the 'fat slow generals' who are 'getting obscene on young blood'.[30] Such pronouncements are themselves always made in Morrison's mythic persona. Figuring himself as reptile, he affects to have achieved the wisdom of the *ouroboros*, the symbolic snake that continually renews its own life by eating its own tail. As 'lizard king' he further affects to be provoking humanity out of its present state of torpor; but paradoxically this means he is really leading them backward, to the moment of origin, so that they may be cured of the disease of linear history – the story of 'the American night'. Like Kerouac, he looks forward to 'the apocalypse of the fellahin'. Unlike Kerouac, however, that apocalypse would have to be purged of its Christian connotations. 'Cancel my subscription to the resurrection', he declares in 'When the Music's Over' (1967).[31] A contemporary Dionysus, Morrison foretells, in a song from *Waiting for the Sun* (1968), a world 'without lament', one of endless, recurrent 'invitation and invention'.[32] A new cosmos is envisaged as proceeding from the vision of the tribal seer – both bard and shaman – who is prepared, like Dionysus, to pay the price of chaos.

The imagery of fertility and renewal, gleaned from mythology, overlaps in Morrison's vision with ecology: the burning question is, how will the planet withstand the assaults which are made upon it in the name of 'civilisation'? The Doors, we may fairly say, are the first rock group to express consistent concern over environmental destruction. In 'When the Music's Over', referring to the earth, Morrison rhetorically asks 'What have they done to our fair sister?' The answer given is that they have 'ravaged and plundered and ripped her' and that they have 'tied her with fences and dragged her down'.[33] For Morrison, his contribution to the restoration of harmony with the earth is his art, his music. As he remarked in the same year as the song just quoted:

> The more civilized we get on the surface, the more the other forces make their plea. We appeal to the same human needs as classical tragedy and early southern blues. Think of it as a seance in an environment which has become hostile to life; cold, restrictive. People feel they're dying in a bad landscape. People gather together in a seance in order to invoke, palliate, and drive away the dead. Through chanting, singing, dancing, and music, they try to cure an illness, to bring harmony back to the world.[34]

The man who made that declaration was speaking the same language as was Snyder, even if he did not explicitly espouse Zen principles.

* * * * *

Another songwriter who has clear affinities with Snyder without having a specific religious practice is Joni Mitchell. Regarded widely as the most important female singer-songwriter to emerge in the sixties, she is interesting for her attempt to maintain Beat values in the midst of the widespread dilution and/or distortion of them in the name of the 'counterculture'. As suggested earlier in this chapter, Snyder embodies the truly countercultural stance, rooted in Beat spirituality; as suggested in discussing Kerouac, Dylan and the Beatles, the expansion from Beat subculture to mass counterculture created as many problems as it solved. Mitchell knows this, so keeps herself grounded in what we might call Beat ecology. One of the most famous of her songs, 'Big Yellow Taxi' (1970) conveys her abiding concern. Mitchell laments the destruction of beautiful, natural landscapes to create arid, artificial worlds dedicated to consumer pleasures. Noting that such constructions often include a 'swinging hot spot' and the customary area for typically large American automobiles, she declares: 'They paved paradise and put up a parking lot.' In full satirical flow, she foresees a time when all the trees will have largely disappeared from nature, so that the remaining few will become curiosities with a commercial value only: deploying a typically sardonic wit, she expects them to be placed in a 'tree museum', for entry into which the people would be charged 'a dollar and a half just to see 'em'.[35] Not only does Mitchell speak up for the land, but she also confirms Kerouac's faith in the earth as 'an Indian thing'. Her songwriting generally is guided by a concern for Native American culture. A much later song, 'Chinese Café – Unchained Melody' (1982), presents the following as intimately related crimes: 'Tearing the old landmarks down / Paving over brave little parks / Ripping off Indian land again.'[36]

We will have more to say about Native American themes shortly. But for now we might pursue the idea of Mitchell as the conscience, not only of a destructive civilisation, but also of the counterculture itself. Her song 'Woodstock' (1970), for example, may sound like unqualified praise for the idea of the pop festival as the gathering of the fellaheen (in Spengler's terms), or as a promise of 'communitas' (in Turner's); but we have to read the lyrics carefully.

The songwriter presents herself as travelling to the festival in order to escape a polluting, soul-destroying system: she wants 'to lose the smog'; she feels herself to be merely a 'cog in something turning'. The song seems simply celebratory, especially when it talks of young men and women trying to get their souls free by getting back to the land. Again, it contains a wonderful image of the possibility of the love generation putting an end to war through the power of song and imagination: the bombers are seen 'turning into butterflies above our nation'. Moreover, it presents us with a powerfully mythic conjecture, that the Biblical 'Fall' of humankind might yet be reversed, through the shift in consciousness represented by the hippies: 'we've got to get ourselves back to the garden.' Nor should we overlook that this intense nostalgia for paradise is a striking instance of what Eliade refers to as the desire to translate profane time into sacred time, profane space into sacred space. Mitchell is careful, however, to make this a declaration of

hope rather than of achievement. The more naïve participants in the
Woodstock festival of 1969 may have believed themselves to have
successfully returned to 'the garden'; but Mitchell makes no such
pronouncement. Indeed, the lingering thought of the song, chanted
ominously in counterpoint to the description of the love generation as
'stardust' and as 'golden' (full of potential for realising the beatific
vision) is that it is also 'a million year old carbon' (still slowly evolv-
ing) and 'caught in the devil's bargain' (inevitably implicated in the
ways of the world from which it desires to escape).[37] For Mitchell's
biographer, Karen O'Brien, 'Woodstock' is 'an ecological protest
against smog, a political protest against Vietnam, and a general protest
against apathy'.[38]

Perhaps Mitchell's most striking critique of the counterculture
comes on her album, *Blue* (1971). We might note the first line of the
first song on the album, 'All I Want': 'I am on a lonely road and I am
travelling ...'[39] This is the language of Kerouac and the early Beats, not
of the communal, gregarious, drug-sharing world of the 'hippie trail'.
In some songs, the critique of the supposedly alternative scene is
restrained. For instance, 'California' has her travelling to Europe and
going to 'a party down a red dirt road' in Spain, where she comes
across 'lots of pretty people ... reading *Rolling Stone*, reading *Vogue*'.
This is a subtle way of suggesting how the line between the conventional civilisation (epitomised by *Vogue*) and its oppositional voices
(epitomised by *Rolling Stone*, originally an 'alternative' publication)
becomes blurred – the latter being effectively incorporated by the
former. That said, there is an admission within the same song of home-
sickness for California, the home of the hippoe ethos – even though
Mitchell herself was to leave there shortly after composing *Blue*, disillusioned with countercultural conformity, and return to California.[40]
A more thoroughgoing critique is made in the title song of the album,
in which she offers a catalogue of the means by which her generation
is seeking oblivion: 'Acid, booze, and ass / Needles, guns, and grass /
Lots of laughs, lots of laughs ...' This last line is sung slowly and
mournfully against the haunting, meditative sound of a solitary piano.
There again, the honesty of the song is self-directed also: having denied
that 'hell's the hippest way to go', she yet resolves to 'take a look
around it though'.[41] The sense of ambivalence and equivocation only
adds to the power of the critique.

The phrase that Mitchell has used herself to describe her kind of
music, in a documentary film about her life, is 'chords of inquiry'.
This captures the tentative but searching nature of her trajectory as a

songwriter. Interviewed for the same film, David Crosby (of Crosby, Stills, Nash and Young), suggests that her work can best be understood in terms of a 'metaphor of flight', a search for 'transcendence' and 'mystery'; he sees her as 'hovering above the culture', looking down.[42] This is an appropriate image for the Beat ideal of a beatific vision, from the perspective of which the existing order of things may be assessed. Certainly, if we go right back to Mitchell's earliest work, we note her first album, *Joni Mitchell* (1968) contains her 'Song to a Seagull', which has the refrain: 'My dreams with the seagull fly / Out of reach out of cry.'[43] The word 'cry' reminds us also of the Beat preoccupation, informed by an interest in Buddhism, with the problem of pain. Mitchell has never flinched from the fact of suffering. As a child in Canada she was struck by polio, and was told she might not walk again, but through sheer willpower managed to recover completely.

This ability to confront the agony of existence is evident in her song-writing. *Blue* in particular seems to have come out of a period of mental torment and spiritual crisis. In the documentary, Mitchell explains that at the time of composition she was going through what might be referred to as a 'nervous breakdown', and felt instinctively that she had to get as close as possible to the natural world. Retreating into rural obscurity in Canada, she found that the 'breakdown' turned into a 'shamanic conversion'. That is, she found the power not only to heal herself but also to heal others through her art. Though the opening line of the title song of *Blue* is 'Songs are like tattoos', her 'chords of inquiry' express far more than her own agony.[44]

Mitchell has made various other statements about that album over the years. They all seem to come back to the idea that it involved a transcendence of her personal and social circumstances. Here is a representative pronouncement: 'I guess you could say I broke down but I continued to work. In the process of breaking down there are powers that come in, clairvoyance and ... everything becomes transparent.' Hence *Blue* is 'a very pure album; it's as pure as Charlie Parker. ... He had no defences. And when you have no defences, the music becomes saintly and it can *communicate*.'[45] The invocation of Parker is signifi-cant: not only was he an icon of the Beat movement, as we know from our discussion of Kerouac, but also his example as a jazz musician specifically influenced Mitchell's development as a folk/pop musician. Indeed, her increasing use of jazz techniques – reaching a peak in her collaborative work with Charlie Mingus in 1979 – was a source of bewilderment to many of her fans. They wanted her to bare her soul; she wanted to perfect her art.

On another occasion, speaking of *Blue*, Mitchell denies that she is a 'confessional' songwriter, despite her reputation: 'It's more like dramatic recitation or theatrical soliloquy.' On that album, she is rather an 'eyewitness reporter', but even as such she realises that mere reportage is not true art: 'Then I find it won't rhyme, or it lacks a certain dramatic quality, and there's a necessity for exaggeration.' This is not deception, but rather 'creative truth'.[46] As Kerouac would say, 'If mind is shapely, art is shapely.' As with Parker's art, the skill lies in informed inventiveness, informed improvisation. Artists have to be dedicated to something greater than themselves if they are to find the 'truth' which exists in 'minute particulars', as Blake proposed.

This capacity to see through and beyond immediate circumstances is evident in Mitchell's remarkably shrewd assessments of the world around her. We have already referred to the songs on *Blue*. We might also mention her first explicitly jazz-oriented album, *The Hissing of Summer Lawns* (1975). The title refers to the sound of the sprinklers perpetually watering the grass in the gardens of affluent America. The album cover depicts tribesman carrying a huge snake in the foreground, with a typical US city standing in the background: the clue to this image seems to lie in the song entitled 'The Jungle Line' which, inspired by the paintings of Henri Rousseau, revels in the idea of the existing civilisation being under threat from 'primitive' forces. If the album were simply a satire on 'square' values, however, it would not be memorable. What makes it so is Mitchell's willingness to challenge the values of those who regard themselves as being in line with the Beat movement, while lacking its integrity of purpose. In other words, she attacks the phoney bohemianism of her contemporaries.

The key song is 'The Boho Dance', in which she queries the commonplace of the artist as outsider. Having visited a 'cellar' in 'the boho zone' and heard 'another hard-time band / With Negro affectations', she is sceptical about the pose of 'artists in noble poverty'.[47] She invokes the image used by the journalist Tom Wolfe in his book, *The Painted Word*: that of the artistic 'mating ritual' which, since the rise of modernism, has kept going through the same two phases. First there is the 'boho dance', during which the artist pretends not to compromise, claiming to be subversive. But then comes the 'consummation', the moment at which all signs of rebellion are incorporated by the art industry, and the 'boho' artist is lauded as a celebrity.[48] It is a cynical thesis, perhaps, but Mitchell draws on it with wit and not a little self-mockery. Perhaps the song shares something of the disillusionment felt by Kerouac in his final years, as he disassociated himself from those who claimed to be latterday 'Dharma Bums'.

It would not be appropriate, however, to end our brief account of Mitchell's achievement without celebrating the positive side of her vision. This is very much in keeping with the early Kerouac's insights and with Snyder's lifelong project. Here we are talking about that which is genuinely countercultural. Perhaps the most important album is *Don Juan's Reckless Daughter* (1977). Very much an experimental, jazz-inspired work, it is also remarkable as a realisation of the neo-shamanic impulse noted already in both Mitchell and Morrison. The title alludes to the books written by Carlos Castanenda in the late sixties and early seventies about his initiation into Native American myth and ritual under the guidance of the elderly Yaqui medicine man, Don Juan. This initiation involved the consumption of hallucinogenic plants, which afforded glimpses into the mysteries of the earth. From his experience, Castanenda had learnt a new respect both for American Indian wisdom and for the environment.[49]

This dual theme appealed to Mitchell, who expresses her vision in the persona of the 'reckless daughter' of the shaman. The album is an affirmation of the mythology of 'Turtle Island', represented by 'Don Juan', the shaman.[50] What is sought is an integral vision, reconciling humanity with itself and with the earth. Her biographer, Karen O'Brien, has offered a useful summary of the title song: 'using the serpent/eagle symbolism of Native America, [she] details her battle to reconcile opposites: the serpent of blind desire and the eagle of clarity, self-indulgence and self-denial, yes and no, woman and man.'[51] Given the long history of exploitation – of men by women, of the Indians by the settlers, of nature by humanity – this battle cannot be easily won. Mitchell, however, is demonstrating on this album certain possibilities of the imagination, which might yet point us in the right direction. Interestingly, Castanenda recounts that, under the influence of peyote, he felt as though he were flying like a bird: this notion must surely have appealed to Mitchell, given what we noted above about her fondness of imagery of flight.

The most ambitious part of this visionary album is a lengthy musical/poetic performance which is hard to classify. Here is O'Brien's summary of 'Paprika Plains':

The cinematic semi-autobiographical stream of consciousness work that is the sixteen-minute part-orchestral interlude, part-vocal 'Paprika Plains' picks up these themes, moving through a

rainy-night bar scene to Mitchell's first childhood memory of
refracted light through a window blind and later, in
Saskatchewan, growing up surrounded by the prairies among
the 'sky-oriented people' for whom reading the skies could
signal either crop devastation or resurrection, and of seeing the
local Indians come to town, dispossessed, with little left to do
but drink and fight and daydream.[52]

It is in describing the plight of these Indians that Mitchell shows her
imaginative empathy. Flying above them, in the role of a tourist in a
helicopter, and observing the Indians' destitution, she asks: 'How came
they to this emptiness? / How came they to this dream?' Then the
vision moves on, and she is floating above the earth itself, represented
by a child's ball which she recalls from childhood. Here she summons
up the guilty history of exploitation which she as a white North American has inherited. She succumbs to 'reckless curiosity' and slashes the
'globe', enabling her to see again the 'Paprika plains', with 'the snake
the river traces / And a little band of Indian men / With no expressions
on their faces'.[53] She may be acting as a 'reckless daughter' here, like
her mother 'Eve', but the guilt transcends sexual division. It is a
compelling moment of terrifying honesty.

In a fascinating chapter of his study of female songwriters, Wilfrid
Mellers makes a point of emphasising the importance of *Don Juan's
Reckless Daughter* and of this particular song:

> The cycle climaxes in a dream of the Plains Indians – a snaking
> turquoise river, wind-swept mesas, the empty ashes of their
> desolate land – which are also the emptiness of Joni's heart.
> This long song, 'Paprika Plains', embraces within its vision of
> aboriginal America a retrospect of Joni's small-town Canadian
> childhood. Like 'late' Dylan, she now senses Amerindian
> culture shallowly buried beneath the glossy surface of her
> American life.[54]

In this light, we see the affinity with Snyder also, whose work may be
seen as a validation of that buried culture, especially insofar as it
carries the memory of a proper, mutual relationship with the earth
and serves as a challenge to the current hierarchy. In the title song
of Mitchell's album, she invokes the 'split tongued spirit', which
reconciles serpent and eagle, 'mother earth' and 'father sky', in her
search for 'clarity'. Such clarity, such balance, is much needed, for in

'Good-Old-God-Save-America / The home of the brave and the free / We are all hopelessly oppressed cowards / Of some duality / Of restless duplicity ...'[55]

While tracing a parallel trajectory in Mitchell's work and Snyder's, we must nonetheless register, as we did with Morrison, the apparent absence of the Zen dimension. True, her biographer, Karen O'Brien uses a quotation from the Zen master, D. T. Suzuki, about the need for modern men and women to wake up and realise that they are 'artists of life', even if they cannot be musicians, painters or poets; and the quotation does prove relevant to O'Brien's account of the revelatory power of Mitchell's work.[56] But it cannot be said that there is a consistently Buddhist influence present in the major songs. The most overt reference to Zen would seem to be negative. I am thinking of 'Roses Blue', from her early album, *Clouds* (1969). This is a song about a woman who has succumbed to the fashion for exotic spirituality: she is pursuing 'mysterious devotions' such as 'zodiac and zen' [sic], and is 'laying her religion on her friends'.[57] But the song is an indictment, not of Zen, but of the superficial, modish interest in it that predominated at that time – particularly among the 'Ladies of the Canyon' (i.e., Laurel Canyon, California) whom Mitchell gently satirises in the title song of her next album. Thus, we are probably on safe ground if we infer a sympathy for all those genuinely seeking a religious practice. After all, Mitchell herself had started researching shamanism by then. Moreover, as a matter of biographical record, we may also note that she enrolled in a course at a Tibetan Buddhist centre in Colorado in 1974. However, as already stated, we are not concerned here with allocating Mitchell to a specific religious practice. Rather, we are interested in the spirit of her work; and that spirit may perhaps be summarised by reference to a song from *The Hissing of Summer Lawns* entitled 'Sweet Bird'.

The allusion would seem to be to Tennessee Williams's play, *Sweet Bird of Youth* (1959), but here the bird is one of 'time and change' – or what Buddhists call 'impermanence'. This is not to suggest that the bird is constrained by time and change: rather, it represents the wisdom that transcends them by experiencing them without attachment. One thinks of Blake: 'He who binds to himself a joy / Does the winged life destroy / But he who kisses the joy as it flies / Lives in eternity's sunrise.'[58] As such, it complements the 'seagull' of her earlier song, symbolising as it does a serenity which lies beyond conventional language. It represents a rich reserve of spiritual potential. Though human beings seem to be trapped in profane time – 'Behind our eyes /

Calendars of our lives / Circled with compromise' – there is always the possibility of 'laughing' with the 'sweet bird' and so gaining a glimpse of sacred time. In learning this lesson of laughter, one sees how to live with contingency, how to bless 'what each set of time and change is touching'.[59] Mitchell is as much concerned with the nature of the beatific vision – and with nature as the stimulus to such a vision – as are any of the other songwriters featured in this chapter.

* * * *

We have used the phrase 'Eco-Zen' to characterise Snyder; we are testing how far it might apply to certain songwriters, while simultane-ously glossing it with Blake's hope of seeing 'a heaven in a wild flower', and the tensions involved in such a prospect. Morrison and Mitchell speak in defence of nature, and of those cultures which revere it. They see nature itself as sacred. With our third songwriter, the ecological emphasis is not so insistent: rather, we may infer a broadly reverential view of nature informed by both mythology and mysticism. There again, he is notoriously difficult to categorise, and it would be advis-able not to try. I am referring to Leonard Cohen.

Superficially, his kind of art seems to form a contrast with the Beats, given his taste for formality and ironic restraint. His work, however, must be of interest to those who take seriously the ideas we have explored throughout this book. In particular, I would emphasise his ability to maintain a Zen-like perspective on the business of living and dying. It is this more than anything that links him with Snyder. That said, Cohen's approach to Zen is very much his own.

Cohen is a Canadian poet and novelist who extended his talents to songwriting in the late sixties, for which he has been mainly known ever since. When his *Poems 1956–1968* appeared, Kenneth Rexroth, the mentor of the Beat movement, wrote: 'Leonard Cohen's poetry and song constitute a big breakthrough ... This is certainly the future of poetry... It is the voice of a new civilization.'[60] Moreover, Cohen began his career reciting poetry to a jazz accompaniment in Montreal in the fifties, inspired by the example of Jack Kerouac; he subsequently moved to New York, where he made sure to attend all the Beat performances he could.[61]

Inevitably, Cohen was touched by the Beat Zen phenomenon. It was through the Beats that he became interested in gaining an Eastern perspective on the faith of his childhood, namely Judaism. That said, he was equally preoccupied with, even obsessed by, the figure of Jesus Christ. Interestingly, his approach to Christianity was in terms of myth:

his first volume of poetry was called *Let Us Compare Mythologies*, a title which gives us a flavour of his spirit of sincere but scrupulous enquiry. His preoccupation only deepened during the sixties. Towards the end of that decade Cohen declared: 'Our natural vocabulary is Judeo-Christian. That is our blood myth ... We have to rediscover the crucifixion. [It] will again be understood as a universal symbol ... It will have to be rediscovered because that's where man is at. On the cross.'[62]

One cannot accuse Cohen of having only a passing interest in this subject. Twenty years later, he reflected on his view of Jesus: 'He may be the most beautiful guy who ever walked the face of this earth. Any guy who said "Blessed are the poor. Blessed are the meek" has got to be a figure of unparalleled generosity and insight and madness.'[63] What is intriguing is that he seems to think of Jesus in terms similar to Kerouac's, identifying him implicitly with the fellaheen. Again, there is the preoccupation with pain, and the appeal to the example of Jesus as a means of comprehending it. However, the difference between Cohen's fascination with Jesus and Kerouac's is twofold. For Kerouac, it comes out of his Christian upbringing and is associated with his idea of himself as a 'crazy Catholic mystic', whereas Cohen is interested in trans-cultural iconography. For Kerouac, the figure of Jesus becomes more and more important as he himself turns away from Zen, whereas for Cohen, Jesus remains a constant referent, which he finds to be wholly compatible with his interest in Zen. For him, Zen is the perfect way of realising the potential he early on finds in Judaeo-Christianity. There is, then, an obvious affinity with Snyder, namely Zen itself; but there is also a contrast, since Snyder consistently associates Biblical faith with the oppression of indigenous communities and the exploitation of the earth.

That does not mean that Cohen is unaware of such associations. His second novel, *Beautiful Losers* (1966), an ambitious work of metafiction which moves between different times and places, centres on the historical figure of Catherine Tekakwitha (1656–80).[64] She was the daughter of a Christian Algonquin woman who had been captured by the Iroquois and then married a Mohawk chief. An epidemic of smallpox left Catherine orphaned; the disease also left her face severely scarred and badly affected her eyesight. Baptised at the age of twenty by Father Jacques de Lamberville, a Jesuit missionary, she was ostracised by her fellow-Indians. She fled, wandering 200 miles by foot to a Native American village in Canada which had adopted the Christian faith. Taking a vow of chastity, she acquired a reputation for asceticism and also for an ability to perform miracles. As she was dying, her scars miraculously vanished. After her death, her grave became a site of pilgrimage; she was regarded by many as a saint, and was subsequently beatified (thought not canonised) by the Catholic church. Cohen's choice of main character gives him, then, plenty of opportunity to explore the connection between Christian myth and Native American myth, and to investigate the way in which the values of a civilisation may be internalised – but also intensified – by a colonised people. The unnamed 'I' of the novel is, by no coincidence, an anthropologist with a special interest in North American Indians: we learn a good deal about their myths, rituals and beliefs, which are given just as much status as the Catholic doctrines which are also explicated. Interestingly, the historical Catherine is known as the (unofficial) patron saint of ecologists, of people in exile and of people persecuted for their beliefs. Cohen in his fictionalised account gives full reign to the possibilities opened up thereby.

Returning to the question of myth, we note that in *Beautiful Losers* there is a comprehensive attempt to 'compare mythologies'. Apart from the allusions to Indian and Christian myths, the novel makes an implicit identification between Catherine and the ancient Egyptian goddess of fertility, Isis, who was believed to have control over both the health of the earth and the fate of the soul in the afterlife. Isis it was who restored her husband, Osiris, after he had been dismembered, and ensured his annual revival in parallel with the cycle of vegetation. Catherine too is credited with a capacity to restore earth, body and soul to a state of harmony. A more obvious association is made between Catherine and the Virgin Mary: surrendering herself to God's will, she is granted mystical insight.

The very title of the novel is worth dwelling on. The 'beautiful losers' are those who achieve that spiritual beauty known as beatitude by surrendering the whole idea of a separate self; in the perspective of materialism, they are absurd, but under the aspect of eternity they are saintly. They voluntarily become victims or scapegoats, suffering on behalf of others so that they too may be granted spiritual release. In this sense, the most obvious 'beautiful loser' is Jesus Christ, crucified and buried as a criminal but bringing redemption by way of his resurrection. Extending the idea, we may remind ourselves that the figure who is beaten down by civilisation is for the Beat writers the one who is most likely to attain, and show the way towards, the beatific vision. We sense this in the paradoxical titles of some of Kerouac's novels, which Cohen's *Beautiful Losers* neatly mirrors: *The Dharma Bums*, for example, or *Desolation Angels*. We might think also of that key phrase from Ginsberg's poem, 'Howl': 'angelheaded hipsters'.

The paradox contained in such phrases and titles takes us to the heart of Zen itself. The Zen lunatic, the holy fool who abandons all material security to wander on 'the Way', is the model for all such figures. One must give up the idea of 'I' in order to have access to the reality of 'the One'. This idea clearly fascinates Cohen, and his fascination only gets more intense as he proceeds. The manifestation of the sacred in the profane is his primary concern, and his major songs articulate this possibility in their various ways.

Though we have stated that Cohen's devotion to Zen is an implicit constant, we should take account of his increasingly explicit association with 'official' Zen. We can trace this quite simply, from his meeting in the early 1970s with a monk called Joshu Sasaki Roshi, with whom he began studying, to his financing of the Mount Baldy Zen Centre, near Los Angeles, to his five-year residence there in the 1990s. Cohen has always denied, however, that his dedication to Zen practice has meant commitment to a new kind of faith, quite other than Judaism or Christianity: 'I never really felt I was studying something called Zen. I never thought I was looking for a new religion. The religion I had was fine. So it was something else' (1993). Again: 'There are Jewish practitioners in the Zen movement. I don't think the two are necessarily mutually exclusive, depending on your position. As I have received it from my teacher, there is no conflict because there is no prayerful worship and there is no discussion of a deity in Zen' (1994). Or again: 'I've never been interested in a new religion ... I just know that [Roshi] has provided a space for me to do the kind of dance with the Lord that I couldn't find in other places' (1994).[65]

It is probably fair to say, then, that no matter which period of Cohen's work we choose, we find evidence of his Zen instinct, if by that we mean the urge to celebrate the here and now as if it were infinity and eternity. Take the first song on his first album, *Leonard Cohen* (1968). 'Suzanne' begins as a celebration of an artistic, eccentric woman that Cohen knew and admired during his young adulthood in Montreal: she had an apartment by the St Lawrence River, near to the chapel of Our Lady of the Harbour, which is dedicated to sailors. These anecdotal circumstances make the account of visiting her and being served tea by her all the more vivid. But the central idea of the song only becomes evident in the second verse, which refers to Jesus as a 'sailor' who waited watching on his 'lonely wooden tower' (his cross, presumably) before addressing 'only drowning men' (those in acute spiritual need). Suzanne and Jesus each offers a sacred gift: a capacity for revelation. The world refuses it: as Cohen points out to Jesus, 'You sank beneath their wisdom like a stone'. But the potential for revelation remains. The third verse has Suzanne as a guide around the harbour, showing us 'where to look among the garbage and the flowers', and alerting us to the 'heroes in the seaweed'. The song, then, is a classic instance of the manifestation of the sacred in the profane: it is one of the most powerful instances of the beatific vision for which one could ask.[66]

The fact that the imagery of the song is insistently Biblical does not detract from its Zen quality. Rather, it intensifies it, Jesus being the archetypal 'beautiful loser' who obtains beatitude precisely by immersing himself in the suffering of this world and thereby sanctifying it. Again, in a later song from *Various Positions* (1984), 'If It Be Your Will', Cohen prays to the God of the Jews and the Christians. He seems to be espousing an orthodox monotheism, the basis of a doctrine of salvation for the righteous; but the imagery simultaneously celebrates the suffering sinners. He speaks for all those 'on this broken hill', dressed in 'our rags of light'; and asks that 'all these burning hearts in hell' be made 'well' at last.[67] A plea for mercy from a God of justice, the song dwells chiefly on the frailty of humanity; but paradoxically, this frailty is the very source of its spirituality. Only in the depths of the profane does the sacred need to be made manifest. The subtlety of such a vision has been preferred by more than one commentator to the more explicit, extensive ruminations of a Ginsberg. Here is one such judgement:

> [U]nlike many Jews who found refuge in Buddhism (e.g. Allen Ginsberg), [Cohen] never lost his monotheistic convictions; indeed, they appear to have become stronger over the years … Ginsberg's dependencies were more often than not drug-induced and escapist. Suffice it here to note that [Cohen] did not force monotheistic (i.e. one-god) doctrines; he did not command theistic (i.e. personal-god) beliefs; nevertheless, those with ears to hear – and many without – could not fail to catch the point, 'directly and immediately'; not out of contrivance or slick devising, but honestly – so that 'everybody knows what's going on.' It was only through that 'gateway' that he could enter, and emerge: with a meaningful word. The songs are 'mystical'; parabolic in their ability to say things at different levels: the sacred and the secular, the human and the divine; projecting the

heavenly by means of promoting the earthly; 'passionate romance' and spiritual truth: an alpha and an omega – 'understanding' now at its peak.[68]

Another commentator celebrates Cohen's ability to use Biblical language while articulating a beatific vision that transcends religious categorisation:

[M]uch of his life has been spent with his nose in the scriptures, whether they be Hebrew, Christian or Eastern, and has conducted his creativity in the form of a meditation, a search for metaphysical meaning, whatever the implications of his more earth-bound predilections. ... Cohen's recent compositions may well be, as Bob Dylan so shrewdly observed, 'like prayers', but the truth is that Cohen's songs have been painted with a Judaeo-ecclesiastical patina throughout his musical evolution. Across the panoply of his hundred songs, from 'Story of Isaac' to 'Anthem', via 'Who By Fire' and 'The Law', there are many more direct examples of his use of the nominally religious form.[69]

This same commentator is impressed by Cohen's capacity for finding the sacred in the profane: 'It is Cohen's ability to locate the redemptive and the spiritually profound within prosaic and sometimes visceral lyrical contexts that gives his work the poignant astringency in which his fans revel and at which his detractors balk.'[70]

One of the songs mentioned above is worth quoting briefly: 'Anthem', from *The Future* (1992). But first we should consider the significance of that title. The OED defines 'anthem' as follows: 'an elaborate choral composition usually based on a passage of scripture for church use'. Cohen would seem to be deliberately subverting that idea, for his song is non-scriptural and non-liturgical; it is, indeed, modest and reflective. It does not make pronouncements in justification of a religious doctrine. Rather, it looks to the minor beauties of this world for revelation: 'The birds they sang at the break of day / Start again, I heard them say.' Having then proceeded to address the horrors of the world – wars, corrupt governments, and so forth – it laments, in language derived from Christian iconography, but not confined to it, that the 'holy dove' will always be 'caught' and 'bought and sold' again. However, the refrain of the song tells us that, despite this, there remains the possibility of spiritual freedom if only we can learn to value profane time and space as if they were sacred, and not torture ourselves in the pursuit of a distant, abstract perfection: 'Ring the bells that still can ring. / Forget your perfect offering. / There is a crack in everything. / That's how the light gets in.'[71] This is pure Zen, comprehending in its simplicity all the subtleties of Judaism and Christianity. We understand now what Cohen meant in the interview quoted, when he said: 'I've never been interested in a new religion ... I just know that [Roshi] has provided a space for me to do the kind of dance with the Lord that I couldn't find in other places'.[72]

'Dance with the Lord' is a neat phrase by which to indicate Cohen's wish to honour the monotheism of his own culture, while being open to the non-theist freedom of Zen. He implies no confinement to any given religion; nor does he imply a spirituality that is entirely without roots. It is a matter of wearing one's beliefs lightly, and being able to let go of those that obscure the manifestation of the sacred. Always the reality which must be faced is that of the profane realm, in which we are born, we live and we die. There is no escape from this obligation. Indeed, according to Zen, enlightenment involves complete acceptance of reality. As Watts would remind us: 'This is IT.'

Finally, then, it is worth pointing to a more recent song whose very title echoes this same idea. 'Here It Is', from *Ten New Songs* (2001), is one of Cohen's most economical presentations of the mystical paradox that is common to Zen and to Blake alike, that 'Everything that lives is holy'. Understanding this involves being able to affirm even the most degraded and demeaning of experiences, being able to grant their validity. One's 'love for all things' necessarily must include 'your drunken fall', 'your cardboard and piss', 'your bed and your pan'. The chorus sums up the Buddhist theme of impermanence with startling clarity: 'May everyone live, / And may everyone die. / Hello, my love, / And my love, goodbye.' But every word of the song – scarcely any of them longer than two syllables – brings home with great economy the meaning of 'samsara' (the wheel of existence, the cycle of living and dying): for example, 'here is your death / in the heart of your son'. Finally, we are struck by Cohen's impulse to bring Jesus, the 'beautiful loser', into the picture. Cohen invokes him in the course of inviting us to embrace pain and mortality, and in so doing to know 'nirvana' (the extinction of ego): 'Here is your cross, / Your nails and your hill; / And here is the love / That lists where it will.'[73] The Biblical vocabulary is informed by Eastern wisdom. The beatific vision could hardly be made more simple (though not, we should add, simplistic). Cohen's instinct that Zen complements rather than contradicts Western religion is borne out by his own work. By that I mean that, right through his career, you can see a wholly consistent attempt to articulate the beatific vision in accessible and compelling language. Though Cohen is a very different writer in many ways from Snyder, they concur on essentials; and the essence is Zen. Nor should his interest in mythology and Native American lore be overlooked.

Whether one would apply the phrase 'Eco-Zen' to Cohen's work is another matter: he certainly celebrates nature in a spiritual, indeed mystical, perspective; but his is not an ostensibly 'green' Buddhism. However, his affirmation of the human potential to find meaning 'among the garbage and the flowers' is a nicely ambiguous echo of Blake's dictum. At the very least, we may say that Cohen's vision complements that of Morrison and that of Mitchell; and all three seem to make more and more sense as we explore their affinities with Snyder. Taken together, all four endorse and extend what we have understood by the term 'Beat'.

* * * * *

As the bias of this chapter has so far been towards American popular song, it might be a good idea to redress the balance by concluding with some British songwriters – three solo artists and one group. We will continue to bear 'Eco-Zen' in mind, though perhaps dwelling rather more on the broader implications of seeing 'a heaven in a wild flower'. Here our discussion will be less detailed, but it is to be hoped that a sense of the depth and breadth of the Beat influence on sixties songwriters will be conveyed.

The first two names came to prominence in what we might call the British 'psychedelic folk' scene: Donovan and the Incredible String Band. The fact that both of them are Scottish may be just a coincidence, though it is worth mentioning that the English folk scene was distinctly non-bohemian and was rather cautious when it came to absorbing literary influences.

Much derided in his early days as a pale imitation of Dylan, Donovan has in fact showed a healthily independent sense of the Beat influence consistently through his career.[74] His latest album, at the time of writing, is entitled *Beat Café* (2005), and it contains several evocations of the time when Kerouac and co were becoming cult figures. Looking back to his early career, it seems astonishing that, apart from acoustic hits such as 'Catch the Wind' (1965), anyone could have perceived him as 'the British Dylan'. I am thinking in particular of

'Sunny Goodge Street' (1965) and 'The Observation' (1967), which are jazz-based meditations on urban life in the England of the sixties, with special emphasis on the transience and sheer strangeness of existence. A brief quotation from the first of these will convey the obvious presence of the Beat sensibility: 'Smashing into neon streets in their stillness / Smearing their eyes on the crazy Kali goddess / Listenin' to sounds of Mingus mellow fantastic. / "My, my", they sigh ...'[75] However, despite his fondness for 'hip' idiom and allusion, Donovan repeatedly displays an ability to detach himself from any modish or pretentious 'scene'. 'Season of the Witch' (1967) evinces an independence of spirit, including as it does a neat jibe at the phonier elements of the counterculture: 'Beatniks are out to make it rich: / Oh no, must be the season of the witch.'[76]

Regarding himself as a true Beat rather than a phoney beatnik, Donovan espoused Buddhism from the late sixties onwards – differing in this regard from his friend, George Harrison, who had become a devotee of Hinduism.[77] Donovan's orientation towards Buddhist ideas and Zen-like imagery is evident in many of his songs. The most striking is 'There is a Mountain' (1967), the chorus of which goes as follows: 'First there is a mountain, then there is no mountain, then there is ...'[78] This is Donovan's cryptic version of the famous statement by Ching-yuan, quoted by Alan Watts in his *Way of Zen*:

> Before I had studied Zen for thirty years, I saw mountains as
> mountains, and waters as waters. When I arrived at a more
> intimate knowledge, I came to the point where I saw that
> mountains are not mountains, and waters are not waters. But
> now that I have got its very substance I am at rest. For it's just
> that I see mountains once again as mountains, and waters once
> again as waters.[79]

Both statement and song are reminding us that it is in building up preconceptions – even, or especially, about Buddhism – that we will usually miss the point of existence. 'This is IT.' They also are reminding us to respect the natural world, and not regard it as a resource to be exploited. Donovan's 'green' orientation is also evident in the significantly titled album, *A Gift from a Flower to a Garden* (1968). Having produced the heavily psychedelic sounds of 'Sunshine Superman' and 'Mellow Yellow', he here demonstrates his capacity for both lyrical and musical delicacy. Returning to his roots in traditional folk, he celebrates the natural world in some of his most intriguing and charming songs. In 'Lullaby of Spring', he uses a telling detail to convey the intricate interconnectedness of nature: 'So begins another spring, / [Of] green leaves and of berries. / Chiff-chaff eggs are painted by / Mother bird eating cherries.'[80] Again, 'Isle of Islay', a celebration of a locality in his native Scotland, is characterised by a Zen-like sense of the beauty of a moment in which discrete phenomena seem to cohere, as in a haiku: 'How blessed the forest with birdsong / How neat the cut peat laid so long / Felt like a seed on your land …'[81] However, it was not until three decades later that Donovan produced an explicitly Buddhist album: that was *Sutras* (1996), the music on which is designed to create a contemplative state in the listener, with repetitive lyrics set against a hypnotic sound. Perhaps he felt he had drawn on ideas and images sufficiently, and now was the time to produce music as a mode of meditation. Certainly, it was the most critically acclaimed of his later albums.

Turning to the Incredible String Band, we note that, as with Donovan, there is a 'green' tendency in their work, which complements their immersion in the wisdom of the East. The two main songwriting members of the band, Robin Williamson and Mike Heron, seemed to have an encyclopaedic knowledge of Hinduism, Buddhism, Taoism and Zen from the start; nor were they indifferent to Christian mysticism. The ISB, as they were often known, was Allen Ginsberg's favourite group apart from the Beatles: their distinctive musical style, drawing freely on traditions from across the world, influenced him in his approach to setting Blake's *Songs of Innocence and of Experience* to music. In turn, they were clearly influenced by Ginsberg in their lyrical experimentation. Many of their songs seem to have been inspired by the idea of 'Spontaneous Bop Prosody', so that lines wander in a wonderfully speculative manner, often without the constraint of rhyme (usually a compulsory factor in popular song) – but always rendered coherent by a rousing refrain.

'The Mad Hatter's Song' (1967), like the Beatles' 'I am the Walrus', is indebted to the 'nonsense' writing of Lewis Carroll. Here the idea of the song is to use the paradox and hyperbole of the *Alice* books in order to orientate the listener towards a moment of revelation. As with the Beats, the dominant civilisation, based on materialism, is rejected: 'Within the ruined factory is the normal soul insane.' The aim is the beatific vision, which is here figured in explicitly Zen imagery: 'Dancing without movement after the clear light … / In the rumbling and trundling rickshaw of time … / Hooked by the heart to the king fisher's line, / I will set my one eye for the shores of the blind.'[82] Profane time and space may be transformed into sacred time and space by virtue of an apprehension of natural beauty and an overcoming of false duality. In a similar vein, 'Keeoaddi There' (1968) contains this striking chorus: 'Earth water fire and air / Met together in a garden fair / Put in a basket bound with skin / If you answer this riddle / You'll never begin ...'[83] Reminiscent of Alan Watts's statement from his preface to *The Book: On the Taboo Against Knowing Who You Are*, it manages to fuse Hindu mysticism with Zen paradox, while suggesting a sense of pantheism – that is, nature as divine. For, if my inference is correct, the idea is that once each of us identifies with the One, manifest in nature, there is no need for the hallucination of the separate ego to take place.

Those two songs are by Williamson; Heron too has his revelatory moments. I would point in particular to 'Douglas Traherne Harding' (1968), which offers another perspective on the Zen and pantheistic elements just noted. What Heron does is invoke two mystics, one from the seventeenth century and one from the twentieth, with added support from the Gospels. It is a bold synthesis, but he carries it off by way of intriguing music which seems to defy Western conventions. To appreciate it, we need to clarify the allusions. Thomas Traherne is the author of *Centuries of Meditations* (1699), one of which includes the following reflection: 'You never enjoy the world aright, till the Sea itself floweth in your veins, till you are clothed with the heavens, and crowned with the stars ...' In being at one with nature, we are at one with the divine: that is, the One.[84] Douglas Harding is the author of *On Having No Head* (1961), which is an account of a Zen-like awakening which he experienced. Suddenly, where he had thought he had a 'head' – an ego, a fixed centre of perception and conception – he attained a state of selfless awareness: there was 'a vast emptiness vastly filled, a nothing that found room for everything – room for grass, trees, shadowy distant hills, and far above them snow-peaks like a row of angular clouds riding the blue sky. I had lost a head and gained a world.'[85] This in turn may remind us that Jesus famously declared: 'The light of the body is the eye: if therefore thine eye be single, thy whole body shall be full of light' (Matthew 6:22).

Impressively, Heron manages to make a coherent song out of this diverse material. It culminates in the invitation to the listener: 'But if you're walking down the street / Why don't you look down to the basement / For sitting very quietly there is a man who has no head / His eye is single and his whole body also is filled with light.' This is effectively an invitation to awaken to the sacred dimension of the profane, which may be manifest in the most unlikely places. The 'basement' detail perhaps echoes Kerouac's *The Subterraneans*. The image of headlessness specifically comes from Harding, but also confirms the Zen ideal of spontaneously losing all sense of separation. Such an awakening brings with it an awareness of the perennial philosophy, that mystical wisdom which lies buried in all the major religions ('One light ...'), as is evinced by the allusion to Jesus's words. To complete the picture, the song ends with an *a cappella* rendition of the words of Traherne quoted above.[86] This is the beatific vision, not only articulated, but placed in the perspective of the visionary tradition. Like all the other songs we have considered in this study, it might never have been written were it not for the Beat influence.

It is tempting to explore the achievement of the Incredible String Band further, and in particular to trace the solo career of Robin Williamson, whose interest in mythology and ecology seems to have originated with his early discovery of the Beats. But I hope that even this brief discussion of the 'psychedelic folk' scene will encourage readers to pay serious attention to the ISB. By way of stimulus, here is an endorsement from, of all people, the current Archbishop of Canterbury, Dr Rowan Williams:

> What is the job poetry is supposed to do? This may be a definition shaped by unfashionably archaic standards, but I think it's meant to do at least four things. It should take us into the realm of myth – that is, of the stories and symbols that lie so deep you can't work out who are the authors of them, the stories that give points of reference for plotting your way in the inner and outer world. It's meant to celebrate; to clothe ordinary experience with extraordinary words so that we see the radiance in the ordinary, whether it in landscape or in love or whatever. It's meant to satirise – to give us a sideways glance on familiar ways of talking or of behaving or exercising power, so that we're not bewitched by what looks obvious and wants us to think it's obvious. It's meant to lament, to give us ways of looking at our loss and our failures that save us from despair and apathy.

If you listen to the ISB's songs, you realise rapidly that they correspond with astonishing completeness to the requirements of poetry. Plenty of songs of that period managed the celebration or the lament, few could do the myth or the satire. Perhaps for a lot of us growing up in the late Sixties and early Seventies, there was a gap in the heart where this very traditional bardic, even shamanic, sense of poetry was looking for expression; and the ISB did just that. Forget the clichés about psychedelic and hallucinogenic vagueness: this was work of extraordinary emotional clarity and metaphorical rigour – an unusual combination. ...

For those of us who fell in love with the ISB, there was a feeling of breathing the air of a very expansive imagination indeed. ... If I go back to the start, I'd have to say again that it was simply discovery of poetry; and as such – risking the embarrassment that so regularly goes with my particular vocation – I'd also have to say that it was a discover of the holy; not the solemn, not the saintly, but the holy, which makes you silent and sometimes makes you laugh and which above all makes the landscape different once and for all.[87]

Though he does not mention him, Blake is a likely source for this ability to affirm the holiness of everything that lives. Certainly, Blake is referred to more than once in the celebratory volume of essays on the ISB to which Williams contributes the foreword, quoted here.

* * * * *

There are two other British songwriters of the same period who cannot, in all fairness, be excluded from an account of the beatific vision in popular song: Van Morrison and Nick Drake. They seem an unlikely pairing at first. On the one hand there is Morrison, the working-class Ulsterman who has played the role of the Irish bard, successfully developing over four decades his 'Caledonian soul' designed to induce a mystical rapture, particularly in public performances. On the other hand there is Drake, the painfully shy Englishman, educated at Marlborough and Cambridge, who could not bear to perform his technically brilliant songs in front of an audience – eventually committing suicide while in his mid-twenties, having failed to have any impact at all on the 'pop' scene. However, as we shall see, the beatific, Blakean connection is undoubtedly there.

Van Morrison's *Astral Weeks* (1968) is interesting musically because of its Beat-inspired acoustic jazz sound and its seeming reliance on improvisation to expand the possibilities of the lyrics. 'Spontaneous Bop Prosody' would describe the poetic technique, as is evident in the title song: 'If I ventured in the slipstream / Between the viaducts of your dream / Where immobile steel rims crack / And the ditch in the back roads stop / Could you find me?' This endlessly shifting, suggestive language owes much to Kerouac and Ginsberg. As the images accumulate, we come again and again towards a moment of mystical revelation: 'To lay me down / In silence easy / To be born again ...' There is an element of Zen here: the impulse to see the world with a beginner's mind, always as if for the first time. Yet working in tension with this openness to life there is a sentiment which is redolent of the later Kerouac. Morrison towards the end of the song repeatedly expresses the desire to be born again 'In another world', and 'In another time', because he feels himself to be 'a stranger in this world' who has his 'home on high'.[88] However, the music, with its quivering, elusive sound, seems to waver between embracing and spurning worldly life. It would seem that Morrison is exploring a state of ambivalence: a choice between what we called, in elucidating Kerouac's development, the mysticism of affirmation and the mysticism of ascesis, the 'Via Positiva' and the 'Via Negativa'. The persona in the song (not necessarily Morrison himself) knows himself to be adrift and alienated, and wishes to find atonement (at-one-ment). But he is uncertain whether the source of his being is to be found by immersing himself in creation or by seeing through and beyond it. It is this sense of tension which gives an edge to his overtly religious music. Unlike Kerouac, Morrison does not opt for one path rather than the other, but proceeds in anticipation of the point where they converge.

Another, related tension in Morrison's art involves the dialectic which we have so frequently invoked in this study: it moves tantalisingly between profane, fallen time and sacred, prelapsarian time, making music of their interplay. Most of Morrison's work is about this very relationship between the beauty of the given world and the desire for transcendence. It is as if apprehending that beauty inevitably suggests an eternity within, behind or beyond it; yet that very suggestion is inseparable from that apprehension. On the same album we find 'Cyprus Avenue', a celebration of an area of Belfast which he used to frequent as a child, and which he saw as a place of enchantment. Brian Hinton explains this 'nostalgia for paradise' by invoking Mircea Eliade's principle of 'eternal return':

[Eliade] describes our lingering sense of being at one with the natural world as a 'profound feeling of having come from the soil, of having been born of Earth in the same way that the Earth, with her inexhaustible fecundity, gives birth to the rocks,

rivers, trees and flowers.' ... Van Morrison's celebration of his
own native ground is also a curiously isolated one. Written
about largely in exile, it comprises the Belfast suburb of his
childhood and landscapes drawn from his imagination:
summertime in England, the fields of Avalon. For all of us, the
landscape in which we grew up evokes an obscure, elegiac
sadness. For [the poet] Jeremy Hooker, it is 'the original
country that can never be re-entered, a condition of complete
being ... a locus of the sacred, a "centre" where wholeness of
being may be found.'[89]

Yet the very intensity of this nostalgia, this sense of loss, is inseparable
from the capacity for vision; thus, paradise is paradoxically regained
even as its loss is lamented. Memory, which would normally bind one
to temporal existence, transcends it when informed by the imagination.
Morrison would seem to have this capacity. Certainly, the songwriter
has himself commented on 'Cyprus Avenue' that the whole of the song
was intended to bring the listener 'to a point where he could go into
meditation'.[90] There is perhaps an affinity, then, between the early
Morrison and the later Donovan.

Consistently, Morrison has celebrated the natural world as a realm
of spiritual healing – though he equivocates on whether it depends on
the cleansing of the 'doors of perception' for its efficacy. At any rate,
his album *Moondance* (1970) contains a song whose title sets the tone
for all his later ones: 'Into the Mystic'. Steve Turner describes this as

> a celebration of mystical union that [Morrison] once stated was
> about 'being part of the universe'. It combined all his main
> themes: nature (sun, sea, wind, sky), a lover, the yearning for
> things to be as they were in 'the days of old', the foghorn
> sounds of Belfast and the promise of redemption through unity
> with the whole.[91]

Again, on a later album, *Beautiful Vision* (1982), there is a song called
'She Gives Me Religion' that refers to walking back down the 'mystic
avenue' – an evocation of Cyprus Avenue, perhaps – and which gives
thanks for having his eyes opened by 'the angel of imagination'. Again,
his celebration of landscape is informed by a strong sense of myth – in
his case, Celtic mythology, as is strongly evident on albums such as
Veedon Fleece and *Avalon Sunset* – which would certainly link him
with Snyder. Nor should we overlook the implications of the way
Morrison performs his songs:

It is Morrison's flexible and highly rhythmic voice, and the musical patterns he and his carefully chosen sidemen (and women) weave around the words he extemporises, which transform them into a wider utterance. *Astral Weeks* is perhaps the finest example in all of rock of how everything can cohere into a highly emotional, charged whole. In an interview with the Irish fanzine *Into The Music*, [the musician] David Hayes declares that Van is the only person he has met in the music business who 'if all the elements are right and everything is in place, can take the music into a totally different realm, where you kind of melt into it.' ... Like any true poet, Van functions as a kind of shaman or high priest, heightening our senses.[92]

The Beat-inspired mode of performance is a means to the beatific vision. Again, if it is thought to be shamanic, we cannot help but note an affinity with Snyder.

However, whether or not we choose to relate Morrison specifically to Snyder, or to Kerouac, or to Ginsberg is not really the issue. The attribution of nature mysticism and the identification with shamanism might encourage us to opt for the first of these. For the record, however, Morrison himself claimed in 1985, after meeting the last of these: 'Ginsberg explains his own visionary experience, not on drugs, and its sounds like the same as mine.'[93] For the record again, when Morrison was invited to appear on a television tribute to a jazz musician admired by all the Beat writers, Slim Galliard, he chose to read a passage from Kerouac's *On the Road*.[94] Just to complicate things even further, he has famously composed a song entitled 'Alan Watts Blues' (*Poetic Champions Compose*, 1987). Nor is the choice of title an idle one: Morrison would seem to have spent a good deal of his time studying not only Watts but also his friend Krishnamurti – whom we quoted in Chapter 1. Krishnamurti's statement might be worth quoting again in full: 'I maintain that Truth is a pathless land, and you cannot approach it by any path whatsoever, by any religion, by any sect.'[95] For the title of Morrison's album of the previous year is *No Guru, No Method, No Teacher* – which would seem to echo not only Krishnamurti's sentiment and Watts's overall message, but also the wisdom of Zen, a 'religion of no religion'. It is also worth noting that this title forms a refrain in a song from the album, 'In the Garden', which is about a paradisal vision recalled from his Belfast childhood – thus confirming the implicit nature mysticism of the *Astral Weeks* album. As with the earlier work, the art seems to hover around the paradoxical relationship between time and eternity, between everyday experience and mystical revelation.

Our concern in this chapter is not, we have said, with the number of specific parallels which may be drawn between a given writer and a given songwriter. It is a question, rather, of shared assumptions and aspirations. On the basis of those, Van Morrison surely belongs here as much as does his namesake Jim Morrison. For, if behind the Beat movement itself lies the figure of William Blake, with his proclamation of the possibility of cleansing 'the doors of perception' and of seeing 'a heaven in a wild flower', then there can be no doubt about Van Morrison's inclusion in the visionary tradition.

Mention of Blake brings us, finally, to Nick Drake, whose posthumous anthology of songs was significantly entitled *Heaven in a Wild Flower*. In a major essay on his work, Ian MacDonald tells us that Drake, having studied English Literature at Cambridge, came to regard Blake as the finest of the English poets. Moreover, reading Blake was for him necessarily complemented by his study of Buddhism – notably by way of the works of Alan Watts.[96] In situating Drake in relation to the Buddha and to Blake, MacDonald hovers about a paradox which has arisen frequently for us:

> The pantheistic aspect of Buddhism – the idea that everything is both illusory and holy – parallels Blake's sense of a way of seeing in which all things become divine: 'If the doors of perception were cleansed, everything would appear as it is, infinite.' ... Here Blake proclaims that everything is sacred and hence profoundly consequential, urging a universal compassion shared by Buddhism. 'Innocence', in Blake's sense, is a state as yet unclouded by experience of the material world. It's the outlook of the child's soul, fresh from heaven and still on the threshold of life. Buddhism, like other mystical paths, seeks to recover this innocent way of perceiving by stilling 'the mind', a tool or faculty we acquire through experience but which comes to dominate our perceptions, among other things subtly creating our sense of time. Time, say the mystics, mysteriously, is the illusion of all illusions.[97]

Again, though, it is necessary to qualify even this modest proposal. MacDonald wants to place Drake in a visionary tradition, but does not want to be understood as labelling him, or translating his art into terms of a doctrine:

Nick Drake wasn't a literal disciple of Blake or Buddha. There are no clear Blake references in his lyrics, nor is he likely to have treated Buddhism as more than a confirmation of concepts he'd arrived at through his own experience. Nevertheless Blake's mystical vision and the tenets of Buddhism illuminate a great deal of his work. Drake's outlook seems to have boiled down to the linked recognitions that life is a predicament and that the world is ultimately an irreducible mystery. Why it exists, why we exist in it, *why there is anything at all*, we haven't the slightest idea. From this sense of predicament and mystery flows all his work, and also his message to us. More than that, the same influences shaped the growth and decline of his life.[98]

MacDonald's instinct to relate Drake to Buddhism is surely a sound one. His account of this relationship is exemplary, except for one major error. He attributes to the Buddha a belief in an eternal soul or 'Self' which is continually reincarnated. He seems to be confusing Buddhism with Hinduism. Once one makes allowances for this error, however, the argument makes perfect sense.

The key album here is Drake's first, *Five Leaves Left* (1969), whose very title suggests a sense of transience. The song 'River Man' is about the river of life – more particularly, in MacDonald's words, 'the realm of material life wherein the senses wander and the mind gets lost in the flow of time and thought'. The song queries the notion of time as mere chronology, personified by the 'river man' (who has aspects of Acheron, the figure in Greek myth who transports the dead across the river to Hades): life to the unillumined mind is a linear process leading only to death. But for the illumined mind, it is always possible to break free from the prison of profane time:

> In reality, there is only *now* ... forever. If we can just *be here now* – mindlessly present, which is very difficult and the goal of all methods of meditation – our Blakeian [sic] 'mind forg'd manacles' will drop off, leaving us free of attachment and beholding reality as it truly is: infinite, holy and illuminated. Some sensitive people – poets and such – are said by Buddhist mystics to experience occasional spontaneous glimpses of this state of 'enlightenment' (called, in Zen, *satori*). To judge from the outlook conveyed in 'River Man', Drake was one of them.[99]

The song turns out to be about this very choice. One may see through
and beyond temporal illusion, as does the narrator – the song being a
narrative about going to see the river man in order to force a moment
of discovery. Or one may surrender to it, even while having doubts
about it – as does another figure in the song, named 'Betty':

> The river of material existence rolls on; only detachment shows
> us the process in motion. Naturally detached, Drake lived on
> the river bank, observing ('If he tells me all he knows / About
> the way his river flows / I don't suppose / It's meant for me').
> Betty is on the verge of leaving the everyday river life for the
> life of detachment, but this is a rather stark – not to say lonely
> – proposition. She's aware of transience and suffering ('Said she
> had a word to say / About things today / And falling leaves'),
> but she doesn't know how to live beyond the incessant current
> of habit, with its clock-driven rat-race fight to win security
> ('Hadn't had the time to choose / A way to lose') – although
> she suspects there must be something better ('But she believes').
> To leave the river, Betty must transcend her mind, with its
> enslaved attachment to time; yet the discomfort of her
> immediate dilemma is too much for her and she returns to the
> river's lulling flow: 'Calling for her mind again / She lost the
> pain / And stayed for more.' Here, string dissonances fret in
> cross-rhythm before relapsing back into sustained chords: Betty
> torn between lives, crying, running back to the world. 'Oh, how
> they come and go,' sighs Drake, watching her recede. 'Oh, how
> they come and go,' he repeats, cadencing fatalistically from his
> wider perspective – lives appearing like bubbles in the flowing
> river of time, travelling for a while and then vanishing.[100]

In this song, the river and the rain are tragic images, for they represent entrapment in profane time. This may strike us as unusual, for
Drake's songs are full of imagery drawn from nature, most of which
are affirmative: he seems especially fond of trees and sky, which for
him are 'symbols of permanence, stillness and peace'.[101] Another song
from *Five Leaves Left* is called 'Way to Blue', in which the 'blue' represents what Zen Buddhists call the 'big sky mind' of enlightenment – the
release into joyous emptiness from the illusion of separate identity. But
even there, the song conveys mainly the desperate yearning for such a
revelation, amidst the pain of the ego's time-bound existence: 'Have
you seen the land living by the breeze? / Can you understand a light

among the trees? / Tell me all that you may know, show me what you have to show. / Tell us all today if you know the way to blue.'[102] As Drake's music developed, his vision became more and more bleak – the bleakness being exacerbated, no doubt, by his growing sense of failure as an artist. What lingers is not so much his relish for the blue of the sky as his sense of desperation. The final album released during his life, *Pink Moon* (1972), consists of stripped-down music (frequently a solitary, acoustic guitar) and disconcerting lyrics which present nature as threat rather than comfort ('Pink moon gonna get you all'). A representative song is 'Place to Be', which uses unrequited love as a metaphor for the sense of spiritual longing: where once he was 'strong in the sun', now he is 'weaker than the palest blue / Oh, so weak in this need for you.'[103] Again, there is a song on the posthumous selection of unreleased material, *Time Of No Reply* (1987), called 'Rider on the Wheel', which expresses disillusionment with the cycle of existence – the wheel of 'samsara' – but offers no certainty of any release other than death.

It is with Drake, then, that we are most forcibly reminded of the power and pull of the Via Negativa, the mysticism of ascesis. With Kerouac, he embraces nothingness; he lets pain be pain, darkness be darkness. As we have acknowledged, this is as legitimate a spiritual path as the Via Positiva, the mysticism of affirmation. Moreover, the two are complementary. Kerouac, we recall, equating Buddhist 'nirvana' with Christian salvation, wishes only to be 'safe in heaven dead'. Snyder stands at the other end of the spectrum, trying to stand within nature as far as possible, addressing it with reverence and defending it with passion; but he, too, does so without forgetting the emptiness which underlies all manifest life. If both Kerouac and Drake know, with Blake, that heaven is manifest in 'a wild flower', then they are surely allowed to celebrate the death which opens onto it. Ginsberg would concur. His favourite of all his own poems was the song, 'Father Death Blues' (1976): 'Hey Father Death, I'm flying home ... Guru Death, your words are true ... Buddha Death, I wake with you ...'[104] The beatific vision must surely comprehend such wisdom if it is to be worth our attention.

That is why this book has not really been a work of musicology, of cultural history or of critical theory: it has been an attempt to gain a perspective on a whole way of thinking, represented by the Beat writers and their songwriting successors. That way of thinking is also a whole way of being – and hence of both living and dying. For the paradox in Blake's line, 'To see a heaven in a wild flower', is that one thing of which one can be sure is that flowers die – which is, after all, intrinsic to their natural beauty. With this in mind, I will leave the last word to Alan Watts. It may be surprising that someone who seemed to enjoy so much the game of life should dwell so frequently on the prospect of death. But as he points out, in a lecture ostensibly on 'Psychotherapy and Eastern Religion', this is the most important subject of all: 'Dying is a splendid opportunity, and the sooner one can realize fully the certainty of death the better.' To embrace the possibility of dying is to be released from the burden of time: 'by acceptance of death, one over-comes the necessity for a future, and that in both senses of the word is a *present.*' We should celebrate the fact that we are bound to die: death is 'the greatest opportunity you'll ever have to experience what it's like to let go of yourself ... than which there is no greater bliss.'[105] We may seem to have come a long way from the question of the influence of certain writers on certain songwriters, but perhaps this final invocation of Watts will remind us of the visionary perspective which compre-hends both life and death, and to which those writers and songwriters might offer access.

Notes

1 Alan Watts, 'Beat Zen, Square Zen, and Zen', in *This is IT and other Essays on Zen and Spiritual Experience* (London: Rider & Co, 1960; 1978), p. 100.

2 Gary Snyder, 'Mid-August at Sourdough Mountain Lookout', in *No Nat-ure: New and Selected Poems* (New York: Pantheon Books, 1992), p. 4.

3 Snyder, 'Front Lines', in *No Nature*, p. 218.

4 Alan Watts, *The Philosophies of Asia* (Boston: Charles E. Tuttle Co., 1995), pp. 41, 57.

5 Patrick D. Murphy, *A Place for Wayfaring: The Poetry and Prose of Gary Snyder* (Corvalis: Oregon State University Press, 2000), p. 108.

6 David Landis Barnhill, 'Great Earth *Sangha*: Gary Snyder's View of Nature as Community', in Mary Evelyn Tucker and Duncan Ryuken Williams (eds), *Buddhism and Ecology: The Interconnection of Dharma and Deeds* (Cambridge, MA: Harvard University Press, 1997), p. 187.

7 For the context of Snyder's ecological activism, see Laurence Coupe (ed.), *The Green Studies Reader: From Romanticism to Ecocriticism* (London: Routledge, 2000), pp. 1–8, 119–22.

8 Murphy, *A Place for Wayfaring*, p. 21.

9 Snyder quoted in Murphy, *A Place for Wayfaring*, p. 21.

10 Snyder, 'Logging 2', *Myths and Texts*, in *No Nature*, p. 35.

11 Snyder, 'Logging 1', *Myths and Texts*, p. 34.

12 Murphy, *A Place for Wayfaring*, p. 23.

13 Snyder, 'Logging 12', *Myths and Texts*, pp. 41–2.

14 Murphy, *A Place for Wayfaring*, p. 28.

15 Gary Snyder, 'The Rediscovery of Turtle Island', in *A Place in Space: Ethics, Aesthetics, and Watersheds* (Washington, DC: Counterpoint Press, 1995), pp. 243–4.

16 William Blake, *The Marriage of Heaven and Hell*, in David V. Erdman and Harold Bloom (eds), *The Complete Poetry and Prose of William Blake* (New York: Doubleday, 1988), p. 39.

17 See Jerry Hopkins and Danny Sugerman, *No One Here Gets Out Alive* (London: Plexus, 1981), p. 45.

18 Jim Morrison, 'End of the Night', in Danny Sugerman (ed.), *The Doors Complete Lyrics* (London: Abacus, 2001), p. 32.

19 Arthur Rimbaud, quoted in Edgell Rickword, *Essays and Opinions 1921–1931* (Cheadle: Carcanet, 1974), p. 126.

20 See Wallace Fowlie, *Rimbaud and Jim Morrison: The Rebel as Poet* (London: Souvenir Press, 1994).

21 See Hopkins and Sugerman, *No One Here Gets Out Alive*, p. 6.

22 Morrison, 'Break On Through', in *Doors Complete Lyrics*, p. 23.

23 Jim Morrison in conversation, quoted in Hopkins and Sugerman, *No One Here Gets Out Alive*, p. 143.

24 Jim Morrison, *The Lords and The New Creatures* (London: Omnibus, 1985), p. 24.

25 Suzi Gablik, quoted by Hans Bertens, *The Idea of the Postmodern: A History* (London: Routledge, 1995), pp. 74–5.

26 Fowlie, *Rimbaud and Jim Morrison*, p. 109.

27 Fowlie, *Rimbaud and Jim Morrison*, p. 109.

28 See Hopkins and Sugerman, *No One Here Gets Out Alive*, p. 179.

29 Morrison, 'The End', in *Doors Complete Lyrics*, p. 35.

30 Jim Morrison, 'An American Prayer', in *The American Night* (London: Penguin, 1990), p. 3.

31 Morrison, 'When the Music's Over', in *Doors Complete Lyrics*, p. 71.

32 Morrison, 'We Could Be So Good Together', in *Doors Complete Lyrics*, p. 91.

33 Morrison, 'When the Music's Over', in *Doors Complete Lyrics*, p. 72.

34 Jim Morrison quoted in Digby Diehl, 'Love And The Demonic Psyche' (1967), in Danny Sugerman (ed.), *The Doors: The Illustrated History* (London: Omnibus Press, 1983), pp. 45–6.

35 Joni Mitchell, 'Big Yellow Taxi', in *The Complete Poems and Lyrics* (London: Chatto & Windus, 1997), p. 56.

36 Mitchell, 'Chinese Café – Unchained Melody', in *Poems and Lyrics*, p. 213.

37 Mitchell, 'Woodstock', *Poems and Lyrics*, pp. 58–9.

38 Karen O'Brien, *Shadows and Light: Joni Mitchell: The Definitive Biography* (London: Virgin Books, 2002), p. 149.

39 Mitchell, 'All I Want', in *Poems and Lyrics*, p. 65.

40 Mitchell, 'California', in *Poems and Lyrics*, p. 74.

41 Mitchell, 'Blue', in *Poems and Lyrics*, p. 72.

42 See *Woman of Heart and Mind: Joni Mitchell: A Life Story*, directed by Susan Lacy, Eagle Vision DVD, USA, 2003.

43 Mitchell, 'Song to a Seagull', in *Poems and Lyrics*, p. 20.
44 See *Woman of Heart and Mind*.
45 Joni Mitchell quoted in O'Brien, *Shadows and Light*, p. 135.
46 Joni Mitchell quoted in Brian Hinton, *Joni Mitchell, Both Sides Now* (London: Sanctuary, 1996), p. 133.
47 Mitchell, 'The Boho Dance', in *Poems and Lyrics*, p. 146.
48 Tom Wolfe, *The Painted Word* (New York: Bantam Press, 1976), p. 19.
49 See Carlos Castaneda, *The Teachings of Don Juan: A Yaqui Way of Knowledge* (Berkeley: California University Press, 1968).
50 The fact that his name is the same as the sexual adventurer of European legend is also relevant. Mitchell is offering a challenge to patriarchal mythology: she is celebrating a female figure to whom is bequeathed the spiritual powers of a shaman and the sexual charisma of a notorious seducer, both of which are conjoined to a 'reckless' spirit.
51 O'Brien, *Shadows and Light*, p. 184.
52 O'Brien, *Shadows and Light*, p. 184.
53 Mitchell, 'Paprika Plains', in *Poems and Lyrics*, pp. 184, 186.
54 Wilfrid Mellers, *Angels of the Night: Popular Female Singers of our Time* (Oxford: Basil Blackwell, 1986), p. 161.
55 Mitchell, 'Don Juan's Reckless Daughter', in *Poems and Lyrics*, p. 192.
56 See O'Brien, *Shadows and Light*, p. iv.
57 Mitchell, 'Roses Blue', in *Poems and Lyrics*, p. 32. To redress the balance, one could point to various invocations of Zen wisdom in other, later songs. For example, 'Moon at the Window', from *Wild Things Run Fast* (1982), echoes a haiku by Ryokan: 'The thief left it behind: / the moon / at my window.' Mitchell's refrain runs as follows: 'Oh, but sometimes the light Can be so hard to find At least the moon in the window – / The thieves left that behind.' See Mitchell, *Poems and Lyrics*, p. 217.
58 Blake, 'Several Questions Answered', in *Complete Poetry and Prose*, p. 474.
59 Mitchell, 'Sweet Bird', in *Poems and Lyrics*, p. 150.
60 Kenneth Rexroth quoted in Loranne S. Dorman and Clive L. Rawlins, *Leonard Cohen: Prophet of the Heart* (London: Omnibus Press, 1990), p. 213.
61 See David Boucher, *Dylan & Cohen: Poets of Rock and Roll* (New York: Continuum, 2004), pp. 15–17.
62 Leonard Cohen, *Leonard Cohen In His Own Words*, ed. Jim Devlin (London: Omnibus Press, 1998), p 11.
63 Cohen, *Leonard Cohen in his Own Words*, p. 11.
64 Leonard Cohen, *Beautiful Losers* (London: Panther Books, 1972).
65 Cohen, *Leonard Cohen in his Own Words*, p. 40.
66 Leonard Cohen, 'Suzanne', in *Stranger Music: Selected Poems and Songs* (London: Jonathan Cape, 1993), pp. 95–6.
67 Cohen, 'If It Be Your Will', in *Stranger Music*, pp. 343–4.
68 Dorman and Rawlins, *Leonard Cohen*, p. 301.
69 David Sheppard, *Leonard Cohen* (New York: Thunder's Mouth Press, 2000), p 115.

70 Sheppard, *Leonard Cohen*, p. 116.
71 Cohen, 'Anthem', in *Stranger Music*, pp. 373–4.
72 Cohen, *Leonard Cohen in his Own Words*, p. 40.
73 Leonard Cohen, 'Here It Is', www.leonardcohenfiles.com/tennewsongs [accessed 3 January 2006].
74 Probably the best account of Donovan's career is his own. See Donovan Leitch, *The Hurdy-Gurdy Man* (London: Century, 2005).
75 Donovan Leitch, 'Sunny Goodge Street', www.lyricsdownload.com/donovan-lyrics [accessed 5 March 2006].
76 Donovan Leitch, 'Season of the Witch', www.lyricsdownload.com/donovan-lyrics [accessed 5 March 2006].
77 See Leitch, *The Hurdy-Gurdy Man*, p. 269.
78 Donovan Leitch, 'There Is a Mountain', www.lyricsdownload.com/donovan-lyrics [accessed 5 March 2006].
79 Alan W. Watts, *The Way of Zen* (London: Penguin, 1957; 1990), p. 146.
80 Donovan Leitch, 'Lullaby of Spring', www.lyricsdownload.com/donovan-lyrics [accessed 5 March 2006].
81 Donovan Leitch, 'Isle of Islay', www.lyricsdownload.com/donovan-lyrics [accessed 5 March 2006].
82 Robin Williamson, 'The Mad Hatter's Song', www.lyricsdownload.com/incredible-string-band-lyrics [accessed 5 March 2006].
83 Robin Williamson, 'Keeoaddi There', www.lyricsdownload.com/incredible-string-band-lyrics [accessed 5 March 2006].
84 Thomas Traherne quoted in Richard Lang, 'Thomas Traherne: A 17th Century English Mystic', http:netowne.com/angels-christian/mysticism/traherne.htm [accessed 5 March 2006].
85 Douglas Harding quoted in Richard Lang, 'Douglas Harding: Introduction', www.headless.org [accessed 5 March 2006].
86 Mike Heron, 'Douglas Traherne Harding', www.lyricsdownload.com/incredible-string-band-lyrics [accessed 5 March 2006].
87 Rowan Williams, 'Foreword', Adrian Whittaker (ed.), *Be Glad: An Incredible String Band Compendium* (London: Helter Skelter, 2003).
88 Van Morrison, 'Astral Weeks', www.lyricsdownload.com/van-morrison-lyrics [accessed 7 March 2006].
89 Brian Hinton, *Celtic Crossroads: The Art of Van Morrison* (London: Sanctuary, 1997), p. 17.
90 Van Morrison quoted in Hinton, *Celtic Crossroads*, p. 255.
91 Steve Turner, *Van Morrison: Too Late to Stop Now* (London: Bloomsbury, 1993), p. 101.
92 Hinton, *Celtic Crossroads*, p. 12.
93 Hinton, *Celtic Crossroads*, p. 251.
94 Hinton, *Celtic Crossroads*, p. 339.
95 Krishnamurti, *Commentaries on Living: Second Series* (London: Gollancz, 1958), p. 64.
96 Ian MacDonald, 'Exiled From Heaven: The Unheard Message of Nick Drake', *The People's Music* (London: Pimlico, 2003), pp. 220, 232. See

also Patrick Humphries, *Nick Drake: The Biography* (London: Bloomsbury, 1997).

97 MacDonald, 'Exiled From Heaven'. p. 233.
98 MacDonald, 'Exiled From Heaven'. p. 233.
99 MacDonald, 'Exiled From Heaven'. p. 235.
100 MacDonald, 'Exiled From Heaven'. p. 236.
101 MacDonald, 'Exiled From Heaven'. p. 238.
102 Nick Drake, 'Way to Blue', www.lyricsdownload.com/nick-drake-lyrics
    [accessed 7 March 2006].
103 Nick Drake, 'Place to Be', www.lyricsdownload.com/nick-drake-lyrics
    [accessed 7 March 2006].
104 Allen Ginsberg, 'Father Death Blues', *Selected Poems 1947–1995* (London
    and New York: Penguin, 1997), p. 295.
105 Alan Watts, 'Psychotherapy and Eastern Religion', in *The Essential Alan
    Watts* (Berkeley, CA: Celestial Arts, 1977), pp. 133, 139, 142.

Postscript

I trust that, as this study comes to a close, readers will feel able to concur with me that, once one has recognised the 'Beat' vision as the 'beatific' vision, the relationship between the fifties writers and the sixties songwriters becomes rather more intriguing than it would be if we relied on some vague notion of a bohemian legacy. Once one takes Beats such as Kerouac, Ginsberg and Snyder seriously as religious writers, exploring possibilities of spirituality with a view to mystical revelation, the achievement of artists such as Dylan and the Beatles appears far more substantial than one thought. For, not only did they benefit from the idea that it is possible to use one's art to help manifest the sacred in the profane, but they also took that idea further than had been possible for the people who influenced them.

While I have said from the outset that musicology is not our concern, it has to be acknowledged that the power of popular song to make the spiritual dimension of existence seem immediate, and to make complex religious philosophies accessible, gives songwriters an advantage. Indeed, it has been the implicit thesis of this book that the Beat vision is not only confirmed by the Beat sound, but that the Beat sound extends the Beat vision. I have even raised the possibility that Dylan and the Beatles are in many ways more successful poets than is Ginsberg – as he himself conceded. The discipline, the craft, the economy of utterance, the sheer beauty of the sound: all these make 'Mr Tambourine Man' and 'Eleanor Rigby' work in a way that 'Sunflower Sutra' and 'Howl' cannot – despite Ginsberg's undoubted skill as performer and rhetorician, which comes across even on the printed page.

My decision to concentrate mainly on Dylan and the Beatles was guided by my intuition that it would be more illuminating to show in detail how one might begin to read popular song in the light of the Beat influence than to offer a broad and equal survey. Moreover, by exploring two bodies of work in such depth, I was able to address the tensions involved: not only within a group of songwriters, namely the Beatles, but within one songwriter, namely Bob Dylan. I have included the work of Jim Morrison, Joni Mitchell, Leonard Cohen and the others in rather less detail, but again with the hope that possibilities of interpretation have been raised. Readers may now wish to pursue the beatific vision for themselves, inspired by our chosen writers and songwriters but not limited to them. For ultimately it is the vision which matters, whether it is reached through sound or through silence.

Select bibliography

Ash, Mel, *Beat Spirit: The Way of the Beat Writers as a Living Experience* (New York: Putnam, 1997).

Barnhill, David Landis, 'Great Earth *Sangha*: Gary Snyder's View of Nature as Community', in Mary Evelyn Tucker and Duncan Ryuken Williams (eds), *Buddhism and Ecology: The Interconnection of Dharma and Deeds* (Cambridge, MA: Harvard University Press, 1997), pp. 187–217.

The Beatles, *The Beatles Illustrated Lyrics*, ed. Alan Aldridge (London: Macmillan, 1990).

Blake, William, *The Complete Poetry and Prose of William Blake*, ed. David V. Erdman and Harold Bloom (New York: Doubleday, 1988).

Boucher, David, *Dylan & Cohen: Poets of Rock and Roll* (New York: Continuum, 2004).

Braunstein, Peter and Michael William Doyle, *Imagine Nation: The American Counterculture of the 1960s and 1970s* (London: Routledge, 2002).

Campbell, James, *This is the Beat Generation* (London: Vintage, 2000).

Chaline, Eric, *The Book of Zen: The Path to Inner Peace* (Gloucester, MA: Fair Winds Press, 2003).

Charters, Ann, *Kerouac: A Biography* (New York: Saint Martin's Press, 1994).

——, (ed.), *The Portable Beat Reader* (New York: Viking Penguin, 1992).

——, *Beat Down To Your Soul: What Was the Beat Generation?* (New York: Penguin, 2001).

Clark, Tom, *Jack Kerouac: A Biography* (London: Plexus, 1997).

Cohen, Leonard, *Stranger Music: Selected Poems and Songs* (London: Jonathan Cape, 1993).

——, *Leonard Cohen In His Own Words*, ed. Jim Devlin (London: Omnibus Press, 1998).

Cook, Bruce, *The Beat Generation* (New York: William Morrow, 1971).

Corcoran, Neil (ed.), *Do You, Mr Jones? Bob Dylan with the Poets and Professors* (London: Chatto & Windus, 2002).

Coupe, Laurence, *Myth* (London: Routledge, 1997).

——, (ed.), *The Green Studies Reader: From Romanticism to Ecocriticism* (London: Routledge, 2000).

Dickstein, Morris, *Gates of Eden: American Culture in the Sixties* (Cambridge, MA: Harvard University Press, 1977; 1997).

The Doors, *The Doors Complete Lyrics*, ed. Danny Sugerman (London: Abacus, 2001).

Dorman, Loranne S. and Clive L. Rawlins, *Leonard Cohen: Prophet of the Heart* (London: Omnibus Press, 1990).

Dylan, Bob, *Bob Dylan In His Own Words*, ed. Barry Miles (London: Omnibus Press, 1978).

——, *Lyrics 1962–1985* (London: Jonathan Cape, 1987).

——, *Chronicles: Volume One* (New York: Simon & Schuster, 2004).

Eliade, Mircea, *The Sacred and the Profane: The Nature of Religion* (New York: Harcourt, 1959; 1987).

Emerson, Ralph Waldo, *Essays* (London and Glasgow: Blackie & Son, 1940).

Farrell, James J., *The Spirit of the Sixties* (New York and London: Routledge, 1997).

Fowlie, Wallace, *Rimbaud and Jim Morrison: The Rebel as Poet* (London: Souvenir Press, 1994).

Fox, Matthew, *Original Blessing: A Primer in Creation Spirituality* (Sante Fe: Bear & Co, 1983).

Freke, Timothy, *Spiritual Traditions* (New York: Sterling Publishing Co., 2001)

French, Warren, *Jack Kerouac* (Boston: Twayne Publishers, 1986).

Furlong, Monica, *Zen Effects: The Life of Alan Watts* (Woodstock, Vermont: Skylight Paths Publishing, 2001).

George-Warren, Holly (ed.), *The Rolling Stone Book of the Beats: The Beat Generation and the Counterculture* (London: Bloomsbury, 1999).

Gill, Andy, *Classic Bob Dylan 1962–69: My Back Pages* (London: Carlton, 1998).

Ginsberg, Allen, *Selected Poems 1947–1995* (London and New York: Penguin, 1997).

——, *Deliberate Prose: Selected Essays 1952–1995* (New York: HarperCollins, 2000).

Gnarowski, Michael (ed.), *Leonard Cohen: The Artist and his Critics* (Toronto: McGraw-Hill Ryerson, 1976).

Gray, Michael, *Song and Dance Man III: The Art of Bob Dylan* (London: Cassell, 2000).

Green, Jonathon, *All Dressed Up: The Sixties and the Counterculture* (London: Pimlico, 1999).

Halper, Jon (ed.), *Gary Snyder: Dimensions of a Life* (San Fransisco: Sierra Club Books, 1991).

Harry, Bill, *The John Lennon Encyclopedia* (London: Virgin, 2000).

Heelas, Paul, *The New Age Movement: The Celebration of the Self and the Sacralization of Modernity* (Oxford: Blackwell, 1996).

Hinton, Brian, *Celtic Crossroads: The Art of Van Morrison* (London: Sanctuary, 1997).

——, *Joni Mitchell: Both Sides Now* (London: Sanctuary, 1996).

Hopkins, Jerry (ed.), *The Lizard King: The Essential Jim Morrison* (London: Plexus, 1992).

Hopkins, Jerry and Danny Sugerman, *No One Here Gets Out Alive* (London: Plexus, 1981).

Horovitz, Michael (ed.), *Children of Albion: Poetry of the British Underground* (Harmondsworth: Penguin, 1969).

Humphries, Patrick, *Nick Drake: The Biography* (London: Bloomsbury, 1997).

Hunt, Tim, *Kerouac's Crooked Road: Development of a Fiction* (Berkeley: California University Press, 1996).

Hutnyk, John, *Critique of Exotica: Music, Politics and the Culture Industry* (London: Pluto Press, 2000).

Huxley, Aldous, *The Perennial Philosophy* (New York: Harper & Row, 1945; 1970).

——, *The Doors of Perception and Heaven and Hell* (Harmondsworth: Penguin, 1959).

Hyde, Lewis (ed.), *On the Poetry of Allen Ginsberg* (Michigan: Michigan University Press, 1984).

Keats, John, *Selected Letters*, ed. Frederick Page (London: Oxford University Press, 1954).

Keightley, Alan, *Into Every Life a Little Zen Must Fall: A Christian Philosopher Looks to Alan Watts and the East* (London: Wisdom Publications, 1986).

Kerouac, Jack, *On the Road* (London: Penguin, 1957; 1972).

——, *Mexico City Blues* (New York: Grove Press, 1959).

——, *The Dharma Bums* (London: Penguin, 1959; 2000).

——, *The Scripture of the Golden Eternity* (San Francisco: City Lights, 1960; 1994).

——, *Lonesome Traveler* (London: Penguin, 1960; 2000).

——, *Big Sur* (London: Flamingo, 1963; 2001).

——, *Visions of Gerard* (London: Penguin, 1963; 1991).

——, *Satori in Paris* (New York: Grove Press, 1966).

——, *Visions of Cody* (New York: McGraw-Hill, 1972).

——, *The Portable Jack Kerouac*, ed. Ann Charters (New York: Viking Penguin, 1995).

——, *Some of the Dharma* (New York: Viking Penguin, 1997).

Kostelanetz, Richard, *Social Speculations: Visions for Our Times* (New York: William Morrow, 1970).

Kramer, Jane, *Paterfamilias: Allen Ginsberg in America* (London: Gollancz, 1970).

Lachman, Gary Valentine, *Turn Off Your Mind: The Mystic Sixties and the Dark Side of the Age of Aquarius* (London: Sidgwick & Jackson, 2001).

Lardas, John, *The Bop Apocalypse: The Religious Visions of Kerouac, Ginsberg, and Burroughs* (Illinois: Illinois University Press, 2001).

Lee, Robert A. (ed.), *The Beat Generation Writers* (East Haven, Connecticut: Pluto Press, 1996).

Leitch, Donovan, *The Hurdy-Gurdy Man* (London: Century, 2005).

Lennon, John, *John Lennon In His Own Words*, ed. Barry Miles (London: Omnibus Press, 1980).

Lopez, Donald S. (ed.), *Modern Buddhism: Readings for the Unenlightened* (London: Penguin, 2002).

MacAdams, Lewis, *Birth of the Cool: Beat, Bebop and the American Avant-Garde* (London: Scribner, 2002).

MacDonald, Ian, *Revolution in the Head: The Beatles' Records and the Sixties* (London: Pimlico, 1995).

——, 'Exiled From Heaven: The Unheard Message of Nick Drake', in *The People's Music* (London: Pimlico, 2003), pp. 210–57.

Macedo, Stephen (ed.), *Reassessing the Sixties: Debating the Political and Cultural Legacy* (New York: W W Norton, 1997).

McNally, Dennis, *Desolate Angel: Jack Kerouac, the Beat Generation, and America* (Cambridge, MA: Da Capo Press, 2003).

Marcus, Greil, *Lipstick Traces: A Secret History of the Twentieth Century* (London: Secker & Warburg, 1990).

——, *Invisible Republic: Bob Dylan's Basement Tapes* (London: Picador, 1997).

Mellers, Wilfrid, *Twilight of the Gods: The Beatles in Retrospect* (London: Faber & Faber, 1973).

——, *Angels of the Night: Popular Female Singers of our Time* (Oxford: Basil Blackwell, 1986).

Melly, George, *Revolt Into Style* (Oxford: Oxford University Press, 1989).

Merrill, Thomas F., *Allen Ginsberg* (Boston: Twayne Publishers, 1969).

Miles, Barry, *Jack Kerouac: King of the Beats: A Portrait* (London: Virgin, 2002)

——, *Allen Ginsberg: A Biography* (London: Virgin, 2002)

——, *In the Sixties* (London: Pimlico, 2003).

Mitchell, Joni, *The Complete Poems and Lyrics* (London: Chatto & Windus, 1997).

Morrison, Jim, *The American Night* (London: Penguin, 1990).

Murphy, Patrick D., *A Place for Wayfaring: The Poetry and Prose of Gary Snyder* (Corvalis: Oregon State UP, 2000).

Nicosia, Gerald, *Memory Babe: A Critical Biography of Jack Kerouac* (Berkeley: California University Press, 1994).

Nuttall, Jeff, *Bomb Culture* (London: MacGibbon & Kee, 1968).

O'Brien, Karen, *Shadows and Light: Joni Mitchell: The Definitive Biography* (London: Virgin Books, 2002).

Parkinson, Thomas, *A Casebook on the Beat* (New York: Thomas Y. Crowell, 1961; 1971).

Phillips, Lisa, *Beat Culture and the New America, 1950–1965* (New York: Whitney Museum of American Art, 1996).

Pichaske, David, *A Generation in Motion: Popular Music and Culture in the Sixties* (Granite Falls, Minnesota: Ellis Press, 1989).

Poirier, Richard, 'Learning from the Beatles', in Jonathan Eisen (ed.), *The Age of Rock: Sounds of the American Cultural Revolution* (New York: Random House, 1969), pp. 160–79.

Polsky, Ned, *Hustlers, Beats and Others* (Harmondsworth: Penguin, 1967).

Portuges, Paul, *The Visionary Poetics of Allen Ginsberg* (Santa Barbara: Ross-Erikson Publishers, 1978).

Rahula, Walpola, *What the Buddha Taught* (New York: Grove Press, 1959; 1974).

Rasky, Harry, *The Song of Leonard Cohen* (Ontario: Mosaic Press, 2002).

Raskin, Jonah, *American Scream: Allen Ginsberg's 'Howl' and the Making of the Beat Generation* (Berkeley: California UP, 2004).

Reich, Charles A., *The Greening of America* (Harmondsworth: Penguin, 1972).

Russell, Jamie, *The Beat Generation* (Harpenden: Pocket Essentials, 2002).

Ricks, Christopher, *Dylan's Visions of Sin* (London: Viking Penguin, 2003).

Roszak, Theodore, *The Making of a Counter Culture: Reflections on the Technocratic Society and its Youthful Opposition* (London: Faber and Faber, 1970).

——, *Where the Wasteland Ends: Politics and Transcendence in Post-Industrial Society* (New York: Doubleday, 1972).

Scobie, Stephen (ed.), *Intricate Preparations: Writing Leonard Cohen* (Toronto: ECW Press, 2000).

Shelton, Robert, *No Direction Home: The Life and Music of Bob Dylan* (London: Penguin, 1987).

Shepard, Sam, *The Rolling Thunder Logbook* (London: Sanctuary, 2004).

Shankar, Ravi, *Raga Mala: The Autobiography of Ravi Shankar*, ed. George Harrison (New York: Welcome Rain Publishers, 1997).

Sheppard, David, *Leonard Cohen* (New York: Thunder's Mouth Press, 2000).

Snyder, Gary, *The Real Work: Interviews and Talks 1964–1979* (New York: New Directions, 1980)

——, *No Nature: New and Selected Poems* (New York: Pantheon Books, 1992).

——, *A Place in Space: Ethics, Aesthetics, and Watersheds* (Washington, DC: Counterpoint Press, 1995).

——, *The Gary Snyder Reader: Prose, Poetry, and Translations* (Washington: Counterpoint, 1999).

Spengler, Oswald, *The Decline of the West, Vols I and II*, trans. Charles Atkinson (New York: Alfred A. Knopf, 1926 and 1928).

Sugerman, Danny (ed.), *The Doors: The Illustrated History* (London: Omnibus Press, 1983).

Thoreau, Henry David, *The Portable Thoreau*, ed. Carl Bode (New York: Penguin, 1975).

Thomson, Elizabeth and David Gutnam (eds), *The Lennon Companion* (London: Sidgwick & Jackson, 1987).

Tonkinson, Carole (ed.), *Big Sky Mind: Buddhism and the Beat Generation* (New York: Riverhead Books, 1995).

Turner, Steve, *Van Morrison: Too Late to Stop Now* (London: Bloomsbury, 1993).

Turner, Victor, *The Ritual Process: Structure and Anti-Structure* (Chicago: Aldine, 1969; 1997).

Tytell, John, *Naked Angels: Kerouac, Ginsberg, Burroughs* (New York: Grove Press, 1976).

Watts, Alan, *Behold the Spirit: A Study in the Necessity of Mystical Religion* (New York: Vintage, 1947; 1971).

——, *The Way of Zen* (London: Penguin, 1957; 1990).

——, *Nature, Man and Woman* (New York: Vintage, 1958; 1991).

——, *This is IT and other essays on Zen and Spiritual Experience* (New York: Rider & Co, 1960; 1978).

——, *The Book: On The Taboo Against Knowing Who You Are* (New York: Random House / Vintage, 1966; 1989).

——, *In My Own Way: An Autobiography 1916–1965* (London: Jonathan Cape, 1973).

——, *Cloud-Hidden, Whereabouts Unknown: A Mountain Journal* (New York: Vintage, 1974).

——, *The Essential Alan Watts* (Berkeley, CA: Celestial Arts, 1977).

——, *The Philosophies of Asia* (Boston: Charles E. Tuttle Co., 1995).

——, *Zen and the Beat Way*, ed. Mark Watts (Enfield: Eden Grove Editions, 1997).

——, *The Culture of Counter-Culture* (Boston: Charles E. Tuttle Co., 1998).

Whiteley, Sheila, *The Space Between the Notes: Rock and the Counter-culture* (London: Routledge, 1992).

Whitman, Walt, *The Complete Poems*, ed. Francis Murphy (London: Penguin, 2004).

Whittaker, Adrian (ed.), *Be Glad: An Incredible String Band Compendium* (London: Helter Skelter, 2003).

Index

Lightning Source UK Ltd.
Milton Keynes UK
23 February 2011
168080UK00001B/13/P